MW00329079

RUGBY BEHIND
BARBED WIRE

RUGBY BEHIND BARBED WIRE

THE 1969/70 SPRINGBOKS TOUR OF BRITAIN AND IRELAND

CHRIS SCHOEMAN

AMBERLEY

First published 2020

Amberley Publishing
The Hill, Stroud
Gloucestershire, GL5 4EP

www.amberley-books.com

ISBN 978 1 4456 9410 8 (hardback)
ISBN 978 1 4456 9411 5 (ebook)

British Library Cataloguing in Publication Data.
A catalogue record for this book is available
from the British Library.

1 2 3 4 5 6 7 8 9 10

Typesetting by Aura Technology and Software
Services, India. Printed in the UK.

CONTENTS

FOREWORD

The year 1969 rocked British rugby and the society around it as never before. The game in Britain was patently unprepared for the explosion of righteous anger that surrounded the tour of Britain by the Springboks.

It's not as if there hadn't been any warning of what was to come. The fires of militant anti-apartheid protest had been burning for several years beforehand and there had been clear indications that sport – rugby in particular – was one of the key levers of change to the entrenched system of racial discrimination in South Africa. Tom Bedford, who had been at Oxford immediately prior to the tour, issued a warning before the team left that they were in for a rough ride but his words were derided as unpatriotic nonsense. How wrong the doubters turned out to be. Peter Hain and the many others who emerged as leaders of the anti-tour movement were well prepared and succeeded in mobilising the biggest anti-apartheid protest then seen in the western world.

An irresistible force was about to collide with an immovable object. Rugby was a sporting fraternity very unaccustomed to being told what to do, particularly by young, long-haired protesters waging urban warfare for a cause in another country that was barely understood in Britain and which represented a very unwelcome threat to the traditional competition between white men around the remnants of empire. The English game, as it had in New Zealand and Australia, dug in angrily and resentfully as a nervous government stood by and watched the contest unfold. For the leaders of the Springboks, and for captain Dawie de Villiers in particular, the tour was little more than a long-drawn-out torment.

Much of this story is the product of reminiscences by players and management, and the events are very clearly seared into the memories of the tourists. The Springboks were expected to win most if not all of their matches and they finished up with one of the most dismal records in their proud history. Would they have done better if there had been no protests? Unquestionably yes.

Chris Schoeman has brought that moment in history back to life very comprehensively. The Springboks were exposed, for the first time, to a relentless, rolling maul of disruption and neither players nor management were ready for what happened. The threat of violence became a daily burden that the team carried with them throughout and it is no wonder that some became increasingly demoralised.

All of us involved in that tour had our understanding of and sympathy for the cries of anguish that the protests represented changed forever. For me, it led to an involvement – at times alongside Tom Bedford and Dawie de Villiers – in the processes of confidence building between the South African government and the ANC in exile in Zambia and Zimbabwe.

We owe a debt of thanks to Chris Schoeman for documenting this ill-fated tour as a precursor of more positive things to come for South Africa; and for the Springboks as a team that has come to represent all of South Africa's people.

Chris Laidlaw

I

APARTHEID AND A TIME OF PROTEST

When Dawie de Villiers' Springboks landed at Heathrow Airport on a grey, cold and damp morning at the end of October 1969 for their tour of the United Kingdom, Nelson Mandela, as a prisoner of the South African government, was pick-swinging and shovelling in the limestone quarry on Robben Island. He had been on the island for five years, serving a life sentence for sabotage and high treason. Just a few miles off, across Table Bay, lay the city of Cape Town – so near and yet so far. News didn't reach the prisoners easily – it was deliberately kept away from them – but Mandela would soon learn about the protests in Britain. The white prison warders, all fanatical Springbok fans, were furious about the *betogers* (demonstrators), and came to see Mandela as the cause of it all.[1]

It's a small world, they say. And the wheel turns. Indeed it does. Twenty-five years later, his rugby career now long past, the former Springbok captain de Villiers was serving under President Nelson Mandela in the country's first Cabinet of National Unity. In time, a deep mutual respect developed between the two, and to Mandela, de Villiers was 'a highly capable and experienced South African who has made an excellent contribution to harmony in our nation.'[2]

De Villiers' first direct opponent of the 1969/70 tour, former All Black legend Chris Laidlaw, who then captained Oxford, later remarked that de Villiers was 'one of the more significant figures in recent South African history, as a highly visible leader of the Springboks at a time when the world was rapidly turning against apartheid. One of the key personalities in the acutely challenging political transformation of his country, his story lies at the heart of that tumultuous period when the world watched, fascinated by the global symbolism of that transformation.'[3]

The events of the tour again focused the world's attention on South Africa's problems, eventually advancing processes to change the South African political, social and sporting landscape. But what exactly was apartheid, where did it actually begin and why the violent protests in Britain and elsewhere?

Contrary to some popular perceptions, apartheid in South Africa did not suddenly come about when the National Party of D. F. Malan came to power in 1948. Its roots go way back to the expansion of Dutch and later British colonial settlements in the Cape, when land and livestock dispossession led to wars between the settlers and indigenous Khoikhoi, San and a number of black ethnic groups. With the increasing conquest of these groups arose the issue of how to deal with them, resulting in what the British colonial government in South Africa termed the 'Native question'.

One of the key legislations that laid down the foundation for a spatially divided South Africa was the Glen Grey Act of 1894. Drafted by the British imperialist Cecil John Rhodes, it was geared towards dealing with the three main issues of land, labour and the franchise. The Act provided for the division of all unalienated land in the Glen Grey district into locations, which were surveyed and divided into portions, while it also implemented provisions to limit the number of Africans who qualified for the franchise.[4]

Then in 1903, the Lagden Commission unanimously concluded that, in the interests of the Europeans, the country should be segregated and that land owned by Africans be held in trust for them, or subject to customary law was to be kept strictly separate in 'white' South Africa. The Commission played a pivotal role in a series of processes that laid down the foundation for the controversial 1913 Native Land Act and spatial segregation in South Africa. The Act, passed three years after South Africa had become the Union of South Africa, marked the beginning of territorial segregation.

The Act affected millions of Africans, its most catastrophic provision being the prohibition from buying or hiring land in 93 per cent of South Africa, closely followed by anti-squatting provisions to stop sharecropping. The effect of the Land Act was to eliminate black tenants and to replace them in white areas by black servants or labourers who would no longer be allowed to lease land in white areas. This alleviated the problem of poor white farm labourers who were competing for employment on farms with black labourers, pressure coming more especially from the provinces of the Transvaal and the Orange Free State. The Act thus went beyond just dispossessing people of their land, also closing avenues of livelihood for Africans other than to work for white farmers and industrialists.[5]

Opponents of the Act rallied to establish the South African National Native Congress (SANNC), which would eventually become the African National Congress (ANC) as we know it today. In 1914, the SANNC chose a delegation of five members, including the well-known black author Solomon T. Plaatje, to go to London, where they met missionaries and members of the Aborigines Protection Society. In spite of the delegation's petition to Parliament, the British government did not intervene in the matter.[6]

Following the passing of the Land Act, white farmers began issuing notices of eviction to black people. The position of African farmers was weakened further when the government began to offer low-interest loans to white farmers, enabling them to make improvements to their farms. African farmers who owned land inside and outside the reserves, on the other hand, did not receive any aid from the government in the form of loans and therefore found it increasingly difficult to compete with white farmers. So, by 1936, nearly half of the African workers living in towns had migrated from white farms.

The Great Depression and the Second World War brought increasing economic pressures to South Africa, and convinced the government to strengthen its policies of racial segregation. In 1948, the Afrikaner National Party won the general election under the slogan 'apartheid' (literally meaning 'separateness'), thereby deposing the United Party of General Jan Smuts. The Nationalists' goal was to separate South Africa's white minority from its non-white majority, as well as to divide black South Africans along tribal lines in order to decrease their political power.

Apartheid was now to be entrenched in legislation. By 1950, the South African government had banned marriages between whites and people of other races. The Immorality Amendment Act of 1950 forbade unmarried sexual intercourse between 'Europeans' and anyone not 'European', while the Population Registration Act, promulgated the same year, classified all South Africans by race, including Bantu (black Africans), coloured (mixed race) and white. A fourth category, Asian (meaning Indian and Pakistani), was later added. In some cases, the legislation split families; parents could be classified as white, while their children were classified as Coloured.[7]

The Group Areas Act of 1950 assigned racial groups to different residential and business sections in urban areas, which in effect excluded non-whites from living in areas which were restricted to whites, such as Sea Point and Claremont. This meant that many non-whites had to commute large distances from their homes in order to be able to work. Non-whites were forcibly removed for living in the 'wrong' areas, of which the old District Six in Cape Town was a prime example.[8] The non-white majority were given much smaller areas to live in than the white minority who owned most of the land. In addition, the Pass Laws required that non-whites carry pass books to enter the 'white' areas of the country.

The reign of Hendrik Verwoerd, who became Prime Minister in 1958, would refine the apartheid policy further into a system that he referred to as 'separate development'. The Promotion of Bantu Self-Government Act of 1959 created ten Bantu homelands known as *Bantustans*. Separating black South Africans from each other enabled the government to claim there was no black majority, and reduced the possibility that blacks would unify into one nationalist organisation. Every black South African was designated as a citizen of one of the *Bantustans*, a system that supposedly gave them full political rights but effectively removed them from the nation's political body. Over the next three decades, more than 3.5 million people were removed from their homes and deposited in the *Bantustans*, where most were plunged into poverty and hopelessness.[9]

By now, Nelson Mandela had emerged as a major political activist, playing a key role in writing the ANC's Freedom Charter, adopted in 1955. The Charter stated that South Africa belonged 'to all who live in it, black and white, and that no government can justly claim authority unless it is based on the will of all the people'. People's resistance to apartheid in South Africa over the years varied from non-violent demonstrations, protests and strikes to political action and eventually to armed resistance. The following year, 156 political activists, including Mandela and several of the ANC's leadership, were arrested and charged with treason. After a trial that lasted four and a half years, all the accused were eventually acquitted.

The so-called 'Sharpeville massacre' of 21 March 1960 was a turning point in the country's history. Following a day of demonstrations against the notorious pass laws, a crowd of an estimated 5,000 to 7,000 protesters descended on the police station in the township of Sharpeville. Just two months before, nine constables had been assaulted and killed during a raid at Cato Manor, and, feeling threatened, the police now opened fire on the crowd, killing 69 people and injuring 180 others. Police reports of the time claimed that young and inexperienced police officers panicked and opened fire spontaneously. The Sharpeville shootings led to a storm of international protest, including demonstrations in many countries and condemnation by the United Nations. South Africa found itself increasingly isolated in the international community and the event also played a role in South Africa's withdrawal from the Commonwealth of Nations the following year.[10]

The event at Sharpeville also contributed to the banning of the PAC and ANC as illegal organisations, and by 1961 most resistance leaders had been captured and sentenced to long prison terms or executed. Nelson Mandela, a founder of Umkhonto we Sizwe (Spear of the Nation), the military wing of the ANC, was sentenced to life imprisonment for organising sabotage at what became known as the Rivonia trial.[11] Along with other key comrades like Walter Sisulu, he was sent to Robben Island jail, where he was incarcerated from 1963 to March 1982, when he was transferred to Pollsmoor Prison in Cape Town. Mandela's imprisonment would draw international attention, and over the years he became a worldwide symbol of resistance to apartheid.

On the sporting front, South Africa's isolation in sport began in the mid-1950s and increased throughout the 1960s to the 1980s. Because of apartheid, which forbade multiracial sport, overseas teams including players of diverse races could not play in South Africa. Whites and non-whites had to organise their sporting activities separately so that there should be no interracial competitions within the country. As early as 1956, the International

Table Tennis Federation severed its ties with the all-white South African Table Tennis Union. South Africa still competed at the 1960 Olympics, but was banned from 1964 to 1988.

Major 'white' sports like rugby and cricket, though, remained relatively unaffected by international sports boycotts during the 1950s and 1960s. New Zealand's All Blacks toured South Africa in 1960 – with no Maori players – while the Wallabies toured South Africa in 1953, 1961, 1963 and 1969, and the British Lions visited in 1955, 1962 and 1968, as did teams like France (1958, 1964, 1967), Scotland (1960), Ireland (1961) and Wales (1964). In return, the Springboks toured New Zealand and Australia in 1956 and 1965, Ireland and Scotland in 1965, and France in 1968. In addition, before the Springboks' tour of 1969/70, tours to the United Kingdom and France also went ahead in 1951/52 and 1960/61. The proposed All Black tour of South Africa in 1967, however, was called off by the New Zealand government, and when the All Blacks finally returned to South Africa in 1970, Maori players were included. But to get around South Africa's racially based laws, star players like Bryan Williams and Sid Going were classified as 'honorary whites'.[12]

When B. J. Vorster took over as Prime Minister after the assassination of Verwoerd in 1966, he signalled a shift in sports policy by stating that South Africa would no longer dictate to other countries how their teams should be constituted. While this reopened opportunities for sporting events with other countries, it did not bring an end to South Africa's racist sporting policies. In fact, two years into his tenure Vorster contradicted his stated policy by refusing to permit Basil D'Oliveira, a Coloured South African-born cricketer, to join the English cricket team on its tour to South Africa. The Marylebone Cricket Club (MCC) had omitted D'Oliveira from the original squad, but following the withdrawal of Tom Cartwright due to injury he was eventually included. Vorster's reaction was to say that the side had been chosen only on political grounds and not on merit, and despite negotiations the tour was cancelled.[13]

Interestingly, D'Oliveira himself did not openly back the Anti-Apartheid Movement. To this Lord Peter Hain explained: 'He described himself as "a cricketer, not a politician", and had huge differences with Hassan Howa, president of the non-racial South African Cricket Board of Control, a rival to the apartheid-accepted, whites-only cricket body with which the rest of the world had traditionally had exclusive relations. Howa backed our protests, D'Oliveira did not.'[14]

Earlier protests against all-white South African cricket teams touring England in 1960 and 1965 were dismissed as 'feeble' by the secretary of the MCC and had virtually no impact on the sport. The 'D'Oliveira Affair', however, again focused wider public attention on apartheid in sport, initiating an international protest movement against the policy. The result was South Africa's exclusion from international test match cricket for more than two decades.

South African rugby managed to hold out longer. Following New Zealand's cancellation of their South African tour in 1967 and Prime Minister John Vorster's proclamation that his government would no longer prescribe rules about the racial composition of sports teams visiting South Africa, pressure on rugby increased from all sides while the majority of the country's white inhabitants were hungry for Test rugby. Blacks, on the other hand, saw the Springboks as a symbol of apartheid, and groups such as the South African Council on Sport (SACOS) advocated for fundamental sporting reform within South Africa.[15]

This was a time of several protest movements around the world, including the civil rights movement, the anti-Vietnam War movement, the women's movement and the gay rights movement, and supporters of these movements questioned traditional attitudes about how people should be treated. This inspired people to begin organising movements to fight against injustice – as against apartheid – and for equal rights for all people. To make their point, these protesters encouraged and engaged in direct action like public marches, picketing, sit-ins, and other measures.

In the United States, activists against the country's involvement in Vietnam became increasingly radical and demonstrations turned violent when the police arrived to arrest protesters. The famous boxer Muhammad Ali was one of those who refused to go to war, stating that he would not aid 'the domination of white slavemasters over dark people'. Other individual athletes also made a stand for their beliefs on the big stage. At the 1968 Olympics in Mexico City, African American athletes Tommie Smith (gold) and John Carlos (bronze) each raised a black-gloved fist during the playing of the US national anthem in what Smith later labelled as not a 'Black Power' salute but rather a 'human rights salute'. At the same Olympics, Czech gymnast Vera Caslavska, who had won 11 medals at the 1960, 1964 and 1968 Games, deliberately turned her head away as the Czech and USSR flags were raised side by side to show her opposition to the Soviet invasion of Czechoslovakia in August of that year.

These protests around the world would spill over to liberal Britain, where apartheid activists, led by Peter Hain (now Lord Peter Hain), actively made their voices heard. Hain came from a family of anti-apartheid activists. His parents, Walter and Adelaine Hain, campaigned against apartheid as members of the Liberal Party of South Africa while living in Pretoria, but they emigrated to the United Kingdom during the 1960s in the face of constant harassment from the South African security forces. Peter Hain was educated at Pretoria Boys High School before continuing his studies at British universities, so he and his family had first-hand experience of South Africa and its racial problems. In the UK he became chairman of the Stop the Seventy Tour (STST) campaign, which aimed at disrupting or halting the Springbok rugby and cricket tours in 1969 and 1970. Not surprisingly, Hain joined the Young Liberals (YLs) and still later the Labour Party. The Young Liberals developed their highest public profile in the 1960s and early 1970s, when they campaigned on issues as diverse as trade union policy, the Middle East and apartheid, while other radical youth organisations such as the Trotskyists and Maoists were more engaged in anti-Vietnam demonstrations than apartheid protests.[16]

The Young Liberals and the Liberal Party were usually in broad agreement on major issues, but they differed over the degree of radicalism and the methods of campaigning, especially the preference of some YLs for direct action, which intensified in the late 1960s. By 1969, the party's annual report noted that, even as the YLs' membership was declining, there was 'new militancy' in the organisation, 'with particular emphasis on campaigns of civil disobedience', specifically protests against international tours by all-white South African tennis and cricket teams.[17]

Prior to the Springboks arriving in the British Isles the demonstrators had already showed their intent with demonstrations and disruptions during the Wilf Isaacs cricket tour in England. The Wilf Isaacs XI, the brainchild of businessman Wilf Isaacs, included former South African Test players like Neil Adcock, Ken Funston, Jackie McGlew, Roy McLean and Hugh Tayfield, as well as three promising young players in Barry Richards, Mike Proctor and Lee Irvine. Before the tour Isaacs stressed, 'We have no intention of being drawn into any arguments. Our aim is to provide some joy for the genuine cricket lovers.'[18]

Led by Hain, the Stop the Seventy Tour activists were determined to protest against a team which included no players of colour. They disrupted the tour, among others ways, by occupying the pitch until removed by the police, digging a furrow through the historic Parks Ground at Oxford, stomping stones into the pitch at The Oval and throwing smoke bombs in Leinster. Wilf Isaacs was cursed as 'Fascist scum' – an ironic insult seeing that he was an ex-fighter pilot who had fought against Adolf Hitler's forces during the Second World War. According to Isaacs, some of the demonstrators told him they had been paid – one even by the BBC – to demonstrate.[19] This would also be the case during the rugby tour later. Legendary Springbok Frik du Preez recalled that during a demonstration in front of their hotel in Dublin, the rain washed off the wording 'Go home Springboks' on one of the placards, only to show underneath 'Ban the bombing in Vietnam'.[20]

Of all the Springboks who had gone on the 1969/70 tour, the outspoken vice captain of the side, Tommy Bedford, who had studied at Oxford for three years before the tour, had the best idea of the extent of the troubles awaiting the team. He recalled that on the evening before their departure from Johannesburg, a massive farewell function was held for the team in Johannesburg and that every VIP, from the State President to the Mayor of Johannesburg, had attended. 'This while the anti-apartheid activist Peter Hain and his comrades in Britain had for several months been busy with plans to disrupt or even halt the tour through protest action.'

'Various patriotic speeches were delivered during the party. Morale was high, because since 1967 the Boks had beaten France, the British Lions and Australia on the rugby field. At the end of the evening I was also given a chance to speak as vice-captain, but I put a damper on the proceedings by warning that events would become rough off the field and that consequently the team may be less successful on the field. My remarks were dismissed as nothing less than treason.'[21] As things turned out during the tour, Bedford's observations were those of a man who knew what he was talking about.

Like Wilf Isaacs and his team, the rugby Springboks were only interested in playing their sport, but they would soon discover it was not that simple. By the time Dawie de Villiers' Sixth Springboks arrived at Heathrow at the end of October 1969, the demonstrators were ready for them. The tour turned out to be the first South African overseas tour to be dramatically disrupted by violent demonstrations in protest against apartheid. The initial focus of STST was the cricket tour, but as the South African rugby team was scheduled to come to England before the cricketers (the rugby Springboks' first appearance in England since 1960/61), STST decided to target the rugby tour as a dry run for the cricket tour the following summer. Hain warned British sporting authorities that 'their complicity in apartheid sport will no longer be tolerated', and one week later the Liberal Party called for the rugby tour to be cancelled. The rugby tour went ahead but was met with sustained protests, as we will see in the chapters to follow. According to Hain, the 25-match tour attracted over 50,000 demonstrators, who had to be controlled by more than 20,000 police officers.[22]

2

A PROUD TRADITION

The Springboks in the UK, 1906/07 to 1960/61

Dawie de Villiers' Springbok touring side was known as the Sixth Springboks, as they were the sixth South African team to tour the United Kingdom and France since the first tour of 1906/07 by Paul Roos' men. The team had big boots to fill, as all the former touring sides to the UK had been very successful, with proud winning records. Over those five previous tours in Britain, the Springboks had in total won 132 matches out of 145, including 19 Tests out of 20, and suffered only eight defeats with five drawn. Their only Test defeat during all those years was to Scotland in 1906 (0-6), their very first Test ever played in Britain.[1]

The British invitation for South Africa to send a team for the first tour of 1906/07 created huge interest in South African rugby circles. Until then, the country had hosted three British touring sides, in 1891, 1896 and 1903, but had never sent a team to tour overseas. The British were easily on top in 1891 (3-0 series win) and in 1896 (3-1 series win), South Africa achieving its first success ever against a British side by winning the final Test. The referee was none other than Alf Richards, the South African half back of the 1891 series. In 1903, the first two Tests were drawn but South

Africa won the final Test to claim a first-ever series victory. South Africa would not lose another Test series – home or away – until 1956, when they were conquered by New Zealand. This final 1903 Test also marked the first time they had worn the green Old Diocesan (Bishops) shirts, which would become the team's national colours.[2]

New Zealand toured the British Isles in 1905 and suffered only one defeat, against Wales. Wales would therefore be the benchmark for the South Africans as to where they stood in terms of international rugby. The Welsh style, however, was unknown to the South Africans, whose game was founded on the lessons taught by the British Isles touring teams. The South Africans therefore had no idea of how successful they would be in Britain.

The 1906/07 Springboks

The South African team was selected at the end of the 1906 Currie Cup tournament in Johannesburg, which was won by Western Province. As could be expected, then, the touring side was dominated by members from Western Province, with 14 players. Transvaal contributed five, Griqualand West five, Border three and Eastern Province one. The side was to be captained by Paul Roos,[3] with Paddy Carolin[4] as vice captain. An interesting coincidence was that Sommie Morkel, who fought with the Boers during the Boer War, was about to 'renew' battle with Britain, so to speak. Taken prisoner by Lord Roberts' forces at Paardeberg, he had been sent to St Helena with other Boer War prisoners. While on the island, the Boer POWs played a lot of rugby after Dutch sympathisers sent eight rugby balls to the men on the island. Two other South African players – Billy Millar, who became captain of the 1912/13 touring side, and William (Rajah) Martheze – fought on the side of the British forces during the Boer War, but now Morkel, Millar and Martheze were teammates. There were also two brothers in the side, Japie and Pietie le Roux.

The South Africans arrived at Southampton on the night of 19 September 1906, where they were greeted by Rowland Hill and Johnny Hammond of the English Rugby Union, and a contingent of reporters and photographers. Hammond was a former member of the 1891 British Isles team that toured South Africa, and acted as a kind of public relations officer. When interviewed about the kind of game they were going to play, captain Paul Roos replied: 'We have not come here to teach you the game; we have not any mysterious tricks to show you; no, we have come here to play a good straightforward, honest, sportsmanlike game; to learn what we can of your methods, and to enjoy good sport.'

Team manager J. C. Carden recalled that the Springbok, as a badge, already existed when they left South Africa. The *Daily Mail* of 20 September 1906 reported: 'The team's colours will be myrtle green jerseys with gold collar. They will wear dark blue shorts and dark blue stockings, and the jerseys will have embroidered in mouse-coloured silk on the left breast a Springbok, a small African antelope which is as typical of Africa as the kangaroo of Australia.' Carden also said that before the London press could invent some funny name for the team, the management agreed to call them the 'Springboks' and to tell pressmen that they desired to be so named.[5]

In the Tests, the Boks started off on the wrong foot, losing 0-6 to Scotland in Glasgow. They took the field without the imposing presence of tour captain Paul Roos, who was too ill to play, and the side was led by half back Paddy Carolin. The big one, of course, was the Wales Test at the St Helens Ground in Swansea. Many years later, Springbok centre Boy de Villiers, one of the so called 'Thin Red Line',[6] still recalled the Test as the most memorable event of his playing days: 'No other crowd in the world is quite like the Welsh crowd at a rugby international, and on that day their pride for Welsh rugby, their fierce enthusiasm, they made the most marvellous picture I have ever seen on a football ground. While they waited they sang, as Welsh crowds always do,

"Land of My Fathers". As the words of that stirring anthem rose into the air they swayed, all 40 000 of them, to and fro in perfect rhythm. It was a wonderful and never-to-be-forgotten sight.'[7]

The Springboks of 1906/07 had an adventurous approach, their slogan being 'attack is the best form of defence', and time and again, when hard pressed, they would launch an attack from their own 25. This was possible due to the great speed and fine handling of their backs; in fact, they had to rely on their backs to a large extent, as their forwards were not yet the powerful scrumming force of later years. They played 29 matches, winning 26, losing only two and drawing one, scoring 608 points with only 85 against. The tour was a great triumph for the Boks' flying wing Bob Loubser,[8] who scored 24 tries in 21 games – still a South African record for most tries by a Springbok on a tour.[9]

The 1912/13 Springboks

The 1912/13 South Africa rugby union tour of Europe was a series of friendly rugby union games undertaken by the South Africa side against England, Scotland, Ireland, Wales and France. The tour also took in several matches against British and Irish club, county and invitational teams. This was the second South African tour of the northern hemisphere after the very successful 1906 tour.

Billy Millar was the tour captain. He was the last person chosen for the tour and was not the selectors' choice of captain, but they were overruled by the South African Rugby Board. Millar did have the advantage of being one of the few players to have toured Britain in the previous tour, but was seen by the hosts as a fiery character and was not as popular with the players or fans as the 1906/07 tour captain, Paul Roos. The other two members of the squad to have played in the 1906 tour were vice captain Fred 'Uncle' Dobbin and Dougie Morkel.

There were two sets of brothers in the touring party: Richard, Freddie and John Luyt; and Gerhard and Jack Morkel. It is interesting to note that Paddy Carolin, who was a keen student of rugby and wrote numerous articles on the sport, attributed the first half back dive-passes to Freddie Luyt, who used the move to protect himself from forwards trying to pounce on him (it surely wasn't Danie Craven, as some people still believe). Gerhard Morkel would have a long career in the Springbok jersey and was still playing for South Africa in 1921. One of the centres in the side, Willie Krige, was the brother of the famous Japie. Their other brother, Jan, who studied at Guy's Hospital, played centre for England in 1920.

The Springboks won all the Tests on tour, beating Scotland 16-0, Ireland 38-0, Wales 3-0, England 9-3 and, after the British leg of the tour, France 38-5. They played 27 matches, winning 24, but lost to Newport (3-9), London (8-10) and Swansea (0-3), scoring 441 points with 101 against. Their runaway victory of 38-0 against Ireland was their biggest of the tour. In the Test, the two Springbok wings Jan Stegmann and Boetie McHardy both scored a hat-trick of tries. McHardy finished the tour with 20 tries.

The 1931/32 Springboks

Apart from the tactical genius of captain Bennie Osler, the 1931/32 side was known for its formidable pack of forwards that included the likes of Boy Louw, Phil Mostert, Philip Nel (the captain of the famous 1937 side that won the Test series in New Zealand), Ferdie Bergh, Lucas Strachan and George Daneel. Also included in the side was young Stellenbosch scrum half Danie Craven, who had not even played for Western Province when he was selected for the tour. He was to become a legend in his own time, known around the rugby world as 'Mr Rugby' for his superb rugby brain and service to the game over decades.

At the time, the Revd George Daneel was already an ordained minister of religion. At their departure by ship from Cape Town, and on hearing that he had to share a cabin with Daneel, the rugged forward Phil Mostert asked the team manager, Theo Pienaar, in jest: 'Uncle Theo, what do you have against me?'

'Why, Phil?' asked Pienaar, somewhat taken aback.

'Well, why do you let me share a cabin with a minister?!'

Revd Daneel also recalled that as captain for the Springboks against the tough men of Swansea, he had a hard time to control his players. Fists and boots were flying from both ends and a few of the Boks threw in some foul language too. After a while this became just too much for Daneel. 'Listen, boys,' he said to his mates, 'hit and kick these guys or even spit at them if you have to, but for God's sake, stop *swearing*!'[10] Daneel served as a chaplain in Europe and North Africa during the Second World War. He was the only Springbok to live to 100 years. He died in 2004.

1951/52 *Springboks*

As the first South African team to visit Britain since Bennie Osler's team with its dour 10-man style, the 1951/52 players was deeply conscious of the fact that they had a special responsibility to improve the image of Springbok rugby created 20 years before. They had an early setback when captain Basil Kenyon suffered a career-ending eye injury in the third match of the tour at Pontypool, but his successor, No. 8 Hennie Muller, turned out to be an outstanding leader.

Their great strength was their continuity and ability to play at pace, which demanded superb fitness, good handling and mobility in the forwards. The Springboks played 31 matches, won 30 (including all the Tests) and lost only one (9-11 against London Counties), scoring 562 points with 167 against. Their four wings – Chum Ochse (15), Buks Marais, Martin Saunders and Paul Johnstone – scored 47 tries, about 40 per cent of their total. The great Welsh and British Lions lock Roy John described these Boks as the best side he had ever played against, saying they had a world-class pack of forwards with 'more than adequate backs'.[11]

The tour will be especially remembered for the 44-0 drubbing of Scotland at Murrayfield, a world record victory that stood for many years. Springbok centre Ryk van Schoor recalled that before the match, Hennie Muller and coach Dr Danie Craven stepped onto the pitch and, feeling the firm surface, Muller immediately declared, 'Doc, we're going to give them a hiding here today.'[12] Craven told him not to be so complacent, but Muller was spot on. The Test match against Wales, won 6-3, proved to be their toughest, and it was only a record fourth successive Test drop goal by Hansie Brewis that sealed the game for them. The match also marked the international debut of the great Welshman Cliff Morgan, a sensation for the British Lions three years later in South Africa.

1960/61 *Springboks*

The Fifth Springbok tourists of 1960/61 under captain Avril Malan played a ruthless, forward-oriented game and were characterised by rigid discipline. The squad included all the players from the series against the All Blacks three months previously, won 2-1 by the Springboks, so they would have arrived in Britain with a lot of confidence in their ability to beat the best the British Isles could offer. The team manager was Ferdie Bergh, with the colourful Boy Louw as coach and assistant manager. Both were forward stalwarts from the 1931/32 Springbok tour to Britain and were therefore familiar with the conditions the Boks could expect.

The great Frik du Preez, then a newcomer on his first overseas tour and the only survivor from this tour among the later 1969/70 squad, recalled that they had hoped to play attractive rugby. They had, after all, exciting runners in their backs like John Gainsford, Mannetjies Roux, Hennie van Zyl, Jannie Engelbrecht and Mike Antelme. And their forwards were all much quicker and showed superior combined speed on to the ball, which had been a key factor in the Boks' victory over the All Blacks. But the tour coincided with one of the worst British winters, with conditions generally unsuited to festival rugby. They nevertheless drew much criticism from the British press for what was perceived as dour rugby.[13]

Like their predecessors of 1912/13, 1931/32 and 1951/52, these Boks completed another Grand Slam, beating Wales 3-0 on a quagmire of a pitch at the Arms Park, Ireland 8-3 in Dublin, England 5-0 at Twickenham and Scotland 12-5 at Murrayfield. By the end of the tour, before their final game against the Barbarians in Cardiff, the Boks were still unbeaten, but they were conquered 6-0 by the Barbarians, with their formidable pack, in an uncharacteristically pragmatic game. They also played four games in France, drawing the Test 0-0 with the *tricolores*.

In the British Isles, they played 30 matches, won 28, drew one and only lost to the Barbarians, scoring 476 points with 110 against. In the Tests, they scored 28 points and only conceded eight points in total.

At the time of the tour, South Africa had already been experiencing problems on the political front because of apartheid, though it did not affect the rugby tour at all. As seen in the previous chapter, the Sharpeville shootings in March 1960 led to a storm of international protest in many countries and condemnation by the United Nations. Finding itself increasingly isolated in the international community, South Africa eventually withdrew from the Commonwealth of Nations in 1961. This happened after the Fifth Springboks had finished their tour of the British Isles and France in February 1961.

But as British rugby journalist J. B. G. Thomas wrote, 'It is the wish of rugby men that the Springboks remain, always, a member of the rugby brotherhood.'

3

THE SIXTH SPRINGBOKS

On 4 October 1969, having watched the Currie Cup final between Northern Transvaal and Western Province at Loftus Versfeld in Pretoria, the five Springbok selectors, Avril Malan, Johan Claassen, Butch Lochner, Ian Kirkpatrick and Tjol Lategan – all former Springboks – sat down at their hotel in Johannesburg to select the Springbok touring team to take on the best of Britain. Northern Transvaal had just hammered Province 28-13 and the Blue Bulls and veteran Springbok lock Frik du Preez had a blinder, scoring a great try and landing a dropkicked penalty from just inside his own half and another 50-yarder from a place kick. Here was one player about which there was no doubt.

When the side was announced, it had eight players from Western Province, runners-up to Northern Transvaal in the Currie Cup final, and only six from Northern Transvaal, much to the dismay of the Blue Bulls supporters; there were also three Natal and two Transvaal players. Rural unions were well represented, with Western Transvaal boasting four players, Griqualand West two and Boland two, including the captain Dawie de Villiers. South West Africa, Eastern Province and North Eastern Cape had one representative each. For once, there were no Free State players in a Springbok touring team.

The Springbok Squad

Notes: Number of Tests as at the start of the tour.

PAUL JACOBUS DURAND (Western Transvaal). Full back. 5 ft 11 in. 182 lb. New cap. Born 21 January 1946 in Benoni. Played 40 matches for the province since 1965. He played at outside half for West Transvaal and kicked four goals against the British Lions on their 1968 tour in South Africa. Injuries later prevented him from completing the tour. Sport instructor.

HENRY OSWALD (HO) DE VILLIERS (Western Province). Full back. 5 ft 9 in. 187 lb. 10 Tests. Born 10 March 1945 in Johannesburg. Humble but fearless, revolutionised full back play in South Africa by attacking from anywhere. Test debut vs France in 1967, became one of the stars of the tour. There were worries about his fitness early on tour, but in all he made 16 appearances, 11 of those consecutive. A likable man, he was one of the happy tourists. His best match was arguably the test against Wales in Cardiff in difficult muddy conditions. He scored 56 points, the second most on tour, which included two tries. Insurance salesman.

RENIER NICOLAAS GROBLER (Northern Transvaal). Wing. New cap. 5 ft. 10 ½ in. 185 lb. Born 14 Nov. 1946 in Luanshya. Nickname of *Rysmier* (White Ant). He had made only five appearances for Northern Transvaal before being selected for the Springbok tour. He played in 11 matches and scored four tries. Unfortunately he suffered a hand injury at Limerick and could not be considered for the team's last five matches. Loves talking and teasing teammates. SA Air Force technician.

ANDREW EDWARD (ANDY) VAN DER WATT (Western Province). Wing. 5 ft. 9 in. 175 lb. New cap. Born 10 October 1946 in Krugersdorp. Played 10 matches for Western Province. He played in the first match and 17 in total. Made his test debut when he came on for the injured Gert Muller in the second half against Scotland. Also played against England and Ireland but lost place to Muller again in the Welsh test. Scored seven tries on tour. Very quick with a powerful handoff, very dangerous on the inside step. Student teacher.

GERT HENDRIK MULLER (Western Province). Wing. 2 Tests. 6 ft. 197 lb. Born 10 May 1948 in Vryheid, Natal. Capped for the first time against Australia in 1969 for the third and fourth tests. A track runner at university, he's a powerful, devastating runner. Before the first match of the tour had to return home to attend the funeral of his father. He missed out on their first seven matches and after injury against Scotland sat out the next 10 matches. In the end he only played in six matches, scoring five tries, including four against the North of Scotland. Student at Stellenbosch University.

SYDNEY HAROLD NOMIS (Transvaal). Wing/centre. 5 ft. 9 in. 175 lb. 11 Tests (all wins). Born 15 November 1941 in Johannesburg, the only Jew in the side. Played 50 matches for Transvaal. Made 16 appearances on tour, and scored three tries which was a poor reflection of his true ability. Missed the first two matches because of injury, but thereafter was never out of the side for more than one match at a time. He played in all four tests. A great team man. His captain Dawie de Villiers said of him, 'Under difficult circumstances it is a great bonus to have positive guys in the team, and I immediately think of someone like Sid Nomis. He was never moody, never complained. He was always open, positive, friendly with a bubbly personality. He loved everyone and everyone loved him. My mother always said that it was a good thing to have Sid Nomis in the team, every team should have a Jew, it would bring luck.' Sales manager.

JOHANN PHILMAN VAN DER MERWE (Western Province). Centre. New cap. 5 ft. 9 in. Born 7 December 1947 in Uitenhage. Quick, hard-running centre. Nickname of *Phantom* because of his ability to glide through gaps. Played 11 games for Western Province, including the match against the 1968 British Lions. He played in

13 matches on tour, the first on the wing against Oxford. He was steady and accurate and made his test debut against Wales, and was one of the successes of the tour. Very popular socially and a close tour friend of Andy van der Watt, his fellow student at Stellenbosch University. Student.

PIETER JOHANNES (JOHAN) VAN DER SCHYFF (Western Transvaal). Centre. New cap. 5 ft. 8½in. 170 lb. Born 19 January 1942 in Ventersdorp. Played 60 matches for Transvaal and 15 for Western Transvaal, also played for the Gazelles, Junior Springboks and SA Barbarians. Played in only three matches before injuries prevented him from completing the tour. Farmer.

OCKERT ANTONIE (TONIE) ROUX (Northern Transvaal). Centre. New cap. 5 ft. 10½in. 165 lb. Born 22 February 1947 in Pretoria. Played in six matches for Northern Transvaal, toured France in 1968 with the Springboks. One of the successes of the tour. Swift around the field and excellent handling and kicking. Along with Mof Myburgh played the most games on tour (19), playing 15 in the centre and four at full back. A happy tourist. Student.

EBENHAEZER (EBEN) OLIVIER (Western Province). Centre. 14 Tests. 5 ft. 8 in. 165 lb. Born 10 April 1944 in Kirkwood. Most experienced three-quarter, having made his test debut in 1967 against France. Made 35 appearances for Western Province. Known for his mesmerising darting runs. First choice at centre until his hamstring injury against England. Played in 11 of the first 14 matches, then two more but missed out on the Welsh test and Barbarians game. A quiet, pleasant tourist. Teacher.

PETRUS JACOBUS (PIET) VISAGIE (Griqualand West). Fly half. 14 Tests. 5 ft. 8 in. 157 lb. Born 16 April 1943 in Kimberley. At the time held the world record for the most points in a Test series (43 vs Australia in 1969). Struggled to adapt to British conditions. Lost confidence as the tour progressed and his place-kicking accuracy deserted him. Being a key player in their tactical approach, his poor form was a blow to the hopes of the side. Nevertheless played in 15 matches, including the Scotland and England tests, and was top scorer with 61 points. Mine paymaster.

MICHAEL JOHN (MIKE) LAWLESS (Western Province). 1 Test, last played for South Africa in 1964 in the one-off Test vs France (lost 6-8). 5 ft 8½ in. 165 lb. Born 17 September 1942 in Cape Town. Made 34 appearances for Western Province. A surprise choice as many thought Transvaal's Springbok Jannie Barnard would be backup to Visagie. Had a very good game against Cardiff that won him a place in the tests against Ireland and Wales. Known as a 'dreamer'. Played in 15 games including a few in the centre. Sales representative.

DAWID JACOBUS (DAWIE) DE VILLIERS (Boland). Captain and scrum half. 5 ft 7½ in. Born 10 July 1940 in Burgersdorp. 18 Tests, Springbok captain since 1965. Made his debut for the Springboks vs the 1962 British Lions. Missed the 1963 and 1964 internationals because of a serious knee injury, but recovered very well to lead the Springboks on their tour of Australia and New Zealand in 1965. Captained the national side in series in 1967 vs France (home), in 1968 vs British Lions and France (away), and vs Australia in 1969 (home). Played in 14 matches on tour, but missed the test against Scotland because of a flu. Proved himself as a world class player on the tour. Showed a swift pass and brilliant blindside breaks to trouble the opposition. Maintained a pleasant dignity on and off the field, easy to approach and willing at all times to meet and answer reporters. A former minister of religion until before the tour, then lecturer in theology in Johannesburg.

DIRK JOHANNES JACOBUS (DIRK) DE VOS (Western Transvaal). Scrum half. 2 Tests. 5 ft 6 in. 165 lb. The shortest man in the side. Born 8 April 1941 in Kroonstad. An experienced player with 47 inter-province matches since 1964 for Western Province, Free State, Transvaal and Western Transvaal. His two Test caps were gained in 1965 and 1969. Known for sniping breaks around the fringes but also a good tactical kicker. Strong and determined but somewhat of an individualist. A quiet man but who can get very excited on the field. Personnel officer.

THOMAS PLYDELL (TOMMY) BEDFORD (Natal). No. 8/flank and vice captain. 19 Tests, 2 as captain. 6 ft. 183 lb. Born 8 February 1942 in Bloemfontein. Studied at Oxford University for three years prior to the tour. An outstanding member of the team, who was very valuable to the side off the field as a kind of technical adviser on British affairs and tactics. Played 52 games for Natal and in England also played for Richmond. A sincere, modest and popular man among the players. Made 16 appearances on tour, of which seven were as captain, including the Test against Scotland when Dawie de Villiers had been down with flu. Missed last match vs Barbarians because of injury. Architect.

MICHAEL WILLIAM (MIKE) JENNINGS (Boland). No. 8. New cap. 6 ft. 2 in. 205 lb. Son of the 1937 Springbok Cecil B Jennings. Born 21 December 1946 in Randfontein. Played under Springbok captain Dawie de Villiers for Boland, and before that for North Eastern Cape. On tour he played in the shadow of the vice captain Tommy Bedford, but developed well in the best tradition of Springbok rugby. A pleasant man who made 11 appearances on tour and scored two tries. Teacher.

PIETER JOHANNES FREDERICK (PIET) GREYLING (Northern Transvaal). Flank. 11 Tests. 6 ft. 2 in. 195 lb. Born 16 May 1942 in Zastron. Part of the formidable Springbok Test backrow with Jan Ellis and Tommy Bedford. Played for Rhodesia, Free State and Transvaal. A tall, lean and strong player with good pace and sure hands; a very hard worker and deadly tackler. Greyling played in 14 matches, including all four Tests and the Barbarians game, in which he proved himself as one of the very best players on tour. He scored tries in both the England and Ireland Tests. Sales representative.

JAN HENDRIK ELLIS (South West Africa). Flank. 18 Tests. 6 ft 1½ in. 215 lb. Born 5 January 1943 in Brakpan. Arguably the fittest forward in world rugby at the time. Toured Australia and New Zealand with the Springboks in 1965. A shoulder injury caused him to make only four appearances in the first 17 matches, and then played in five more matches, in which he scored two tries apiece in the games against Llanelli and the Barbarians. In his 10 appearances he became top try scorer with eight. Deceptively fast, Ellis could run and handle like a back. Finished the tour as the star of the Springboks vs Barbarians game at Twickenham. Business executive.

PIETER IGNATIUS (PIET) VAN DEVENTER (Griqualand West). Flank. New cap. 6 ft. 197 lb. Born 6 June 1946 in Krugersdorp. Played his first match against the Eastern Counties at Leicester and scored a try on debut. He made 12 appearances and scored five tries. Had speed and a good positional sense. Another young player who developed well on tour. Mine compound manager.

ALBERT JACOBUS (ALBIE) BATES (Western Transvaal). Flank/No. 8. New cap. 6 ft 3 in. 206 lb. Born 18 April 1941 in Germiston. Tall and energetic, could also play lock if the need arose. He played well in Aberavon and in Cardiff in Wales and won a starting place against England in the absence of Jan Ellis. He made 12 appearances, but never really regained his best form after the England Test. After the tour he went on to play in the first two Tests against Brian Lochore's All Blacks at No. 8. Mining shift boss.

GABRIËL (GAWIE) CARELSE (Eastern Province). Lock. 13 Tests. 6 ft. 4 in. 240 lb. Born 21 July 1941 in Port Elizabeth. Had been playing for Eastern Province since 1961 and captained the province from 1967 to 1969. Big and powerful in the true Springbok tradition and had to stand in as prop against the Southern Counties at Gloucester at the end of the tour. He played in 11 matches on tour and also took on place-kicking duties on occasion. A likeable gentle giant and a good tourist. Motor garage owner.

FREDERICK CHRISTOFFEL HENDRIK (FRIK) DU PREEZ (Northern Transvaal). Lock/flank. 26 Tests. 6 ft 2 in. 230 lb. Born 28 November 1935 in Dwaalboom. Played for Northern Transvaal for 12 seasons. The man BBC commentator Bill McLaren said can 'leap like a salmon and run like a stag'. Very fast for a forward, he ran on the Air Force relay team in his day and made his debut on the flank against England in 1960 on the Springbok tour of the UK. Played in 14 matches on tour, including three tests. Destined to become South Africa's Player of the Century. Air Force lieutenant.

ANDRÉ ELOFF DE WET (Western Province). Lock. 6 ft 4½ in. 225 lb. Two caps (3rd and 4th Tests vs Australia 1969). Born 1 August 1946 in Kokstad. Played for Western Province for two seasons before the tour. He started the tour with cartilage trouble and could never gain his best form, although he won another Test cap against England. He played in 10 matches on tour, and made way for replacement lock Sakkie de Klerk in the next Tests. Student.

MARTHINUS COENRAAD (MARTIN) JANSE VAN RENSBURG (Natal). Lock. New cap. 6 ft. 5 in. 228 lb. Born 29 December 1944 in Ladysmith (Natal). He played for Natal for four seasons before the tour. He was seriously injured at Swansea and had to be hospitalised with a bad back injury, and therefore missed the major part of the tour. He only played in six matches and never had the chance to push for a Test berth. Also took on place-kicking duties at times. Market agent.

JOHANNES LODEWICKUS (MOF) MYBURGH (Northern Transvaal). Loosehead prop. 6 ft. 1 in. 250 lb. 13 Tests. Born 24 August 1936 in Senekal. One of the most experienced players in the team as he had toured with the Springboks through the UK in 1960/61 and played 98 matches for Northern Transvaal. Along with

Tonie Roux he played the most games on tour (19). He scrummed well and supported well at line-out time, and was a very powerful, hard but clean player. A very close friend of Frik du Preez, had a dry sense of humour and was a happy tourist. Police lieutenant.

RONALD (RONNIE) POTGIETER (Northern Transvaal). Tighthead prop. New cap. 6 ft. 240 lb. Born 18 November 1943 in Thabazimbi. Played 30 matches for Northern Transvaal before being selected for the Boks. Very powerful tighthead who ran out in seven matches on tour and may well have gained a Test cap if not for badly torn knee ligaments early in the match against the South Western Counties at Exeter. His leg was put in plaster and he returned home on 7 January 1970. A happy tourist who made the most of it. Engineering student.

JOHANNES FREDERICK KLOPPER (HANNES) MARAIS (North Eastern Cape). Tighthead prop. One of the stalwarts in the squad with 16 Tests. 6 ft. 217 lb. Born 21 September 1941 in Somerset East. He had played provincial rugby since 1963 for Western Province, Eastern Province and North Eastern Cape. A very mobile prop who is excellent on the cover defence. He made 16 appearances and scored three tries. Captained the side on two occasions in the absence of Dawie de Villiers and Tommy Bedford. Destined to become captain of the undefeated Springbok side in Australia in 1971 and the Springboks vs Willie John McBride's formidable British and Irish Lions in 1974. Agriculture lecturer.

JACOBUS BURGER (TINY) NEETHLING (Western Province). Loosehead prop. 6 ft. 1 in. 228 lb. 5 Tests. Born 6 July 1939 in Rawsonville. A mobile and skilled prop who could also play at lock or No. 8 when needed. An experienced and versatile player who had been playing for Western Province since 1961. Neethling made 12 appearances, even one at hooker against the North Western Counties when injuries demanded drastic changes. A cheerful and pleasant tourist. Sales representative.

GYSBERTUS (GYS) PITZER (Northern Transvaal). Hooker. 5 ft 11 in. 195 lb. 12 Tests. Born 8 July 1939 in Louis Trichardt. He had played 40 matches for Northern Transvaal before the tour and was familiar with the Blue Bulls props Mof Myburgh and Ronnie Potgieter. A good, robust forward and a quick striker of the ball. Having already suffered back trouble during the 1969 Australia series, he unfortunately injured his back after only two matches at Leicester and Newport and had to be detained in the hospital at Swansea for treatment, and then had to return home after the Scotland Test. He never played for the Springboks again. Electrical contractor.

DONALD CAMERON (DON) WALTON (Natal). Hooker. 7 Tests. 6 ft. 185 lb. Born 5 April 1939 in Durban. He had played 73 matches for Natal since 1961 before the tour. A very mobile hooker and a fast striker of the ball. In one match he suffered a cracked rib, and having recovered suffered a depressed fracture of the forehead in another match and had to be operated on, but he nevertheless managed to play in 10 matches, including the Test against England. He was an excellent tourist with a keen sense of humour. Like Pitzer, he never played for South Africa again.

REPLACEMENTS:

IZAAK JOHANNES (SAKKIE) DE KLERK (Transvaal). Lock. 6 ft. 4 in. 229 lb. Played his first game in the eighth match of the tour, vs New Brighton-North of Ireland, after the injury to Martin van Rensburg. He made 10 appearances on tour. Not being fit yet for the first Test, he did play in the next three against England, Ireland and Wales. Public relations officer.

FRANCOIS DU TOIT (MANNETJIES) ROUX (Griqualand West). Centre/wing. 5 ft 7 in. 170 lb. 22 caps. Toured with the Springboks through the UK in 1960/61 and one of the most experienced players. An unorthodox, instinctive player about whom an opponent once remarked, 'You never know what he's going to do next', to which a teammate of Mannetjies replied, 'Don't worry, we never know either!' Roux played his first game in the 17th match of the tour, vs Northern Counties at Gosforth, and made five appearances in total, including the Ireland Test. Farmer.

ROBBIE BARNARD (Transvaal). Hooker. New cap. 5 ft. 10 in. 196 lb. A longstanding servant of Transvaal rugby and the brother of the mercurial Springbok fly half Jannie, who played in five Tests for South Africa during 1965. He played his first game in the 20th match of the tour, vs Munster at Limerick, having flown over as replacement for the injured Don Walton. He made three appearances on tour.

CHARLES COCKRELL (Western Province). Hooker. 5 ft 11 in. 193 lb. Played his first game in the eighth match of the tour, vs New Brighton-North of Ireland, replacing the injured Gys Pitzer. He had made 62 appearances for Western Province before joining the touring team. Cockrell played in 10 matches on tour, including the Tests against Scotland, Ireland and Wales. Phone technician.

Of this squad, only eight players were familiar with the demands that such a long British tour would hold for them – captain Dawie de Villiers, Jan Ellis, Don Walton, Frik du Preez, Sid Nomis, Tommy Bedford, Hannes Marais and Mannetjies Roux, although Roux would only arrive later as a replacement. They had experienced a similarly long tour to Australia and New Zealand in 1965, which lasted three months. That was a long time to be away from home and loved ones. A long time spent in hotels, airports and practice sessions, day in, day out, in sometimes cold, miserable conditions. Players have to absorb everything that is thrown their way – pressure, tension, disappointment, injuries, bad news from home – all these things and more. It is a tough test of character. What they did not bargain for was the power of political demonstration.

4

SURPRISE, SURPRISE

In the weeks leading up to the first match of the tour against Oxford University on 5 November, a lot of trouble had been brewing for the Springboks and their tour. The treasurer of the Liberal Party and MP for North Cornwall, John Pardoe, called on Liberals to do all they could to disrupt the tour. In a speech of the Anti-apartheid Movement in Brighton, he described the tour as 'a test case', and urged Liberals, 'Sit down all over the pitch if you have to.'

'The anti-apartheid movement has been fighting for a long time the idea of visits to Britain by South African sports teams selected on a racial basis,' Pardoe said, 'We have not been 100 per cent successful, but I was delighted to see that a South African team was barred from the British surf lifesaving championship. In cricket, of course, there has been a tremendous row on this issue, and the M.C.C. has made a fool of itself.'

Pardoe encouraged all Liberals to join a huge demonstration planned before the Springboks' first match against Oxford University, which was being organised by the Oxford Fireworks Committee. The latter was an ad-hoc organisation responsible for a protest in July earlier that year when the Oxford University cricket side played the Wilf Isaacs side from South Africa. 'If we can make enough row, be a big enough menace and be bloody-minded enough, we may be able to destroy totally the concept of sporting exchanges between South Africa and this country,' Pardoe said. 'We may even be able to stop the M.C.C. from going ahead with the planned South African tour.'[1] Other organisations such as the Oxford Committee against Apartheid (largely trade union supported) and the Joint Action Committee against Racial Intolerance were also planning to support the demonstrations.[2]

At Oxford University itself, Vice Chancellor Alan Bullock issued a public statement officially disassociating the university from the match. In response, the full Oxford University Rugby Football Club (OURFC) committee, senior members and the team's captain, Chris Laidlaw (then All Blacks scrum half), convened a meeting to discuss the issue and then issued a statement on 10 October declaring that, as far as they were concerned, the match was still on. Greig Barr, senior treasurer of the club, said, 'The club has never practised, and does not approve, any form of racial discrimination. Obviously individuals inside and outside the University have widely differing opinions on the propriety of playing against South African teams. The opinion of the RFU [England Rugby Football Union] of which this club is a member, and of the governing bodies of the game in Ireland, Scotland and Wales, is that it is appropriate. These four governing bodies are responsible for deciding whether or not to invite teams from abroad to tour the British Isles and for organising major tours. The detailed fixture list was published by the RFU more than two years ago.'[3]

One of the first signs of trouble at Oxford was noted when, on 23 October, it was discovered that weed killer had been used to spray the message 'Oxford rejects apartheid' in 5-foot-high letters on the rugby pitch. Fortunately, no real damage was done, according to Oxford skipper Chris Laidlaw.[4] No real damage to the pitch, no, but some ten days before the match it was reported that the game might be called off because of the threat of anti-apartheid demonstrations. 'Certainly it will not take place at Iffley Road,' wrote the *Liverpool Echo*. Oxford Rugby Union officials were to attempt to switch the venue to another, less exposed ground where the danger of violence and incidents would not be so great. Following an appeal by the police, who feared extreme danger to persons and property if the match was to take place, the club had to consider whether it was right to play in the circumstances. They were told by the police that it would be inadvisable to stage the match at Iffley Road because of danger to the spectators and the club facilities.

The university's representative on the RFU, Alec Ramsay, said, 'It is a bitter disappointment to those people involved who do not mix politics with sport.'[5] He also pointed out that there were a great many undergraduates at the university who felt very strongly against South Africa's policy of apartheid, and that it was widely believed that they would follow the Oxford fixture wherever it was held. 'If the match is to be held elsewhere, it is certain to prove a worrying burden to the Rugby Union.'[6] And so it would later prove to be.

Ramsay's father, Bill Ramsay, who was treasurer of the RFU, was nonetheless adamant that the tour would go ahead. 'I can assure these anarchists that every one of the remaining 24 matches will be played. The Rugby union is determined to see this through, come hell or high water. Naturally, we are very worried about a situation inspired by what can only be described as absolute anarchy. It is monstrous that mob violence can prevent other people from going about their pleasures. It is a hell of a thing and there is no telling whether it will develop to the point of Government intervention – but we shall go through with our programme.' He also stressed that they had advised their players not to use any violence against demonstrators.[7]

Speaking at the Right-Wing Conservative Monday Club during a week-long visit to Britain, South Africa's Foreign Secretary, Hilgard Muller, urged goodwill over South African sports tours, saying that efforts to disturb sporting relations between Britain and South Africa were most regrettable. He also claimed that Britain had become the operations centre for those wanting to subvert the accepted order and progress in South Africa. Muller told the meeting that during discussions with the British Foreign Secretary, Lord Michael Stewart, the latter had told him that the British government regarded sporting relations 'as a matter for sporting bodies and not for governments'. At the time, however, it was a well-known fact that the British Minister of Sport, Denis Howell, was an opponent of racially selected South African sporting teams coming to Britain.[8]

In the meantime, back in South Africa, the Springbok touring team had been announced following a week-long series of trials in Johannesburg. British newspapers carried reports on the composition of the side. The team assembled again in Johannesburg on 27 October 1969 to prepare to leave for Britain on a Viscount 10 two days later.

During the South African tour, several British internationals would rekindle friendships forged earlier that year during the British Barbarians tour of South Africa and Rhodesia (now Zimbabwe). These included Scotland's Rodger Arneil, Alastair Biggar and Frank Laidlaw, England's Dave Duckham, Bob Taylor, Rod Webb and Keith Fairbrother, Ireland's Alan Duggan and Barry McGann and John O'Shea of Wales.

Springbok captain Dawie de Villiers recalled their anticipation:

Our players were all very excited about the tour to the United Kingdom. What we did not foresee were the massive demonstrations that awaited us. By the time we arrived in the British Isles, the demonstrators had already had a good deal of 'practice' of demonstrations and disruptions gained shortly before during the Wilf Isaacs cricket tour in England.

The team assembled in Johannesburg a week before our departure for the UK to prepare for the tour. Mr Corrie Borman was appointed as manager of the team and the former Springbok captain Avril Malan as the coach. We arrived in London at the end of October 1969. The first demonstrators already made an appearance at the airport when we arrived. Although one could not always physically see them, you were aware of them throughout because of the police presence in our immediate vicinity and the special arrangements that had to be made to try and prevent targeted the rugby grounds, but afterwards also the hotels where we were accommodated.

Of all the players in the touring side, Springbok vice captain Tommy Bedford was by far the best informed and prepared for what might be coming. On the Springboks' short tour of Ireland and Scotland in 1965, some Springboks and Irish players were standing on the first floor of the Shelbourne Hotel in Dublin for the post-Test cocktail party when they saw a small group of anti-apartheid demonstrators gathered outside the hotel. Some of the Irish players thought nothing of it and, laughing, started throwing eggs at the protestors below. When the Springboks toured Australasia the same year, Bedford noticed more pockets of anti-apartheid protestors when they played in Australia en route to New Zealand. After Prime Minister Verwoerd's Loskop Dam speech, when he said Maoris would not be welcome in South Africa, they started to see more demonstrators. What frustrated Bedford was that the team management did not bother to reply to the protestors at all.

Eighteen months before departure I had been at Oxford. I had been at the University for three years, having been back in South Africa for just a two-week spell following the (long) 1965 three-and-a-half-month Springbok tour of Australia and New Zealand, which itself followed some six weeks after the three-and-a-half-week (short) Springbok tour of Ireland and Scotland. In other words I had seen something of the outside world beyond the confines of South Africa, geographically isolated at the bottom end of Africa and thus from the way the democratic world functioned beyond the Limpopo, compared to the increasing narrowness of our world south of the Limpopo thanks to the increasing powers of the governance of the National Party in its dedicated implementation of apartheid and the various states of emergency resulting from it, with its restrictive conditions of reporting in the media allowing in effect only skewed 'news' to be disseminated, and broadcast via radio by the organisation it too controlled, the SABC.

These adventures, particularly the experience of being a student in Britain during the latter half of the 'swinging 60's' – which saw the way dissident protests were debated, accepted, orchestrated, campaigned for and allowed – were in such a very different way from what one had seen of these being put down as a student in South Africa. There was then, of course, the news about Sharpeville but for me especially was seeing the protests squashed at the time of the Cato Manor riots since these had taken place right around the University in Durban, where the army had been called up to assist the police and had based themselves on the campus unmissably right in front of Howard College. Seeing those first very differently handled protests against Ian Smith's UDI taking place along Oxford's St. Giles and later the huge demonstrations against the Vietnam War both in Oxford (where there were many American students also with strong feelings about South Africa) and in London marching on the American Embassy in Grosvenor Square, as well as those organised demonstrations and marches by trade unions about all and sundry, plus the anti-apartheid ground swell gathering pace also through the churches, could leave one in no doubt that such gatherings in Britain were disruptive and if organised on the scale one saw across three years of them, would be exceedingly difficult for a bunch of elitist South African rugby players who had no experience of this sort of climate to cope with – let alone doing so in a rugby community in the British Isles itself by and large removed from these kind of challenges.

At the farewell function given for us at the Casa Mia Hotel on Johannesburg's Berea the night before we flew to London, a fair number of speeches were made by the great and the good present. The news was out there that there were going to be demonstrations against the Springbok team, the news for some time that Peter Hain and the anti-apartheid movements (of which there were a number) were organising demonstrations. It was unclear what the position of Oxford University would be, the first game of the tour, because of the strong student and academic staff views of apartheid South Africa come 1969, yet the Rugby Football Union (England) apparently felt it would not be a problem which could not be handled by the Police and the rugby fraternity and their stewards at the grounds. So the speeches from the great and the good, the Government, the Transvaal Provincial Council, the Johannesburg City councillors, the South African Rugby Board, the Transvaal Rugby Football Union, the touring team's hierarchy – Mr Corrie Bornman, Avril Malan and Dawie de Villiers – were without exception all gung ho of the 'we shall overcome' kind and do our stuff as usual as Springboks. It was as if demonstrations were going to be irrelevant and that the form the Boks had maintained throughout 1968 in first beating the British Lions and then the French on tour to France, and the Wallabies in South Africa earlier in 1969, was already a *fait accompli*. I could simply not believe the confidence exuded by every one of the many who spoke and wished us well.

Well, at the end of all this speechifying, amazingly I was asked to say a few words. How then to put it as politely as one honestly could to such a gathering and to one's own team mates from the 1968 campaigns to the 12 or so new Springboks; to a team manager who might be sociably acceptable to the white South African rugby fraternity especially in Transvaal rugby circles, but could he put the case for the team confronted by robust political as opposed to rugby questioning in English in front of an inquiring media with television at the forefront seeing we had none of this in South Africa; an assistant manager in Avril Malan who had been given the job of team coach instead of the then customary Johan Claassen and serious as he was as a person and a former Springbok and captain (under whom I last played on the 1965 Irish/Scottish tour); how would he manage the players under sustained international playing and demonstration pressures – the latter which he nor any of the team had ever seen or experienced – and Dawie de Villiers, captain and like Malan of similar mould and background having also come out of Stellenbosch University and thus of favoured Western Province rugby stock but also of Afrikaner stock.

With my rather different upbringing and background, and having since my return from those years out of the country realised how different my direction in life had gone compared to the country in those years having moved in an opposite direction, a direction where the Afrikaners had become noticeably dominant in so many things South African, including even more when it came to rugby as the ostracization of white sport like the Olympic sports and cricket attracted universal boycotts, and isolation from the world stage. There was nothing to do in these circumstances but to say my piece and spell it out as I saw the situation. Fifty years ago is a long time to remember exactly what I said. What I do know is that I pointed out to that gathered throng, and to my team mates, that playing international rugby is difficult enough at the best of times. From my time in the England left one and a half years ago I did know that the rugby in Britain and Ireland where I played many matches across three seasons is on the up and up. Although the nucleus of our touring team had played together successfully a fair number of times, in my view it would not be an easy tour, and not a foregone conclusion that we would do as well as every speech made had indicated we would do. There was a real chance we would not do that well. No one in the room had seen the power of demonstrations as they have taken place throughout Britain. Without television this was understandable and hence the feeling that we would easily overcome them and their potential influences on matches and on the team, and that we would not lose come what may.

But having seen what these organised demonstrations could be like, against South Africa, Vietnam, Rhodesia, and subsequently the demonstrations leading to the riots in Paris, it might be that they too could be well organised against the Springbok tour and if they were and kept up for the three months of the tour, it could be they would affect the outcome of the tour. So if we did not win all our games or even lost Test matches because of the unknowns none of us would have had any idea of how to cope with this additional demonstration phenomenon, the people back home and those in the comfort of the function room should remember this. That went down like a lead balloon. The final speech after mine made light of what I had tried to convey by implying what I said was in effect disloyal, as if in my position as vice-captain it was not patriotic and was to be dismissed. It was unthinkable that we would lose. Gung-ho was what the team was all about and ready to take on everything coming its way.[9]

It was not only the demonstrators that may have been a shock. Three years before the tour, Bedford had spoken to Peter Laker of the *Daily Mirror* about the state of rugby in Britain. At the time, Bedford had skippered Oxford to victory over Cambridge in the Varsity match. He was very critical of the dirty play that had become common in the British game. 'When I go down on the ball at home, I know I will be walked on. But I will not be kicked hard in the back and kidneys, as I usually am over here,' Bedford told Laker. 'In most matches that I have played in or seen here there've been incidents between two players, usually caused by one troublemaker. Why they must stand up and fight instead of getting on with the game, I don't know, but it is always happening. It is up to referees to stop it. They ought not to speak to a man three times. They ought to send him off.'[10] Len Elliott, president of the Cambridge University and District Referees Society, told Laker: 'I agree with Bedford. Something is dreadfully wrong with the game. An unpleasant feeling has crept in. What used to be a pleasant afternoon has too often become a stupid punch-up.'[11]

Prior to their departure for Britain, the Springboks were to be briefed on the political climate and given advice as to their behaviour in the event of demonstrations, but according to Johann van der Merwe not much was said, except that the players should under no circumstances become involved: 'There was talk that the tour would be cancelled, but the management and Doc Craven decided to go ahead. We as players obviously all wanted to go on tour. To be honest, we did not have much of a clue what the demonstrations had been about except that it had something to do with apartheid.'[12]

Springbok full back Henry Oswald (HO) de Villiers had been educated at Dale College in King Williamstown in the Eastern Cape and the University of Cape Town, which in those days was already regarded as a liberal institution. Asked about the team's preparation for the tour, he said, 'We had obviously been made aware, to an extent, that we were heading into a tour that was being frowned on/criticised by a certain percentage of the U.K. population, and that this anti-tour group would make their voices heard by way of possible public political demonstrations. South Africa had accepted the invitation to tour, and as such we would attempt to do our best, and not deliberately wish to have confrontation with the demonstrators (this may not always have played out in exactly this manner though!).'[13]

Eben Olivier, who made his debut for the Springboks in the centre in the series against France in 1967, says that they were not prepared for what was to come. 'At that stage we had no idea what a demonstration was like because it was something very rare in South Africa [outside the black townships]. We have heard that Peter Hain was against the tour and that they can disrupt it, but I thought it was just an individual and that it would not be so organised. As far as I can recall it was not a point of discussion. It may be that Tommy Bedford had mentioned something about it, but then it would be from one ear to the other? All I could think of was a nice tour for three months through Britain. We did not have TV in South Africa yet, so demonstrations were something foreign.'[14]

The team arrived at Heathrow on the morning of 30 October 1969 on a BOAC jet, with Corrie Bornman, Avril Malan, Dawie de Villiers and Tommy Bedford first off the plane onto the tarmac. A video of their arrival shows some demonstrators but also enthusiasts who formed a guard of honour and clapped for the arriving Springboks as they entered the building.[15] To the team, the large police presence was something strange. Getting on to the team bus outside the airport, the players were greeted by demonstrators' insults such as '*Boere, julle moere!*' (loosely translated meaning 'Boers, f*ck you!') and 'Go home, you fascist pigs!' and chants of 'Sieg heil!'

The players were surprised by the demonstrations when they arrived, Springbok coach and assistant manager Avril Malan said. 'Tommy Bedford did mention to individual players and to myself that we could expect demonstrations. The intensity thereof had been totally underestimated. I think the South African Rugby Board depended on their knowledge of previous tours, where there were no or very few demonstrations, consequently there was no advice conveyed to us that I had been aware of.' The scale and intensity of the demonstrations did surprise them. 'We who had been on previous tours realised that these were not the old demonstrations. The intensity was much greater.'[16]

'To us it was quite odd, a bunch of long-haired demonstrators carrying placards and chanting "Paint Them Black and Send Them Back" and the Nazi "Sieg Heil" sign and other slogans,' Johann van der Merwe recalled. 'I can't say the demonstrations at Heathrow really bothered us.'[17]

Eben Olivier said that it was something that he never really expected. 'We have all along been told, "Don't worry about these demonstrators. They are only a small minority." When we got off the bus, and arrived at our hotel, the liaison officer told us to hold our togbags above our heads to prevent anyone from being hit if something would be thrown at us. That was the first time that I had become aware of demonstrations and some of us found it amusing. In time we also discovered that many of the demonstrators were the same people who had moved from town to town to make themselves heard.'[18]

To HO de Villiers, the demonstrators were something he's never seen before. 'In my own case, I had been part of the Springbok rugby team that toured France the year before, in 1968, where I cannot recall having been exposed to demonstrations against us,' he says. 'I found the circumstances and activities in Britain / at Heathrow on arrival were totally new to me. I could not really assess the magnitude of the protesting or the intensity thereof, and I had nothing to compare it to!'[19]

Tommy Bedford recalled little trouble with the demonstrations when they arrived at Heathrow. 'The demonstrators were there, of course, but the police got us straight away into a coach virtually off the plane and we were secreted off to a hotel south of London on a golf course without seeing a demonstrator.'[20]

5

A SHAKY START

At noon on the day of the Boks' arrival, a press conference was held at the Park Lane Hotel in London with the management and home union officials on the platform. They were facing a large group of pressmen, mainly news reporters, cameramen from both TV services and sound radio men. 'Having arrived in London, Mr Bornman and I had to face the media at the first press conference,' Springbok captain Dawie de Villiers recalls. 'It was immediately evident that they did not want to ask questions about rugby, but only wanted to talk about apartheid and the demonstrators. It was not what we were prepared for and it upset me quite a lot, but of course one cannot show your anger out there. We had to control our emotions. But I told them that if they did not want to talk about rugby, they should go and talk their politics on the streets.'[1]

Most of the questions asked were of a political nature and to these the manager, Corrie Bornman, replied, 'We have come to play rugby and not engage in politics. We want to mix socially and create a favourable impression among the British people. We have a well-balanced side with no particular stars and we will try to run with the ball at every opportunity. However, should the situation alter in any one game, or the playing conditions change, we may have to revert to a wholly forward pattern. We hope to do a good job and better relationships between South Africa and Great Britain. We have had no advanced instructions on how to approach the tour and I feel sure all matches will be played.'[2]

Asked about their broad approach in terms of playing the game they wanted to play on the tour, should conditions have allowed it, Springbok coach Avril Malan replied, 'You win the ball up front and the backs score the tries. That, I would say, was our approach, but things don't always go in your favour on the field. There is the game plan of the opponents, your own players' skills to succeed, and the referee, that had to be taken into account. My view is that if you can succeed in inhibiting the emotional condition of the players, then one is much less able to play as you wanted to. The demonstrations at the rugby grounds contributed to a large extent to inhibit even our experienced players. I believe that the Barbarians game, which was the team's best performance, was played in the knowledge that the tour had come to an end, tomorrow we are going home and then we will be rid of all the demonstrations.'[3]

In the evening a crowd of about 40 demonstrators had gathered outside South Africa House but they were outnumbered by television camera crews, radio men and news reporters. As the Springboks' bus arrived the police made an avenue for them to walk through into the reception. There was a further demonstration when the Springboks left South Africa House but they appeared unmoved by it.

The Springboks experienced their first taste of 'fake news' soon after their arrival in London. Once settled into their hotel, some of them went out to explore the city (doing their best to be as unobtrusive as possible in everyday civilian dress), and in one of the shop windows noticed a large poster depicting blacks allegedly shot dead by police in South Africa. These 'corpses' were lying on a lawn in a park. The Transvaal members in the group immediately recognised the location as Joubert Park in Johannesburg and it was clear that these 'dead' people were merely sleeping in the sun.[4] Every South African familiar with the city would have known that this is a perfectly normal phenomenon. The lawns around the Government's Union Buildings in Pretoria were equally known as a popular venue for taking naps during lunch hours.

At the first practice of the Springboks at the Richmond Athletic Ground the rugby writers and British TV personnel showed up as expected, and for a short while it was thought and hoped that the promises of disruption to the tour had been little more than idle threats. But soon a group of long-haired youths showed up with placards and tried to run in between the players on the field. However, they were quickly spooked by the secretary of the Richmond Athletic Club, a former Metropolitan policeman, rugby forward and referee, the 61-year-old David John, some of them at the end of his boot. He smashed a couple of banners over his knee, made a diving tackle and told the invaders, 'This is private property. Clear off!' After that the Springboks spent nearly two hours training.[5]

Oxford University

The first match of the tour between the Springboks and Oxford University at Iffley Road coincided with the celebration of the centenary of the Oxford University Rugby Club, but unfortunately it turned into a more political than sporting event. Oxford captain Chris Laidlaw did not recall any pressure being put on the team members to pull out of the game, in spite of the political build-up to the tour. 'My college authorities probably didn't even know the game was on. The matter was certainly never raised with me. The university didn't discuss it as such but several prominent academics publicly questioned the wisdom of the Oxford name being associated with a racially selected team.'

Oxford flanker Steffan Jones, however, admitted that he did consider pulling out of the game and recalls the reaction of a friend opposed to him playing. 'I nearly didn't play because I sympathised with the demonstrators but came to the view it's better to play, or else where do you draw the line, and which teams don't you play against? ... A year before the game I was in the High Street in Oxford asking people to boycott Cape Fruit, but I did feel a little bit guilty I must say. A good friend came to see me later and told me she was disgusted. She had been one of the demonstrators and it took quite a lot of time to rebuild our friendship.'

Because of the threat of violence from the Stop the Seventy Tour campaign an alternative venue to Iffley Road, Oxford, had to be found. 'There were doubts the game could be played,' Laidlaw said. 'There were direct threats to disrupt it if we played at Iffley Road and those were taken seriously. I was asked by the RFU if I thought we could handle this and was obliged to say I didn't know. All I did know was that determined protesters from around the UK were intent on stopping it. A few days beforehand the words "stop the tour or else" were sprayed onto our pitch in weed killer.'[6]

A few years later, in his popular book *Mud in Your Eye* (1973), Laidlaw wrote, 'The world, it seemed, had gone mad. Who, the rugby community asked, could have the affrontery to disrupt an international rugby tour? Rugby is, after all, simply rugby, and nothing to do at all with South Africa's domestic scene. As a rugby player at Oxford I was incensed that anybody, no matter how committed, could throw weed killer on the pitch, smash the windows of the clubhouse, and lay down an open challenge to play the game and see what happened. It was all so sudden and so irrational that it could not fail to antagonise the rugby world.'[7]

Disruptions were not to be confined to the playing field. For their first match on Wednesday 5 November against Oxford, the Boks' accommodation was cancelled. They had heard that the match would indeed take place, but no one could say where.

They were driven by bus to the seaside resort of Bournemouth, just over 100 miles away.

The decision on the venue was left in the hands of RFU President Dudley Kemp, who wanted the game played at the United Services Ground in Portsmouth with a Royal Marines armed guard to keep the peace. However, this idea was rejected on the Monday evening by Prime Minister Harold Wilson, who stated that it was the democratic right of people to protest. It was not until late on the Tuesday evening, the night before the match, that it emerged that the game would be played at Twickenham.

So at this very late stage the Springboks had to get on the bus again for the long trip to London. Along the way they had a 'picnic lunch' of hardboiled eggs, chicken, sandwiches and fruit from Spain. Near their destination the players were told to cover their Springbok blazers with their coats so that they wouldn't be recognised, and to keep their hand luggage on their laps so they were ready to jump off when called upon. Two hours before kick-off, the players found themselves waiting nervously behind closed doors in the changing rooms at Twickenham, the grounds swarming with police. Not the ideal start to a three-month rugby tour.

Stop the Seventy Tour campaign chairman Peter Hain, in the meantime, had stood ready to mobilise his fellow demonstrators. 'The new venue was kept secret but Bob Trevor, a friendly Welsh sports journalist with the *London Evening News*, had promised to phone us immediately the press were informed. At 9.30 the night before [the game], our phone rang and his familiar voice said, "Twickenham, 3pm". I immediately relayed the news. Over 1,000 rushed to the ground and we all purchased tickets, grouping together in the main stand. The match took place under siege. Midway through I spotted an opening in the police cordon and tried to jump over the spectator fence, but was immediately grabbed, carted out and dumped on the pavement.'[8]

Outside the ground there were hordes of protestors chanting slogans. Springbok captain Dawie de Villiers remembers those anxious hours before the match very well. 'The main problem for us was that we never knew what to expect at any moment and it was impossible to really plan anything. As our bus arrived at Twickenham we saw hundreds of police. We were rushed through to the changing room and told to wait there and we just sat around. And when we finally did run out onto the field, there was this general mood of chaos and conflict between the spectators who had come to see rugby and the shouting minority who had come to protest and try to disrupt. Some protestors ran across the field persistently during the game and it was extremely difficult to concentrate on the game. The players just couldn't focus their minds on the rugby. I don't think Oxford was a particularly strong side, yet we still lost. We were sort of paralysed. I think many average teams would have beaten us that day.'[9]

Oxford University centre Doug Boyle also recalled that the team were not told until almost the very last minute that they would be playing the match at Twickenham, and that there had been time to mobilise 500 policemen, who managed to ensure the match was completed. 'We didn't know pretty much until the day of the match. We got on a coach and somebody said it's going to be Twickenham. They only told us at the last minute because if they broadcast the news they would have had even more demonstrators. And when we got there at least 50 per cent of the crowd were anti-apartheid demonstrators. And only the West Stand was full.'[10]

One of the Springboks' issues was that fly half Piet Visagie had to play full back, with both full backs HO de Villiers and Paul Durand carrying injuries. No. 8 Mike Jennings made his debut in the Springbok jersey, and became the second Springbok after Harry Newton Walker (1953–56) to follow in his Springbok father's footsteps. Harry's father, Alfred, played for South Africa in New Zealand in 1921, while Mike Jennings' father, C. B. Jennings, was a member of the famous 1937 Springboks tour to Australia and New Zealand.

Centre and new cap Johann van der Merwe recalled: 'Gert Muller would have played on the wing against Oxford but his father passed away and he suddenly had to return to South Africa. I had originally been selected as centre but Avril and Dawie came to ask me if I would mind playing on the wing. They need not even have asked, I would have played in any position. I played some matches on the wing at school as well as one game for Western Province. Chris Laidlaw was a very good player, possibly the heart and soul of Oxford, and he was a great captain for them.'[11]

Just a few days earlier, Oxford had beaten Cardiff 13-9 and therefore went into the clash with a great measure of confidence. Oxford prop Richard Griffiths believed that the university caught the tourists off guard at the right time. 'I don't want to downplay what we did. But we were lucky. It was the [Springboks'] first match of the tour and I don't think they were completely match fit. And because of the politics surrounding us playing them, and them being so grateful that Oxford University had agreed to play them, that they were told behave themselves.'[12]

Oxford hooker Julian Malins stressed the work that skipper Chris Laidlaw had put into drilling every mistake out of the university game. 'The captain was the coach and the captain chose the team and there was none of this management business. We trained as a team. Chris was the best scrum half in the world at the time and he drilled us and everything that was done was done perfectly. And the Springboks made the mistake of having Tommy Bedford on the sidelines and not playing. They underestimated us … The Springboks were unfit and thought that the first game was going to be a piece of cake and by the time they woke up and needed to roll over us they started to make mistakes.'[13]

Oxford captain Chris Laidlaw recalled that it was only at half-time that they believed they could win. 'We didn't really expect to win it but we knew we had as good a team as Oxford had had for decades and realised that by half-time we had a real chance. It was one of the best games I have ever played and the rest of the team desperately wanted to strike a blow against the Springboks partly because of the misgivings we all had about what that team represented. And our forwards were a highly underrated outfit. The Springboks were genuinely shocked by the extent to which we ran them round. We had a variety of other innovative tactics including short line-outs and the use of a double backline using blindside wing and two loose forwards on defence and this caught the Springboks off balance.'[14] Laidlaw also believed that the 1969 Oxford and Cambridge teams were possibly two of the strongest post-war teams to be fielded by either university.[15]

When the two teams took the field, there were boos from a group of demonstrators at the south end of the West Terrace. The referee, Mike Titcomb, could not be blamed for being a bit nervous when he blew for kick-off and Piet Visagie started the match. The Springboks were first to put points on the board when Piet Visagie landed an easy penalty goal from 25 yards after Oxford infringed at a line-out, but that would be it for the day. Hereafter the demonstrators chanted and blew whistles and kept this up for the rest of the half. Even when Oxford full back Mike Heal replied after seven minutes with an easy penalty to equalise, they booed just as loudly as when Visagie had taken aim. They were clearly just there to disrupt proceedings. The Boks were clearly tense, holding back and fumbling. On the other hand, Oxford, so skilfully led by Chris Laidlaw, played with great spirit. After 32 minutes the Boks were penalised at a maul, and Oxford took a 6-3 lead when Heal kicked another easy 20-yard penalty – even this attempt was jeered by the troublemakers. The score remained 6-3 until the players trudged off for half-time.

During the interval a strange, almost amusing, incident took place. An elderly gentleman had somehow slipped the police cordon and now emerged from the dressing room, appearing to be some kind of ball boy or reserve touch judge. But he made for the centre spot and kicked the ball away from the halfway line, before taking off his pullover and displaying a white jersey with the bold red letters 'A.A.' (Anti-Apartheid) on the front and back. He was led off the pitch, and play restarted with Oxford kicking off. Again the Boks looked apprehensive and Oxford mostly in control, and at the end the visitors, desperate to pull the match out of the fire, surged upfield and won a ruck in the opponents' 25. The ball came to Piet Visagie, but his hurried drop goal attempt went wide. The final whistle blew and Oxford had won 6-3.

The first match of the tour had ended in huge disappointment for the tourists. The only 'consolation' was that the demonstrators had failed to stop the game. And by the time it began to look as if Oxford was going to win this game, the crowd's cheers were drowning the shouts and chants of the demonstrators.

Back home in South Africa, the post-mortems questioned why the 'Test team' was not fielded for this first and highly important game, and suggested that the Boks were not match fit and also that their forwards did not 'climb in', especially at the rucks. But that was all water under the bridge, and the best the visitors could hope for was to salvage what was left of their tour.

Midland Counties East

From Oxford and a first defeat it was on to Leicester, the world of Simon de Montfort, 6th Earl of Leicester and a progenitor of English parliamentary democracy. The Springboks' match against Midlands Counties East was to be played at Welford Road, home of the Leicester Tigers RFC. After the Oxford match they returned to their hotel at the edge of the New Forest in Hampshire, obviously disturbed by what had happened but too proud to admit it. The Springbok team manager, Corrie Bornman, had praise for Oxford and conceded they were the better side on the day. Their pack was terrific, he said, and skipper Chris Laidlaw was quite outstanding. On the Thursday morning (6 November) they left their hotel and set off for Leicester via Moseley, where they trained. While at Leicester, the tour party stayed at the Abbey Motor Hotel, seven stories up on the roof of a multi-storey car park. They were happy with their accommodation, and moved fairly freely about Leicester, undeterred by the threats of the demonstrators who promised a total stop of the tour. But the police and the Leicester Rugby Club had prepared an elaborate plan to beat the demonstrators and see the match through.

It was reported that a hand-picked anti-riot squad would be on duty at the match. *The Birmingham Post* said, 'It has a reputation for keeping soccer rowdies in order and will work with 150 Scotland Yard "commandos", a mobile group that was at Twickenham for the Springboks' game against Oxford University. It is understood that about 1,000 policemen will be on duty.'[16]

Police Chief John Taylor said that they had catered for 'all foreseeable eventualities' and that ten forces would form a security screen for the match. Throughout the night before the match, police with dogs kept watch at the ground, while the South Africans spent a quiet evening at their hotel in Leicester. In addition, 'scores of burly young rugby players from local clubs' had volunteered to act as stewards.

According to the police chief, students from Leicester University had asked permission to stage a protest march and he had agreed. He did not expect any trouble from them but it was his duty to ensure that any troublemakers either on the march or in the ground be dealt with. The day before the match, anti-apartheid activity was building up in Leicester, with thousands of leaflets being distributed, calling for a boycott of the match and urging people to join the protest march through the city to Welford Road. Over the same weekend, in faraway New Zealand, police dogs were to be used to guard the golf course when the South African golfing legend Gary Player competed in the international golf tournament at the Hutt Golf Club near Wellington.[17]

The Springboks at least had some supporters among the media – especially the Welsh – so the reporting would not be one-sided. 'We journeyed back to Wales [after the Oxford match], concerned and worried, but determined to support the Springboks because they were our guests and always played the game the way we expected it to be played,' wrote the well-known Welsh scribe Bryn Thomas. 'We had watched them apprehensively trying not to offend anyone. Again, we felt that in Britain it was our privilege to be allowed to play matches against anyone we desired, of whatever nationality, creed or past record. We would no more think of protesting against Russian ballet dancers, Japanese jugglers or German chess players, if they came as sportsmen. Thus, we felt that the tour must go on and be completed, because if rugby men wished it so, they should be allowed to carry out their intention. Only the Government could stop the tour, or the South African Board recall their team.'[18]

To the argument that British teams had been criticised for playing against South African rugby teams while nobody seemed to condemn the staging of the Olympic Games in a repressive country like Russia, Lord Peter Hain replied, 'Unlike South Africa the Russians did not choose their national sides on a racist basis. The former was unique in doing so.'[19]

There was a feeling that sometimes the demonstrators' antics at the matches had received more publicity than the game. In a letter dated 10 November 1969 and addressed to the editor of *The Times* in London, former Member of Parliament Sir James Pitman expressed his disappointment in the presentation of a news report by the BBC on the actions of demonstrators at a certain match. He objected to the encouragement given to them to proceed with their interference in the rights of those who wanted to play and watch the game of rugby. 'If the BBC were by propaganda, even in programs concerned with politics, to encourage those who thus protest, and by its encouragement enable them to succeed, it will have itself most largely to blame if tyranny based on anarchy becomes the general rule.' Copies of this letter were also addressed to Lord Wakefield, president of the Rugby Football Union, and Corrie Bornman, team manager for the Springboks.[20]

Only three players who played Oxford at Twickenham made the selection, while three players were not considered: HO de Villiers, Sid Nomis and Gert Muller, the latter having returned home for his father's funeral. The side was captained by No. 8 Tommy Bedford in his first appearance on the tour. The East Midlands was to be led by Pat Briggs of Bedford, an outside half. Their pack fielded no less than four British Lions, of whom three had toured South Africa the year before: Larter, Powell, West and Bob Taylor. Precautions suggested that the match would be played in comparative peace, while the fact that it was an all-ticket occasion would further assist in helping the police maintain order.

On a fine and sunny day on a good ground, the Boks took on the Counties in front of about 15,000 spectators at Welford Road, to be refereed by Ron Lewis from Maesteg. There were scenes outside the ground before kick-off, but spectators were carefully screened by police at the entrance. The rule of no ticket, no admission was strictly enforced. The police were well organised with 30 mounted policemen charging from one street to another to keep the demonstrators at bay. The latter shouted slogans, distributed leaflets and exchanged rude words. Rugby fans expressed their disgust and the police had a hard time keeping the protestors under control; their job here was generally more difficult than at Twickenham. Nine people were arrested and twelve taken to hospital for treatment, of whom three were police officers. But it was a triumph for law and order, nevertheless.

The legendary BBC rugby commentator Bill McLaren was on his way to the commentary box when he witnessed some unpleasant scenes. He thought apartheid was 'unacceptable', but 'some of the

actions adopted by those aiming to stop tours were despicable ...
I remember having to walk the gauntlet up a narrow channel lined
on each side by policemen holding back the mob. Those policemen
were covered in spittle, had hats knocked off, were kicked in places
where no man should be kicked, and yet took it all with stoic calm.
I couldn't believe that people in the British Isles would behave in
that manner ... Constant noise outside the South Africans' hotels to
try and prevent them sleeping was another unbelievable ploy that
sickened decent people.'[21] (Ten years later he and his wife, Bette,
were referred to as 'racist scum' on their way down to Mansfield
Park to see the South African Barbarians play, when the touring
team comprised equal numbers of coloureds, blacks and whites.)

The Springboks made heavy weather of winning the match,
and only just, 11-9. But it was a considerable improvement on
their game at Twickenham. Ten minutes into the match, Hannes
Marais pulled a calf muscle and was replaced by giant Mof
Myburgh. Around 15 minutes later the Boks suffered a further
setback when their star flanker, Jan Ellis, injured his shoulder and
had to leave the field. He was replaced by Don Walton, one of the
Springbok hookers on tour, as there was no reserve loose forward
on the bench.

The Springboks were first on the scoreboard when Piet Visagie
landed a superb penalty goal into the wind from 50 yards out.
This score was soon cancelled out by a penalty by Peter Larter. At
halftime South Africa was trailing 6-9, after two good unconverted
tries for the Counties, one by Robertson following a neat grubber
by Sweet and one by Sweet himself, who received the ball from
Taylor; Small had dribbled through, and with Springbok full back
Durand unable to gather, Taylor took the opportunity to send
Sweet in for the try. The Springboks added to their tally with a
good dropped goal by Visagie.

In the second half the Springboks had a lot of possession, but
their half backs' kicking was not very accurate, and good positions

were wasted. The Counties nevertheless had to defend bravely as several potential Springbok scores went abegging, but 20 minutes into the second half they got the try they wanted. Visagie got quick position, moved to the right and ran between two defenders to the right corner. As he was held, he passed inside to his Griquas teammate Piet van Deventer who went in for the try. Visagie converted and the Springboks now took the lead. They held on to this lead until the final whistle blew, and the Springboks were warmly applauded by the spectators as they left the field.[22]

One of the Counties players was Northampton Saints man Bob Taylor, an England international who had toured South Africa in 1968 with the British Lions and played in all four Tests. A highly competent administrator, he later became president of the RFU. 'My first recollection of the match at Leicester is that we played in front of a full house of spectators crammed into every possible viewing space. The large demonstrations outside the ground and threats to disrupt the match were again dealt with particularly well by the police. I remember the match being close and played in a good spirit between the players.'[23]

England teammate and lock Peter Larter recalled that the English players generally were unhappy about the disruptions by the demonstrations. 'As players we just wanted to play rugby against very good opposition. Having seen the apartheid situation in South Africa during the 1968 British Lions Tour, I could understand that peaceful demonstration would show that many people in England were against apartheid. However, we weren't happy with the disruption to your team and their travel arrangements; we just wanted to get on with playing.'[24] Anticipated antagonism from sections of the public towards Larter or other players for playing against the Boks, seen by many as 'ambassadors of apartheid', did not materialise, he says. 'Our team that day at Leicester was a composite of the counties in the East of the Midlands. I was not aware of any ill feeling towards us as players.'[25]

While the Counties men lost narrowly, for Larter it was a good day on the Welford Road paddock, adding a penalty to his side's total. 'My main recollections of the game? I remember the match being physically very hard, as were all matches against South African players. One incident I do recall was at a scrum close to the Springbok's try-line, when a male spectator leapt over the fence and ran onto the pitch and suddenly found himself amongst the forwards who were about to scrummage. He found himself close to Mof Myburgh, who as you will know is a huge man, and he suddenly thought to himself, 'What the hell am I doing here!' He then raced back to the stand and leapt over the fence and a few seconds later his trousers were thrown onto the pitch by the disgruntled crowd! I vaguely remember kicking a penalty, which was probably a long-distance effort as we had a short-range kicker in the backs.'[26]

From the Springboks' point of view, the day belonged to the men from Griquas. As mentioned, their livewire flanker Piet van Deventer scored a try while fly half Piet Visagie kicked a penalty and a conversion and also landed a drop goal, the two Griquas men therefore scoring all the Boks' points. The Boks were to enter Wales the next day and they would have felt much for comfortable than before, even though there was still a fair amount of room for improvement.

At this point news broke of more protests being planned for future matches. Two days after the Midland Counties game, *The Birmingham Post* reported that stronger protests were being planned after the failure of 2,500 anti-apartheid demonstrators to stop the Saturday's match at Leicester. The report said that the demonstrators' clash with police proved that it would be difficult to disrupt any of the matches during the three-month tour. However, the 19-year-old Peter Hain anti-apartheid leader of the STST told the newspaper: 'We learned how hard it is going to be, but we don't think it will be easy for the police to stop us at other rugby grounds.' As described earlier, Hain was now organising much of the anti-Springbok tour protest. Hain went on to say: 'We failed to achieve our initial object at Leicester. But the police were aided by the location of the ground; other matches will be played on pitches which will be harder to defend. Our motive is not the violence. We are determined, however, to do a lot more than we did when the Springboks played the Midland Counties East. More effective protests are being planned.' Hain also said he hoped at least as many of the demonstrators who turned up at Leicester would be there to protest when the Springboks return to the Midlands on 6 January to play Midland Counties West at Coventry. 'That is if the tour is still on by then,' he concluded.[27]

The newspaper said that the 1,000 police present had handled the situation well at Leicester, and described the scenes of the unrest:

Police were kept at full stretch for most of the afternoon. Twelve people, including three policemen, were slightly hurt. Nine arrests were made and those arrested will appear in court tomorrow. Many of the more ugly scenes of the demonstration were played out 100 yards from the ground outside the roller skating rink at the junction of Welford Road and Ayleston Road. As a pop music spilled out from inside the rink, 500 policemen faced the main body of demonstrators. Hooves repeatedly clattered across the cobbled forecourt of the rink as a dozen mounted police raced to disperse groups of students making frequent attempts to break through cordons. Punches were swopped, dozens of students took off their shoes and threw them at police barriers. Others hurled 'bombs' of red paint. While the second half of the match was being played, the atmosphere cooled, with several policemen mingling with the crowd and with banner carriers. But violence flared again at the end of the match as spectators left the ground. There were many scuffles between the two groups and police were forced to build an avenue of men to escort spectators.[28]

But there was more disturbing news for the visitors. At this early stage there were already moves afoot to try and stop the Springboks match against Ulster – the world of the famous Willie John McBride – scheduled for 29 November and still some 18 days away. The *Belfast Telegraph* reported that Queen's University deplored any attempt to stop the match between Ulster and the Springboks. After a meeting in Belfast the rugby club issued a statement: 'The club appreciates the right of the individual to express his feelings about apartheid by way of non-violent protest, but deplores any attempt to stop the match between Ulster and South Africa being played.' The spokesman said: 'This is something that the rugby students decided for themselves. It is a policy statement from the committee. We think that any rugby player who comes to Northern Ireland should be given normal hospitality. The South Africans are not coming over to preach politics. They are pure sportsmen.'

The report also mentioned that the People's Democracy had committed in the meanwhile to holding Harold Wilson responsible for any disturbances arising out of his decision to allow 'the ambassadors of racialism into Belfast'. This statement read: 'At the moment British troops occupied the streets of Belfast. Does Wilson intend to use them to prevent protests against the South African racialists? Wilson should understand very clearly that racists are not welcome here.' According to the report, the United Nations Student Association at Queen's University had denied that it would support an attempt to sabotage the Ravenhill pitch, home of Ulster, in an effort to prevent the match.[29]

On the same day as this report, the *Press & Journal* brought further bad news for the touring party: a group of Labour town councillors in Aberdeen were making a bid to have the let of the municipally owned Linksfield Stadium cancelled for the Springboks' clash with the North of Scotland, scheduled for 2 December. The report read that a special meeting of the city's parks and recreation committee had been called for the Thursday morning when the let would be discussed, and that Labour councillor Thomas Paine was prepared to move that the let be cancelled. In addition, another member, councillor Robert Hughes, a prospective Labour candidate for North Aberdeen, had indicated that there were several Labour councillors who wanted the let to be stopped. Councillor Paine had described the tour as 'most undesirable'.

A number of protests about the match had been sent to the town clerk and Councillor Hughes said he had been inundated with phone calls asking what could be done to stop the match from being played. 'I am hopeful of getting the let cancelled,' Hughes said. 'I do know a number of my Labour colleagues are in favour of this.' He said he was objecting to the tour because the Springboks represented only white South Africa. The booking was made by the North District Rugby Union in May 1968 but it was done at administrative level.

Councillor John Parkinson, the leader of the Progressive group on the town council, said that he would resist any move to cancel the let. The Progressive group were not in favour of apartheid, but felt action of the sort proposed was not going to have any effect. Parkinson also added that the Labour councillors were not making the protest from an idealistic point of view.[30]

6

A WELCOME IN THE VALES

Newport

The Springboks arrived in Cardiff from Leicester on a typically quiet Sunday. At their hotel, team manager Corrie Bornman told reporters: 'We are very happy to reach Wales, because all we know that Welshmen love rugby and we are proud to play against the leading sides in the Principality; but we know that they will be hard matches.' He also spoke about Leicester, saying that the Springboks were quite happy having beaten the Eastern Counties but added that many players were still not fully fit and that they were some way off normal Springbok test standards. And of course injuries were a problem, especially those to Ellis, HO de Villiers and Nomis. They would all be treated in Wales for their injuries.

The Springboks prepared for their match against Newport at the Glamorgan Wanderers ground instead of the University College ground in an effort to sidestep possible demonstrations. On the Tuesday morning, the side selected for the match against Newport played a friendly against a Glamorgan Wanderers XV for an hour. The Springboks beat them 9-0, but of course it was a match that the Wanderers players would remember for ever and a day.

The Newport club had made elaborate arrangements with the police to counter the expected demonstrations. The secretary for Newport, Nick Carter, put out a warning to demonstrators the day before the match: 'If anyone tries to interfere with the ground or the pitch in any way, they will get more than they bargained for. A lot of people are taking good care to see that the game goes on.' It was also reported that rugby supporters in the Newport area had formed vigilante patrols to help the more than 100 policemen who would be on duty at Rodney Parade. The police under chief superintendent Fred O'Connor, a Newport wing three-quarter of the 1930s, anticipated their task to be made easier because the ground was totally enclosed and the game was all-ticket.[1]

The Springbok management showed the traditional respect of touring sides for Welsh rugby by choosing a team of near-Test standard – only five of the players did not appear in the recent series against Australia, won 4-0 by the Springboks. The side showed four changes from the side that scraped a win at Leicester, including the return of skipper Dawie de Villiers, who teamed up with his regular Test fly half Piet Visagie. It was the first time on the tour that De Villiers and Visagie would combine at halfback. The experienced wing Sid Nomis had recovered from a neck injury and was to play his first game on the tour. On the Newport side, the former North Midlands full back John Anthony was passed fit to lead Newport, which freed up the Welsh international Billy Raybould – also a British Lions tourist in South Africa the year before – for the outside half position. Newport had to make a change at the last minute when their vice captain, John Jeffery, failed to pass a fitness test. He was replaced by Paul Watts. On the Springboks side, their lock André de Wet also had to withdraw because of knee ligament trouble, and he was replaced by Martin van Rensburg.

Prior to the game, an interesting letter to the editor of the *Press & Journal*, written by the Lord Provost R. S. Lennox, appeared in the newspaper. It concerned an invitation to the Lord Provost to write a foreword for the match programme for the Springboks vs Newport game. It read as follows:

To the Editor

On November 5, I sent the following letter to Mr. David F Phillip in respect to his invitation to write a foreword in the programme for the Springboks match:

Dear Mr. Phillip

I regret the delay in replying to your letter of 25 September, but as you would appreciate, there is very considerable controversy concerning the visit to this country of the South African rugby touring team.

In these circumstances it seems to me that politics and sports cannot be kept apart, and what ever I might say in the form of a welcome would be the subject of controversy. In the present climate of opinion therefore, it would perhaps be better that I should not write foreword to the programme on this occasion. As requested, I returned herewith the copies of previous programmes which you were good enough to send me.

Yours sincerely,
(Signed) R S Lennox.
Lord Provost.[2]

Newport felt quietly confident for this match. They had started their preparations in July with commando training and fitness and ball training twice a week at Rodney Parade. Just the previous Saturday they had come off a draw with Cardiff, but that did not dampen their spirit at all.

On the day of the match, the police kept good control outside the ground, ensuring that the demonstrators were more orderly than for most of the tour. Entrances to the ground were cordoned off and guarded by the police as well as stewards. Only one demonstrator ran on to the field during the match, but he was quickly marched out of the ground.

The weather at Rodney Parade was dry and windy, with a slippery ground which probably suited the local side better. Watched by a crowd of 22,000, the Springboks started impressively and Bedford crossed for a 'try' but was recalled by the French referee, Robert Calmay. Visagie also failed with a penalty attempt. Newport grew into the match as Billy Raybould and John Anthony's clever tactical kicks found full back Paul Durand wanting at the back in slippery conditions, the very opposite of the dry fields of Western Transvaal. Then, from a line-out near the Springboks' line, the ball was sent down the Newport back line and centre David Cornwall sent an overhead pass to Taylor; Taylor drew Springbok wing Renier Grobler inside and then passed to Alan Skirving, who managed to run around the turning Grobler for a fine score. Although the conversion went wide, the Newport men were leading and they must have felt their confidence surging. Visagie failed with two more penalty attempts, one from 45 yards and another easy one from 25 yards – valuable points that could have made a difference at that stage of the game. South Africa nearly conceded a second set-piece try eight minutes from halftime when from a similar build-up, Cornwall cross-kicked and Newport just failed to get over in the same corner. When halftime arrived, Newport was leading 3-0. They looked better organised, their forwards were holding their own and their halfbacks were using their possession judiciously to keep the Springboks at bay.

The Springboks were lacking their hard rucking and driving game, and it was no surprise when Newport took the lead soon after the interval. Newport set off with Anthony joining the line and he put through a grubber. As the ball bounced back off one of the Boks, it was gathered by Cornwall who charged through before turning inside and scoring under the posts. Anthony converted and Newport led 8-0. Visagie kicked a fine goal from 45 yards out soon after, but a few minutes later Anthony cancelled out that score with a penalty of his own, making it 11-3. The score became 11-6 when Visagie landed an easy 25-yard penalty some 25 minutes into the second half, and now the Bok forwards got stuck in and Newport had to defend for their lives. But the Black and Ambers held on for a glorious and historic victory over the Springboks.[3]

The Springboks had no excuses and management and players all agreed that they had been beaten by a better team on the day. It was Newport's second victory over the Springboks in their history, the previous time having been in 1912 against Billy Millar's Springboks. After the match the players enjoyed a happy time at the Newport clubhouse with the dance going on till after midnight.

The next day's *The Journal* newspaper carried a match report under the heading 'Springboks beaten to a frazzle', and from a South African point of view it did not make for good reading. 'The 1969 Springboks were outclassed before a crowd of 26,000 at the Rodney Parade, Newport, yesterday,' it began. 'The crowd was astonished and delighted in about equal parts at the manner in which Newport dictated the game very nearly from first to last. They were the first Welsh side to beat the Springboks for 56 years. During its 94-year history, the Newport club has defeated all the major touring countries, but it has never gained a more convincing victory than this. Not since 1912 when they won 9-3 have Newport inflicted such a hiding on a South African side. Piet Visagie, the South African fly half, failed to get his backs into action and when Newport began to make their first serious raids into the Springboks half, the tourists showed a marked dislike for dealing with the ball when it was on the ground. They were slow in getting to it and slower to deal with it as they floundered in the mud.'

It goes on to describe how the points were scored and concluded: 'The packed ground kept waiting for the South Africans to cut loose, but not until Visagie got a second penalty 15 minutes from the end for an offside offence was there anything remotely resembling a rally.

In the final 10 minutes South Africa did more or less pin Newport in their own half, but their somewhat uninspired bids to reach the home line were well contained. The only anti-apartheid demonstrations inside the ground were confined to two sole invasions of the playing pitch in the seventh and 65th minutes of the game, but they were about as effective as the tourists' display.'[4]

Swansea

The day after the Newport match, the Springboks trained at Glamorgan Wanderers and then set off to the Dragon Hotel in Swansea, the venue for their second clash with a Welsh club. Here they were not only met by club officials and players, but also by a few demonstrators carrying banners. Still struggling to recover from the most disastrous start in their country's proud tour history, they had another setback when they were forced to switch centre Tonie Roux to full back for the clash with Swansea. They had little choice but to improvise in this key position because of the continuing absence of number one full back HO de Villiers – nursing a hamstring injury – and the poor form of deputy Paul Durand against Newport. There were also changes to the back row, where vice captain Tommy Bedford moved to the flank to accommodate Mike Jennings at number eight. Otherwise there were eight straight changes, four of them forward, from the side beaten by Newport. The Boks also had to make a difficult decision in resting fly half Piet Visagie after three hard matches, his first at full back and then two at fly half. Mike Lawless, who played at fly half in the first match against Oxford, therefore returned to the side to partner skipper Dawie de Villiers. Springbok coach Avril Malan gave the squad a two-hour tactical talk at Cardiff. The *Daily Mirror* commented that 'whatever his observations, there can be no denial that these players have been grossly misled about the standard of British rugby, which has soared as the result of closely supervised squad training'.[5]

Stuart Davies, Swansea's centre and captain for the day, recalled that the match made news bulletins around the world not for the rugby that was played but for the massive anti-apartheid demonstrations. 'The match was the first major Saturday fixture of the tour and Swansea's accessibility by road and rail promised to attract many demonstrators. It would be true to say that I, as captain, the rest of the team, the club and indeed rugby in general chose to ignore the moral issue, a stance which my daughters would not be happy with, if it happened today!'[6]

On the Friday afternoon before the match, several of the Springbok party visited Brangwyn Hall and Stuart was invited to be there as well. The Springboks had come to see the well-known Sir Frank Brangwyn panels and Dawie de Villiers, with an impressive knowledge of art to this day, explained that these were indeed world-famous works of art, a fact of which the Swansea captain had been blissfully unaware at the time.

'The day itself was obviously marred by the demonstrations culminating in a pitch invasion,' Davies recalled. 'During the course of the day, some 70 people were arrested and over 100 people were injured, including 10 police officers. There was an eerie feeling on the field throughout the match which affected us all and it would be true to say that the Springboks were saddened by the experience.' While he remembered very little about the game itself, a humorous incident in the build-up to taking the field stuck out in his mind. Following an early light lunch in the clubhouse, the team members went for a walk on the beach, turned around at Sketty Lane and by the time they arrived back could hear noise coming from the Guildhall area where the demonstrators were holding a rally. Coach Morrie Evans and Davies ushered the players into the dressing room from where they heard the increasing chanting from the demonstrators parading in Mumbles Road. The coach and captain spent the next hour trying to keep the players calm and focused on the match ahead.

'We had emptied the dressing room of all but the players and had convinced ourselves and them that the noise and the crowd were nothing really. Everyone was sitting in total silence when the dressing room door was flung open to reveal the infamous Tommy Clement, the long-serving team bus driver. He took one look at the silent gathering before uttering the immortal words – "They are going f.......g mad out there!' Despite the increasing tension, we all had to laugh.'[7]

The Swansea side that day was still in an unsettled stage of their 1969/70 season, with both their half backs, Hylton Bowen and Tom Pullman from Mountain Ash, only playing in their third game for the club. Lyndon Jones, David Morgan, John Joseph and Malcolm Henwood were all newcomers who had played very little for the club and by the end of the season only half of the team that played against the Springboks were still at St Helens. The side nevertheless played above themselves and restricted the powerful Springboks to just one try and no points at all in the second half. 'The one real memory I have of the match itself was the audible gasp from the crowd in the stand when the gargantuan figure of Mof Myburgh, the Springbok prop, took the field as a replacement for the injured Martin van Rensburg,' Davies remembers. 'It was an awesome sight and certainly sent shivers down the backs of our young team. The headlines over the next few days were regrettably all about the violence off the field and the knock-on effects of the trouble. I was surprised on the Sunday morning to receive calls from the news desks of the leading newspapers seeking our reaction to the events of the day before, my views on apartheid and what we should do now as a rugby community.'[8]

Also, on the Friday, in the evening, some players and pressmen from the Springbok party, headed by Tommy Bedford, went to talk to the demonstrators outside the Springboks' hotel. They tried to put across their views and listened to those of the demonstrators, and it was clear that the latter had little or no knowledge of the conditions in South Africa.[9]

Swansea represented the demonstrators' biggest attempt to disrupt the Springbok tour in Wales, and with a heavy police presence it was bound to lead to unpleasantness. A South African radio commentator described the scenes at St Helens:

> On our arrival at St Helens it was clear that the police were going to have their hands more than full. Outside, behind the main pavilion, mauling hordes taunted the police, surged forward time and again and tried to break through the police cordon. I can still see the police mercilessly pulling the ringleaders by their long hair from amongst their comrades. Within the playing area the police were deployed all around the field, and between them were men with yellow armbands, the 'vigilantes' as the British press called them. In contrast to other matches, no mercy was shown. The yellow armbands of the 'vigilantes' were to be seen everywhere. There was grabbing, hitting and dragging. There was none of the usual slow, authoritative little step by the police, they simply got hold of the intruders and worked them over. To add insult to injury, two of the 'victims' when exiting through the players tunnel were attacked by an old lady who hit them over the head with her umbrella. Her fury was symptomatic of the feeling amongst the rugby-loving crowd at the ground.[10]

Springbok centre Johann van der Merwe, who partnered Eben Olivier in midfield on the day, recalled the role of officials in containing the demonstrators. 'A lot of officials stood ready during the match to look after the demonstrators and they showed no mercy in removing those who ran onto the field. I can remember that one of the 'marshals', as they were called, tackled a nice-looking girl with long hair right next to me and he dragged her over the touchline by her hair.'[11]

The *Belfast Telegraph*, among others, ran a graphic report of the vicious clashes between the police and demonstrators:

Fighting broke out between police and the anti-apartheid demonstrators outside Saint Helens ground, Swansea today where the Springboks were playing the fourth match of their tour. Police clashed with demonstrators, mainly anarchists, and fighting grew as attempts were made to enter the ground. Several arrests were made. Banner poles were used as weapons and police helmets went flying. The scenes came after a march by the police-estimated crowd of between 800 to 1,000 along the 400 yards from the Guild Hall to the Saint Helens ground.

The demonstrators chanted 'Apartheid out' and linked arms in runs. All was peaceful until they reached the stadium. Then attempts were made to move from the left-hand side of the road to the stadium side. Police shoulder-to-shoulder were supported by rugby fans as they drove the demonstrators back.

Girls were led weeping from the melee. When one officer fell almost beneath the wheels of a bus he was rescued by rugby spectators who immediately crashed with a demonstrator. The outbreaks spread with bunches of people being carried on to the pavement where the first arrivals for the game were waiting to pass through the doors. More than 20 demonstrators were led away by police. Heavy police reinforcements moved the main body of demonstrators from a position near the Saint Helens ground.

Traffic was stopped except for ambulances going through. Three smoke bombs were thrown with billowing orange smoke pouring from them. Inside the ground police ringed the pitch, helped by about 200 volunteer stewards. A silver band drowned the shouting and chanting of the demonstrators outside.[12]

But as they said, there was also some rugby. Regarding the match, the *Coventry Evening Telegraph* reported that the tourists had been in excellent form. 'Encouraged by a prolonged ovation from the crowd the visitors showed the best form of their tour so far. They stormed into the lead after 15 minutes and by halftime had a commanding lead. After four days of almost continuous rain, however, the pitch appeared soft and likely to cut up early on ... The South Africans received a prolonged ovation when they appeared.'

Swansea kicked off into a breeze on a dry and cold day in front of a crowd of 20,000. Soon the Boks got a penalty from their third line-out, but van Rensburg hooked his attempt. But after 15 minutes he put his side in the lead with a 40-yard effort after Swansea was penalised at a ruck. About 24 minutes into the first half, he succeeded again with a fourth attempt to increase the lead to 6-0. Then, 34 minutes into the half, the Springboks took a commanding lead when they worked an excellent try. Tiny Neethling peeled off from a line-out and the ball went down the line all the way to Andy van der Watt on the left wing who went over for the try. Van Rensburg could not convert from the difficult angle.

Shortly afterwards van Rensburg fell awkwardly with several players on top of him, and he was stretchered off, to be replaced by Mof Myburgh. He was taken to hospital in Swansea where it was discovered that he had a form of concussion of the spine. Dawie de Villiers had to take over the kicking and just before half-time succeeded with a third penalty for the Springboks to take them into a 12-0 lead.

The expectation was that the Boks would now win by a fair margin, but just after the restart about 100 demonstrators invaded the pitch, with double that number of police in pursuit. They were quickly removed and play could resume. The crowd cheered the police and the stewards for their 'efficiency'. After this interruption, however, the players seemed to have been unsettled and play was a bit scrappy, and the tourists failed to add to their score. So the game ended in a 12-0 victory for the Boks, but it has to be said that they had left quite a few points out there through inaccurate place-kicking and poor finishing.[13]

After the match the Boks were entertained at the Dragon Hotel by the Swansea club and returned to Cardiff the next day. Here it was revealed that van Rensburg would not be able to play for six weeks, while Gys Pitzer was put to bed in the hospital in Swansea and special traction treatment applied. It meant that he would not re-join the party or play again during the tour. He was due to have played against Gwent but had to be withdrawn, with Don Walton taking over his duties. Van Rensburg was to be replaced by Transvaal lock Sakkie de Klerk, flying over from South Africa as soon as possible. Another setback was the withdrawal of Tommy Bedford in the side against Gwent because of a cold, and he was replaced by Mike Jennings at No. 8.[14]

The violence at St Helens led to allegations of police brutality in handling the threat of the demonstrators. The *Evening Chronicle* reported two days after the match that the Home Secretary, James Callaghan, had received a report on Saturday's violence between the anti-apartheid demonstrators, the so-called 'vigilantes' and the police at the Springboks' rugby match at Swansea. It was submitted by Frank Williamson, a Home Office inspector of constabulary, and his report dealt with the allegations that police handled demonstrators with unnecessary violence. Williamson was a Home Office observer at previous Springboks' matches, and was likely to be attending others during the tour.

Hugh Jenkins, the Labour MP for Putney, said that he would ask the Home Secretary to hold a formal inquiry into the violence. 'If this violence continues someone is going to get killed,' Jenkins said, adding that he tabled a Commons question for the Thursday, asking Callaghan for a full inquiry and to consider the possibility of abandoning the tour. 'It is my personal view that it should be abandoned. I do not think the Springbok tour should have taken place at all. Reports show that what happened at Swansea was a combined assault on demonstrators by strong-arm rugby fans and the police. The Home Secretary has got to take action, not on the part of any one side, but in order to keep the peace,' he concluded.[15]

The events at St Helens in Swansea surely led to lively discussion, not just among the public but also in the British House of Commons. Two days after the match, James Callaghan had a lot to answer in the House. Quoting from a preliminary report from the Inspectorate of Constabulary on the disturbances and casualties at the match, he said that disturbances took place at Swansea both outside and inside the ground, and that a number of people were injured, including 11 police officers. Charges had been brought against 63 people, who would appear in court on 19 November. Complaints have also been made about a number of police officers, and these were to be investigated under Section 49 of the Police Act 1964.[16]

Callaghan said that the leaders of the demonstration had previously agreed with the Chief Constable of the South Wales Constabulary that a meeting should be held outside the Civic Hall, and they had also agreed a line of route that should be followed by a procession from the Civic Hall past the ground to the foreshore where they were to hold a further meeting. The meeting outside the Civic Hall passed off peaceably and the procession itself was peaceable until the ground was reached, but it was when the head of the procession halted that disturbances began. Inside the ground, a number of demonstrators broke away on to the pitch just after half-time. Stewards had been engaged by the Swansea Rugby Football Club to remove demonstrators from the pitch, and the task of the police in such circumstances is extremely difficult, Callaghan stressed. They have a duty to assist the stewards where physical force is necessary to remove intruders, but at the same time they have a duty to preserve the peace.[17]

'These developments are placing a very heavy responsibility on the police service. I have, therefore, decided to call a conference of chief constables in those areas where games are still to be played in order to discuss the best way in which the responsibilities of the police can be carried out. Among the questions that I shall ask to be examined is the extent to which stewards are helpful. At two previous games, there was little or no complaint of the activities of stewards, but it is clear that their behaviour at Swansea caused a great deal of public disquiet. In the meantime, outbreaks of disturbances can be limited inside the grounds if matches are by admission by ticket holders only.' With regard to the South Africans' forthcoming match against Gwent, to be played at Ebbw Vale, one of the inspectors of constabulary was already consulting the Chief Constable of Gwent.[18]

Callaghan also pointed out that there was a joint responsibility upon the clubs and upon the protesters. 'If the newspaper is correct, I observe that one of the chairmen of the "Stop the '70 tour" has said: "The match at Ebbw Vale could make Swansea seem like a tea party." It is for the demonstrators themselves to consider how far that attitude is likely to advance the cause of anti-apartheid to which they are, I have no doubt, sincerely devoted. The question of cancellation of the rest of the tour gets us on to very difficult ground. If the police or the Government were to be called in to stop events that people did not like for various reasons, this would be the first step on what could be a dangerous and slippery slope. I ask the House to appreciate the very difficult circumstances in which those who are trying to prevent a breach of the peace are being placed at the present time. It is unwelcome, no one will want it, and it is also inevitable that there will be occasional examples of roughness. If people break on to a ground, certainly a Rugby ground, the prospects in such circumstances of trying to prevent a breach of the peace are extremely slim and I must ask support for the police who, I believe, could carry out this task. That is what I want to discuss with the chief constables.'[19]

Callaghan also pointed out: 'I must say that those who do not enjoy a game against the South Africans are free to stay away. If I may express my own personal view, I shall not go to see them, because I object to their sending a totally white team to this country. But, having expressed that personal view, I do not think that it would be right for the Government to step into this matter and to try to ensure that the tour was not played. It is for those who organise the tour to judge what the public reaction is and how far they go towards helping the cause to which the hon. Gentleman referred.'

Regarding the alleged strong-arm actions of the stewards, he said: 'It is not the job of a steward to assault people; he should escort them from the ground, if such a thing is possible, and, if physical force is required, it is his duty to call upon the police for that purpose. If any demonstrator feels that he has been assaulted by a steward, he has a remedy in the courts and it is for him to apply. I doubt whether any general inquiry would produce anything new that we do not already know.'

But he also pointed out the risk of interfering with the game in a rugby-loving country such as Wales. 'On this occasion the anti-apartheid demonstrators agreed the route and agreed both meeting places. However, as we all know from experience, although the leaders or the organisers may wish to carry out agreements, these demonstrations are sometimes taken over by other people, or at least they attach themselves to a demonstration. This is one of the difficulties of free assembly, but it is one that we have to live with and in which we must try to ensure, as the police did, what their obligations are in the matter – they will do their best to carry them out. However, I am bound to say that anybody who rushes on to the middle of a rugby football pitch, even in a minor game in a Welsh valley, is likely to suffer a little trouble. It will be difficult if spectators allow themselves to give way to this, but I appeal to spectators not to give way. They will make the task of keeping order, and, if they want to see the game completed, the task of playing the game, much more difficult if they do not leave these matters to the police to handle.'[20]

Gwent

Events at Swansea really shook up the authorities and they quickly took measures to counter any possible trouble expected in the Springboks' match against Gwent at Ebbw Vale. The *Coventry Evening Telegraph* reported on 19 November – four days after the Swansea incidents and on the day of the Gwent game – that a strong police force would be present at the ground:

Police were at strength at Ebbw Vale Welfare Ground today to meet expected trouble from anti-apartheid demonstrators protesting against the Springbok rugby side playing the Gwent County team. Between 400 and 500 officers from all parts of Monmouthshire moved into the steel town today to take control. The Gwent Socialist Charter have cooperated with the police in organising a peaceful demonstration involving the distribution of leaflets at a point outside the ground. But there is fear that a violent protest may develop with the possibility of students with strong anti-apartheid feelings coming up from Swansea, Cardiff and Bristol.

Police have a strong guard at the bridge which provides the only access to the ground. Demonstrators were not allowed to go over it. Police will also be in strength inside the ground to stop any attempts to interfere with the game. Inside 50 voluntary stewards, members of the Ebb Vale Rugby Club will be on duty to prevent demonstrators going on to the pitch.[21]

Ebbw Vale, where the big steelworks provided employment to the townsfolk, was definitely pro-rugby and the Springboks were made to feel very welcome. On the field, however, there would be no hospitality. The Gwent team was coached by the former

England No. 8, Derek Morgan. Morgan had gone to university in Newcastle, and represented Northumberland in the County Championship. Asked how it happened that one born in Wales, bred in Wales and with an accent to match had come to be capped by England, Morgan – a dentist by profession – said, 'Well, let me answer that question with a question, if you were born in a stable, does that make you a horse?"[22]

Apart from Morgan's acumen, the Gwent players were further motivated by captain Dennis Hughes' instructions: 'Tackle, tackle, tackle, and let young Robin Williams kick the goals.' So while the Boks were the slight favourites, the Welshmen fancied their chances. Oxford and Newport had shown that the South Africans could be beaten, so why not Gwent?

The Springboks started the match at a tremendous pace with the forwards on the rampage, winning scrums and line-outs and possession at the rucks. They took the lead in the first minutes with a simple penalty by Piet Visagie, but 19-year-old Gwent full back Robin Williams levelled the score with a penalty from 20 yards halfway out following an infringement by the Springboks at a line-out. Only four minutes later Williams landed a second penalty attempt from the right-hand side of the field, 30 yards out and near touch. Remarkably, having landed his first penalty with his right foot, he kicked this one with the left. This penalty took the home side into the lead by six points to three.

Unfortunately for the Springboks, Visagie failed with three 30-yard penalty attempts in the space of three minutes – one was even in front of the posts. When the Springboks took the lead a few minutes later, this turned out to be the turning point in their fortunes. With the Springbok forwards on the run again, Frick du Preez was bundled into touch near the corner flag, and from the following line-out, Mike Jennings jumped to collect the ball and crash over the line. His try was converted by Visagie. When halftime arrived, the Springboks were leading by two points.

In the second half the young Williams failed with a left footed penalty attempt, but then compensated by landing a beauty all the way from the halfway line after the Springboks had gone offside at a restart. This took the Welshmen into the lead again and really lifted their spirits. To complicate matters for the Springboks, Du Preez and Visagie both failed with penalty attempts, from the halfway line and 30 yards out respectively. In addition, the tactical kicking was not accurate enough to threaten the home side. On the other hand, the Gwent backs covered and a defended well while full back Williams drove the Springboks back with long, raking kicks to touch.

At this stage the match was still delicately balanced, with only point separating the sides. An excellent try by right wing Roger Beese, however, sealed the match for Gwent. From a scrum just inside the Springboks' 25 the ball went from Evans to Grindle, and then to Lewis; Lewis got a little gap and passed to flanker Geoffrey Evans, who sprinted away diagonally before throwing a long pass to Lewis who sent Beese away. As the winger crossed over in the corner, his teammates were jumping in the air. To put the cherry on the cake, Williams converted left-footed from touch, the ball sailing high between the posts.

With only seven minutes remaining, the Springboks had their work cut out. No matter how hard they tried, the Gwent defence was solid and the Welshmen held out bravely till the final whistle. While the young full back Williams was the hero by kicking Gwent to victory in an amazing display of left- and right-footed placekicking, the role of the Gwent pack leader, Dennis Hughes, should not be forgotten. Hughes was a member of the Welsh national squad at the time.

The Springboks were probably wondering how they had lost this game, because they had a great deal of good possession from the set pieces and the loose. But this possession was not well applied, and to make matters worse they succeeded with only two goals, including the conversion, from eight attempts. On the other hand, Robin Williams succeeded with four from five attempts – a vital statistic in the end result. The points difference – six – would be the biggest of any match the Springboks lost during the tour.

After the match, Corrie Bornman said that the Gwent full back was the best they had seen so far, describing him as 'magnificent'. He also conceded that they had thrown the chances away, that the forwards had played well and won a lot of ball, but that it was wasted. The conditions were good, he said, and there were no demonstrators inside the ground to cause any disruptions. For this he gave credit to the police and the club officials.[23]

At a local rugby dance after the match, the Welsh had a lot to celebrate. The Springboks, meanwhile, could be forgiven for looking a bit depressed; a third loss in five matches did not make for good reading. The Welsh selectors had to choose the teams for the national trials that evening, and young Robin Williams was included in one of the teams. Unfortunately, an injured shoulder kept the prodigious kicker from playing in the trials. He went on to play 117 matches for Pontypool and scored 1,158 points. He sadly passed away in 2018.

7

LONDON & NORTH WEST COUNTIES, NO ULSTER

London Counties

The Springbok lock forward Sakkie de Klerk, the replacement for Martin van Rensburg, who was injured in the match against Swansea, flew into London from Johannesburg on 20 November. When he arrived at Heathrow and was asked about South African views on the anti-apartheid demonstrations, De Klerk told reporters: 'There was some surprise at home at the anti-apartheid demonstrations, but no one is terribly worried and there certainly has been no suggestion that the team should come home.' De Klerk had not played rugby since the end of September. With him on the flight was Springbok wing Gert Muller, who had now buried his father.

Meanwhile, on the London Counties front, Alistair Biggar, the London Scottish centre selected on the right wing by London Counties, had to withdraw because he was needed for the first Scotland trial at Murrayfield. The England captain, Bob Hiller, was kept out of his normal position at full back, instead providing backup as a utility back when the side to face the Boks was selected.[1] Other notable selections were J. P. R. Williams at full back,

John Dawes, the captain, at centre, Nigel Starmer-Smith at scrum half and Mervyn Davies in the back of the scrum.

In London, the Springboks were accommodated in the pleasant Park Lane Hotel, from where they could explore the sights of the West End. On the first evening they were the guests of the Rugby Writers Club and hosted at the Royal Air Force Club in Piccadilly. The occasion was attended by several well-known rugby players including Tom Kiernan, captain of the 1968 British Lions in South Africa, legendary Irishman Tony O'Reilly and Cliff Morgan, the Welsh fly half who in 1955 had entertained South African crowds with his scintillating play for the British Lions.

The chairman of the RWC, Pat Marshall of the *Daily Express*, reminded people that many brave South Africans had used the RAF Club during the Second World War while fighting in the Battle of Britain. It was also recalled that when the formidable 1951/52 Springboks toured Britain, the London Counties were the only side to beat them on the entire tour (11-9).

On the Friday before the match against the London Counties, the players toured London by bus to enjoy the sights, including the Tower of London.

The London Counties XV was led by John Dawes, who had been captain for the London Welsh Club for the fifth successive year, and included seven internationals. But there was doubt about the pack of forwards. The Counties fly half Campbell Hogg was the son of a former New Zealand rugby union president, Cuth Hogg. The exciting Welsh full back J. P. R. Williams would be wearing the no. 15 jersey for the Counties. At the time they were coached by Gerwyn Williams, who in 1951 played full back for the victorious London Counties.

As far as demonstrators were concerned, the big concern was that it was not an all-ticket match and that the demonstrators would be present in force, which would mean a larger police force as well.

It was a rainy Friday but the weather was fine on the day of the match as the two teams ran out in front of a crowd of 25,000 spectators. As soon as the teams appeared on the field, the whistling and chanting started. Bob Hiller put the first points on the board for Counties with a fine penalty kick that flew high between the posts. This was met by boos from certain parts of the ground. Once again, Piet Visagie had left his kicking boots at home, missing two penalty attempts to draw level.

After 11 minutes, the 'great charge of Twickenham', as some referred to it, began. Demonstrators ran from several parts of the ground and occupied the middle of the field. All the players could do was stand still while the police hurried on to the field. They were assisted by a few stewards, and in five minutes nearly 100 demonstrators were removed from the field under loud cheers from the crowd. As play resumed, extra police from reserve positions marched into the ground.

The players did not seem to have been put off by the demonstrations as both sides attacked strongly and with skill. HO de Villiers brought the teams level after 26 minutes with a penalty from 30 yards out after Visagie had been off-target again with the penalty attempt. Then came the Springboks' first try, scored by Andy van der Watt. The Springboks had caught John Williams in possession and got the ball from the ruck, where Dawie de Villiers gathered, scooted off on the blind side some 30 yards from the Counties' line and fed Van der Watt. The speedy wing darted inside past Bucknall and ran in for a well-worked try to put the Springboks into the lead. HO de Villiers could not convert. In the meantime, Hiller had missed with three attempts from 50 yards and more, but a fine drop goal by centre Lloyd from a line-out drew Counties level with the Springboks, 6-6. The teams went in at half-time with honours even.

The second half saw a better effort from the Springboks, and after 13 minutes they won a maul 15 yards out and moved right with Dawie de Villiers running well before handing an inside pass to Tonie Roux, who crashed over with John Dawes unable to stop him. Visagie converted. Five minutes later they scored again when Tommy Bedford gathered from a set scrum and passed to Dawie de Villiers, who sped down the blindside, kicked ahead past Williams and gathered again before being tackled. The ball was released quickly for Bedford to gather and fall over for an unconverted try.

The Springboks' fourth try came five minutes later. With players like Frik du Preez, big Gawie Carelse and Albie Bates pounding away, something had to give and eventually Tonie Roux crossed over for his second try. Again Visagie could not convert. Wave after wave of green jerseys now followed, and no matter how hard the Counties tried to defend, the Boks could not be denied their fifth try. De Villiers again snuck around the blind side, passed inside to Bedford and Bates took the final pass to score in the corner. Lock Gawie Carelse converted from the touchline, and afterwards probably teased Visagie about how it should be done. The final score was Springboks 22, London Counties 6.[2]

Looking back, the Springboks' tight five were the key to their success. Their opponents could not hold them and this gave the Springbok back row of Tommy Bedford, Albie Bates and Piet Greyling freedom to roam. Behind the dominant pack, scrum half Dawie de Villiers was quick to set moves in motion and the opposing loose forwards had great difficulty in cutting him off on the blindside.

When they left the field at Twickenham, the Springboks were treated to a resounding cheer around the ground. They had shown Britain what they were capable of, and the only negative was the injury to hooker Don Walton, who had cracked a rib and would be out of action for six weeks. This meant they had no fit hooker. Corrie Bornman described the match as 'the first one in which the Springboks had delivered a very good performance, especially in the second half'.

After the match there was an assault on the Twickenham police station by a large group of demonstrators in an effort to release their arrested comrades. People were thinking, where would it end? When would there be a backlash from rugby followers? In all, 191 demonstrators were removed from the rugby ground and 15 were taken to Twickenham police station, while six policemen were injured and three civilians were taken to hospital. One British rugby writer, the well-known Bryn Thomas, who for 36 years wrote for the *Western Mail*, was disgusted with what he saw. 'Indeed the policeman's lot, nowadays, is not a happy one. He is sandwiched between the demonstrators and the do-gooders and idealists, trying to maintain law and order so that idealists can dream, the demonstrators perform and militants act like dangerous hooligans. My sympathy after this tour is firmly with the police. They deserve medals and the full thanks of a sometimes ungrateful nation.'[3]

After this resounding win over the London Counties, the Springboks left for Manchester where four days later they were to meet the North Western Counties at the White City Stadium. They were accommodated in the pleasant Stanneylands Hotel in Wilmslow, some 10 miles south of Manchester, where a replacement hooker had to be called. The choice fell on the 30-year-old Charlie Cockrell from Western Province, but the big question was whether he would be fit in time for the first Test against Scotland. The best they could hope for was for him to be ready to play at Aberdeen against the North of Scotland side.[4]

North Western Counties

In the week of the Springboks' match against the London Counties, a meeting was held in Liverpool. Three hundred students attended the event, during which Peter Hain, organiser of the Stop the Seventy Tour, and Aziz Pahad, a member of the African National Congress, spoke of the reasons why they objected to apartheid. Under the apartheid regime in South Africa, Pahad was given a banning order in 1963, and in 1966 he left South Africa and lived mostly in London, also spending some time in Angola and Zimbabwe, before he started working full-time for the ANC, developing the anti-apartheid movement in the United Kingdom and Europe.[5]

Plans were also discussed for 200 Liverpool students to join the 'Stop the Seventy Tour' demonstration at Manchester on Wednesday when the Boks would play the Northern Counties. 'There are now 80,000 political prisoners in South Africa and all chance of bringing about change is no longer possible. We must submit or fight,' Pahad declared. 'We feel that confrontation with South Africa will involve not only them but the whole world. Armaments are supplied by Western Europe and North America and foreign investments are about 26% of total investment capital.' He also claimed that the rugby team was there under false pretences: 'It is a white South African team whose members have the best of both worlds here and at home, and they are far from being innocents – they are collaborators.'

Peter Hain then emphasised Pahad's words, adding that the aims of the Stop the Seventy Tour committee were to isolate white South Africa from all international sport and to sever South Africa's last cultural link and force them to compromise. He also spoke of peaceful demonstrators being beaten up by vigilantes, virtually a private army of 'toughs' who wear orange arm bands for identification. 'What kind of sport needs to guard players and spectators with hundreds of police?' Hain asked. 'Let me tell you that South Africa brought politics into sport, not us.'[6]

The weather was fine and on-field conditions good when the Springboks took on the North Western Counties at the White City Stadium. It was a modest crowd of about 6,500 spectators. Outside the ground there were fierce clashes between the demonstrators and the police and there were several arrests, but in the end the police had won the day. Some 2,000 policemen were in action and about 70 people arrested. Of the latter, about 40 were grabbed inside the ground as they attempted to invade the pitch. Some forged tickets were also found.

The Springboks started well, being solid at the scrums where makeshift hooker Tiny Neethling won several tightheads. In the first 25 minutes Piet Visagie kicked two penalties and centre Tonie Roux dropped a goal to give the Springboks a 9-0 lead. Then flanker Piet van Deventer, Visagie's teammate at Griquas, ran well for a try after he had been sent away by Neethling. Visagie failed to convert, but the Springboks would have felt comfortable with such a handsome lead. Just before half-time, they were leading 12-0 and looked set for an easy victory.

But the Counties were not content to roll over, and before the interval they replied with a try by their no. 8, Lyon. Full back O'Driscoll failed to convert and the players went into the interval with South Africa a leading 12-3. In the second half, O'Driscoll landed two penalty goals to reduce the deficit to just three points. It was anybody's match with 10 minutes to go. In the final moments, the Counties nearly scored twice: first, flanker Tony Neary held on to the ball with two players unmarked outside him, and a golden chance was lost; then an overhead pass from Robinson to the lock Michael Leadbetter went astray when the latter was going for the line at full speed. Finally, replacement back Toone took aim for a drop at goal, but backed into one of his own men and another chance was lost.

The tourists held out for the win, but they could not feel too happy about the way it had been achieved. After a good start, they had slacked off and allowed the Counties to get back into the game in a big way and nearly blew it. Along with the disappointment of their game, they also received the depressing news that the Ulster match in Belfast had been cancelled.[7] Most of the Springboks must have looked forward to playing the likes of Willie John McBride, Mike Gibson and Roger Young – all survivors of the 1968 British Lions – but it was not to be.

New Brighton/North of Ireland

On 11 December, it was announced that the Springboks' match at Bournemouth, due to be played on 28 January, was off. It was cancelled by the Rugby Football Union, who informed Brian Savage, secretary of the Dorset and Wiltshire Rugby Union. Their official reason was that the ground was 'not now available'. Efforts were made to find another ground for the game. It was known that the police had been worried about the security at the ground in King's Park, Bournemouth, where there was a small stand on one side but only a thin wire mesh fence protecting the other three sides.

Finding another venue was proving difficult. An attempt was made to have the match played at Poole's football ground, but the club refused to stage the match.[8] This was now the third match of the 25-game tour to run into trouble, and it was a similar problem to the tourists' first fixture, which could not be played at Iffley Road in Oxford as the Thames Valley Police could not guarantee that the game would be played in safety.

With the cancellation of the match against Ulster, another match was organised against a New Brighton/North of Ireland XV. The match was only attended by a few hundred spectators, due to no publicity. At first it was announced that the Springboks would play a seven-a-side competition among themselves to give any potential spectators something to look at, but late on the Friday night in Blackpool a fixture was arranged between the South Africans and a combined XV from New Brighton and the North of Ireland. The latter two clubs were due to play against each other that Saturday.

The Springbok team quietly entered Blackpool, the seaside resort on the Irish Sea coast of England, before they were transported in great secrecy to a field in the seaside town of Leasowe near Liverpool for the unofficial match. It was to be the first match for replacements Sakkie de Klerk (lock, Transvaal) and Charlie

Cockrell (hooker, Western Province), who had joined the side following the injuries to Martin van Rensburg and Gys Pitzer.

On Saturday morning, Bornman told the press that the Boks were going for a training session and that they should travel in the same bus as the team, which the press members found unusual. The bus then travelled on to the New Brighton Club, where the press discovered that it was going to be a real match, albeit unofficial. And spectators rocking up at the ground expecting to see an ordinary club match were excited to see a full Springbok side take the field against a team that included some of the New Brighton players, including the captain, D. Ibison, in the centre. There were only around 500 spectators because of the absence of advance publicity, which also meant there were no demonstrators present. It was still an important match in the sense that it gave an opportunity to the two replacements, Sakkie de Klerk and Charlie Cockrell – both short of match fitness – to get into action, and for star flanker Jan Ellis and lock André de Wet to return from injury. It was also the first appearance of the strong-running Gert Muller on the wing. Muller showed great pace, scored an excellent try and covered well; he looked ready to take on Scotland a week later. Ellis, who captained the side, celebrated his return with a brace of tries, and he too, would be ready to take his side on the scrum against Scotland.

In the end, the Boks had little difficulty in beating the combined XV and ran out 22-6 winners, with tries by wingers Renier Grobler and Gert Muller, centre Johan van der Schyff and flanker Jan Ellis (2), who also captained the side on the day. Full back Paul du Rand kicked a penalty and two conversions. The Combined side replied with a try by their prop D. J. K. Wilson and a penalty by fly half S. Kirkwood. While it was an unusual match, organised at very short notice, it was nevertheless some consolation after the cancellation of the Ulster fixture.[9]

Ulster

Some three weeks before the Springboks' match against Ulster, hopes were high that the South Africans would run out at Ravenhill. 'Ulster stars WILL play the Springboks,' read a headline in the *Belfast Telegraph* on 6 November. The report said that Ulster's rugby stars were not expected 'to follow the example of a Welsh international [John Taylor] by withdrawing from the team which meets the South African tourists at Ravenhill, Belfast, later this month'. The newspaper quoted Ballymena and Ireland legend Willie John McBride as saying that he would definitely play if selected.

'The thing is – apartheid is South Africa's problem and not ours,' McBride said. 'I don't think the majority of people understand it. With eight years of international rugby behind me I am completely against politics being mixed with sport. Even in Ireland politics could have crept in – thank God it hasn't.'[10]

Many years later, in a documentary on his life and commenting on the famous 1974 British Lions tour to South Africa, McBride reiterated, 'There was never any question in my mind that we should go, and I don't think that politics should be using sport, whether it's rugby, any sport, politics should not be using any sport in any way, because sport is about people. And it's about bringing people together, it's not about isolating people.'[11]

In the same documentary, Peter Hain strongly disagreed with him. Commenting on the 1974 British Lions tour, Hain said, 'I think they should have said no. I don't think they should have gone. I cannot defend any player who participated in that team and went to apartheid South Africa and where rugby was infected with apartheid. I don't see how you can justify that.'[12]

Nevertheless, the Irish international and Ulster captain Mike Gibson agreed that there would not be any reluctance on the part of Ulster players to play against the Springboks, while Irish scrum half Roger Young was quite firm that he would play if selected.

'The Springboks are 30 rugby players, not politicians. They are here to play rugby, not get involved in politics.' Colourful Irish international Ken Goodall, who was to switch to rugby league soon after the tour, also stressed the point: 'I want to play sport, not talk politics. It does not make any difference to me whom I play against.'[13]

At the same time, the Irish government refused an opposition demand that it declare the South African team unwelcome in Northern Ireland. The matter was raised in the Commons by John Hume, who stated that it was the responsibility of all to show their objection to South Africa's policy of apartheid, and to show their solidarity with the people of the country who were struggling for equality. But it was pointed out by the Minister of Education, William Long, that the team would be visiting not at the invitation of the government but the Irish Rugby Football Union.[14]

More pressure was then put on the Irish government by opposition MPs to call off the Springboks' visit to Belfast. In the Commons, Independent MP for Mid-Derry Ivan Cooper asked the Minister of Home Affairs, Robert Porter, if a decision had been reached to cancel the match between the Springboks and Ulster. At the same time, Austin Currie, the Nationalist MP for East Tyrone, urged a ban on the game because of the possibility of serious disturbances. The joint security committee chaired by Robert Porter had preliminary talks on the issue, and was expected to make a decision on whether the game should go on.

An Ulster police chief was expected to go to Twickenham on 22 November for a personal study of security precautions. District inspector John Hood, head of the RUC Special Patrol Group, was in London for the Home Office meeting at which police chiefs from various parts of Britain discussed the tour with Home Secretary James Callaghan, who was to attend the London Counties vs South Africa game at Twickenham to see for himself what could happen during the matches. It was also planned that a large force of stewards would patrol Ravenhill to help quell any disturbance at the Ulster vs South Africa match, should it take place.[15]

Following the criticism about the stewards employed at the rugby matches, on 24 November, after he had met 15 chief constables to discuss ways of handling demonstration troubles on the tour, Callaghan announced curbs on the policing of the events. Rugby stewards were to be banned from the pitch at all future Springbok tour matches, and they would not be allowed to stop demonstrators in the crowd from chanting anti-apartheid slogans. 'Everybody in this country is entitled to demonstrate,' said Callaghan. 'This is a traditional right and I don't intend to interfere with it, whether the cause is popular or unpopular.' However, he also had a warning for protesters: 'There is a difference between demonstrating and disrupting. I do not intend to let the police be made the butt of mischief-makers or those seeking violence when they are trying to carry out their duties.'

Under a plan hammered out at the Home Office meeting, stewards would simply show people to their seats and carry out similar duties. Only the police would be entitled to remove demonstrators from the field. Police and stewards were to be briefed about their respective duties before all future Springboks' matches, which would be all-ticket where possible. Where arrests were made, a senior officer would be on hand to hear any complaints.[16]

On 25 November, news reached the Springbok camp that their visit to Northern Ireland had been called off. This followed after an hour-long meeting of the Ulster Security Committee at Stormont. A statement from the Security Committee, comprising army and police chiefs and members of the Stormont Cabinet, read: 'The Security Committee were not satisfied the match would be played without prejudicing the preservation of peace and order.' Robert Porter, who was chairman of the committee, would make an order under the Special Powers Regulations prohibiting the holding of the match, the statement added.

Reports from police chiefs on disturbances at matches held in England during the tour were put before the committee. Commander John Gerrard of Scotland Yard presented a report which was also discussed. The general officer commanding troops in Northern Ireland, General Sir Ian Freeland, was opposed to the match, arguing that it might mean an end to the peaceful situation achieved in Ulster over the preceding six weeks.

W. J. Patterson, the secretary of the Ulster branch of the Irish Rugby Football Union, commented: 'It was almost certain the game would be a sell-out and Ulster rugby fans will be bitterly disappointed. Now we have a lot of paperwork to do, money must be returned, gatemen cancelled, and so on.'[17]

The game was not switched to an alternative venue, with the Springboks instead playing their makeshift fixture against a combined New Brighton and North of Ireland team at New Brighton. A newspaper report on the issue said that the decision had come as a surprise to the tourists, who were then staying in Cardiff in preparation for the game against Cardiff at Cardiff Arms Park.[18]

8

TROUBLES IN SCOTLAND

With the London Counties and North Western Counties games and the makeshift match at Leasowe out of the way, and the Ulster game cancelled, the first match in Scotland awaited the touring side. Flying to Aberdeen, the players enjoyed the sight of a snowy landscape below and on arrival in Aberdeen playfully started pelting each other with snowballs. Secrecy had to be maintained, however, and they were transported in a roundabout way from the airport to their hotel under police escort. They arrived at the Station Hotel in Aberdeen not really knowing what to expect by way of demonstrations in the city, which had a large student population.

On 2 December, shortly before the first of the Springboks' matches in Scotland started, hundreds of students began marching on Linksfield Stadium in Aberdeen as part of the anti-apartheid demonstrations. About 20 police gathered at the start of the demonstration to keep an eye on the students on their half-mile walk to the stadium. Many of the students carried banners and posters calling for an end to apartheid. It was claimed that some 200 of them had obtained tickets for admission to the ground and threatened to run on to the field during the match between the Springboks and a combined XV from the North and Midlands of Scotland. The marchers were accompanied by a small grey van displaying a large poster bearing the Nazi sign and the message 'Springboks go home'.

One of the demonstration organisers, Kenneth Chew, who was secretary of Aberdeen Students' Representative Council, said that they were warned by Aberdeen's Chief Constable, William Smith, that anyone who went on to the pitch would be arrested. Chew added that this has made it a personal decision for each protestor: 'If he or she is arrested it will be a separate selfless action rather than the normal sort of demonstration.'

A large contingent of 600 police from six counties converged on the stadium, supplemented by about 120 stewards recruited from local rugby clubs. The stewards were told that they must not become involved in any physical violence towards any person, and that pitch invaders would be dealt with by the police.

North & Midlands of Scotland

At the time that the Springboks were preparing at New Brighton, the Welsh were playing trials to pick a side to face Scotland. One Gareth Edwards was superb during the matches, and when the selectors announced to the team Edwards had been appointed as captain. The squad, consisting of 29 players, had a good look about it.

The side that the Scotland selectors picked showed four new caps, including full back Ian Smith, centre Alistair Biggar, Duncan Paterson at scrum half, and lock Gordon Brown. The latter, affectionately known as 'Broon of Troon', was to become one of the heroes of the legendary 1974 British Lions team in South Africa. The selectors also recalled the 6-foot-9-inch lock Peter Stagg, who toured South Africa with the British Lions the year before.

When they arrived in Aberdeen, the Springbok side was announced to play the North and Midlands of Scotland at the Linksfield Ground. Although the fixture was regarded as one of the easier games of the tour, the Springboks selected a strong, almost Test side. Mike Lawless was given a chance in the place of Piet Visagie at fly half, and Charlie Cockrell had an opportunity to prove that he was ready to play against Scotland only ten days after arriving in Britain. Unfortunately for the Springboks, their inspirational captain Dawie de Villiers developed a cold but it was nevertheless decided that he would play. They were all holding thumbs that it would not become worse.

The most notable player in the North of Scotland side was the prop Dave Rollo, who had already played for Scotland a record 40 times. Rollo was no stranger to South Africa, having toured there with Scotland in 1960 and again in 1962 with the British Lions. At the time he was sharing the record for the most caps for Scotland with Hawick legend Hugh McLeod, who had represented the Scots from 1954 to 1962. A farmer from Fife who always played with his stockings rolled down to his ankles, Rollo was a strong and skilful front row who could pack on either side of the scrum. The Scots had another international in Ian McCrae at scrum half, but otherwise they did not look like a side who could match the Springboks. They also did not have many opportunities to practise as a squad.

The demonstrators were there again, and it had become evident that they were trying to put up a better showing than at their last outing. The chief constable of Aberdeen, William Smith, said on the day before the match that there were two official demonstrations and that one was organised by students outside Murrayfield in peaceful protest. The match was interrupted for about 12 minutes when demonstrators ran onto the field. One of the radio commentators recalled that 'there were some great tackles executed by the police. If some of them had played for the Scots, there probably would not have been so many tries.'[1] But they had come to play some rugby. In their ninth match of the tour, the Springboks' scored a runaway victory of 37 points to three in front of a small crowd of 4000 spectators, and in good weather and on a good ground. It was their biggest victory over any team on the tour. The North of Scotland was arguably the weakest side the Boks came up against, and it showed in the scoreline, the visitors scoring eight tries, four of them by their pacy, strong-running wing Gert Muller. Were it not for two forward passes, he could have had six to his name. Centre Eben Olivier scored two, and Jan Ellis and Hannes Marais one each, while full back HO de Villiers landed five conversions and a penalty. For the Scots, wing J. F. Craswell scored a try.[2]

At this stage, with the first Test only four days away, a new threat reared its head among the Springboks: the dreaded flu. The Springboks arrived in the beautiful southern Highlands of Scotland three days before the Test in Edinburgh. Here they could enjoy some of the most magnificent natural beauty in the whole of Britain. In peaceful Peebles, the main centre in Peeblesshire, the squad could prepare for their first Test of the tour. However, Edinburgh was only some 20 miles away and through TV and the newspapers they were still aware of the demonstrators' plans and threats. The team left for Edinburgh on the Saturday morning of the Test, and would remain there until they had to travel to Wales again.[3]

The Birmingham Post reported extensively on the demonstrations and arrests at the Linksfield Stadium:

Ninety-eight demonstrators were arrested yesterday after mass invasions of the Linksfield Stadium pitch, Aberdeen, in the Springboks' first Scottish match against the North and Midlands of Scotland XV. Play was stopped three times – once for 7 minutes – as students shouting 'Sieg heil!' swooped down from the terraces and swarmed over the ground. Demonstrators defied a direct police warning that they would be arrested if they set a foot over the fence. Two protesters perched on a goalpost crossbar for 5 minutes giving the Nazi salute.

The second invasion stopped the game for 2 minutes. The third, when two men sprinted onto the ground about 15 minutes before the end, stopped play for about a minute. Those arrested during the game were photographed and charged at a temporary police station in the stadium. A further 20 people taken from the ground but not charged were loaded into a police bus and left at nearby Aberdeen beach.

Policemen took off their tunics and ties to join the wild chase over the pitch. A special squad of uniformed men waited under the grandstand but they were powerless to stop the crowds leaping the fence. Mr. William Smith, chief constable of Aberdeen, said that 29 women and two juveniles were among the 98 arrested. They had been charged with a breach of the peace and would appear in court in 2 to 4 weeks.

Mr. Smith said that a police constable had received a broken collarbone during a scuffle in the second invasion of the pitch, which stopped play for 2 minutes. He would be off duty for at least four weeks. There were 300 police among the 3,200 who watched the game, and the chief constable had a special word of praise for 16 of them. They were members of the Aberdeen police football team who stripped off their jackets and put on football boots to get a flying start on the pitch invaders.

I thought the police did extremely well considering the difficult circumstances and the small and the 7-minute invasion came shortly after the kick-off. Protesters leaped the fences and sat down or lay on the pitch waiting to be hauled away. The Springboks won the match 37-3. Yesterday's 98 arrests topped the tour chart. Seventy-seven demonstrators were arrested during the match at White City, Manchester, on November 27 and 67 were arrested on November 15 during the Swansea game.[4]

Of course, many people were quite upset about these actions and it may be worthwhile to give a view or two in the form of letters to newspaper editors. One, under the title 'Why the double standards?', read:

> It is surely significant that one of the recent letters to the *Evening Express* calling for a ban on the proposed rugby game at Linksfield was written by the chairman of the Aberdeen University Socialist Society. Some readers may remember how the *Evening Express* reported a demonstration held to outside the students in union in protest against the appearance within the union of a troupe of Russian dancers. This took place less than a year after the Russian rape of Czechoslovakia in the interests of socialism and at a time when feeling on the subject was still strong. Yet there were only four people who thought this issue worth protesting about.
>
> Where, we may all ask, were the hundreds of outraged moralists on that occasion? Why the double standards? I have no sympathy with the policies of a nation which discriminates against citizens on the ground of color or race, but until I see our student demonstrators rising to condemn Russian totalitarianism in the same spirit in which they oppose South African racism or American aggression, I will remain convinced that far from being the champions of morality and freedom, they are merely a band of Marxist yobs; the enemies of all they claim to uphold. *AC Rennie, Bucksburn.* [5]

Another appeared in the same newspaper under the heading, 'Most would vote for apartheid':

> I was amused to read the fiery letter contributed by a Mr. Alan Grant of Aberdeen University's Socialist Society, regarding the visit of the Springboks to Linksfield Stadium.

Firstly, it is interesting to note that he candidly assumes that 'most of us in Britain abhor apartheid', as this is practiced in South Africa. Now, frankly, I don't know of any referendum on this matter, and I doubt whether this socialist does either.

Of course the annual immigration of 16,000 Britons to South Africa might deplete the number of votes here in favour of South African racial policies, but personally, I feel that a fairly massive majority of people here would still give votes approving apartheid as a positive policy promoting harmony and prosperity among the races in South Africa.

Mr. Alan Grant, it appears, seems to think that those who shout loudest, that is the leftists, are the most numerous. Let him be disillusioned. The people of America voted for Mr. Nixon, the Conservative candidate, for all the din created in the streets by rowdy left-wing factions about Vietnam. Likewise, in Britain, the crowds attending the Springbok matches have enormously outnumbered the troublemakers in their midst, and have each time given the South Africans a most hearty welcome. *Trevor A Mitchell, Aberdeen.*

Trouble seemed to be brewing already for the touring party in Ireland. On 2 December, the *Daily Mirror* reported that pilots and seamen might be called on to stop the team from travelling to Ireland. This was revealed by Michael Mullen, general secretary of the Irish Transport and General Workers Union. The Irish Congress of Trade Unions had already urged union members to refuse to supply services or support for the Springboks. Mullen said, 'All our ports and airports are trade union manned, and I would expect the union concerned to act on the Congress request.' He also added, 'I would like to see the Springboks kept out at all costs.' Individual trade unions were to hold emergency meetings to form an overall policy for the Springboks' visit in January to play two matches against Ireland and Munster. It was also reported that officials of the Irish Rugby Football Union were to hold talks with trade union leaders in Dublin about the 'blacking' of the Springboks.[6]

Scotland

Scotland and British Lions flanker Rodger Arneil, now living in the Cotswolds village of Adlestrop, had no qualms about playing the Springboks, for whom he had great respect.

> As a young lad from Scotland it was a great honour to be picked to go with the Lions in 1968 to South Africa and our focus was on rugby. I was even more thrilled to be selected for all four tests and was so impressed with the hospitality and friendship we received in South Africa. Playing on the firm grounds of South Africa suited my game well and I enjoyed every minute of it. Playing against the likes of Jan Ellis, Tom Bedford and Piet Greyling was a great experience and for me they were world class.
>
> Whilst aware of the apartheid situation and the many problems my view was that politics had no place in sport. Sport is a way of making friends and reaching people of all classes and colour. Courtesy of the SARU we were asked back in 2018 with our wives for a most wonderful visit being 50 years ago in 1968. What was evident was the enormous sporting talent in the townships we visited from the youngsters we met and talked to. They saw sport as a way forward and the work being undertaken by various organisations was absolutely marvellous. The future for South Africa through sport will be formidable.[7]

During the demo tour, Arneil not only played against the Boks for Scotland, but also for Northern Counties and the Barbarians. When asked if he experienced any antagonism from sections of the public for playing against the Boks, seen by many as 'ambassadors of apartheid', he said, 'When the Boks arrived in

UK in 1969 they seemed subdued on the field in comparison with the fantastic rugby they played in South Africa in 1968. Apart from a certain (now Lord) person throwing nails onto the pitch before the international and trying to prevent the matches taking place, I experienced no ill will or bad words from anyone about South Africa or the tour. The Boks were made most welcome and friendships renewed.'[8]

The Springboks' suffered a serious setback when captain Dawie de Villiers was laid low by flu and had to withdraw from the Test side. His place was taken by Dirk de Vos, while Tommy Bedford took over the captaincy. Two players made their debut for South Africa, namely Tonie Roux and Charlie Cockrell. Otherwise it was a fairly experienced side. The outstanding flank Jan Ellis had been injured and had only started playing again in the previous match at Aberdeen, while Hannes Marais was still struggling to shake off an ankle injury.

The Springbok side to face Scotland was: HO de Villiers, Gert Muller, Eben Olivier, Tonie Roux, Sid Nomis, Piet Visagie, Dirk de Vos, Hannes Marais, Charlie Cockrell, Tiny Neethling, Piet Greyling, Frik du Preez, Gawie Carelse, Jan Ellis, Tommy Bedford (capt.). The Scotland team: Ian Smith, Sandy Hinshelwood, Chris Rea, John Frame, Alistair Biggar, Ian Robertson, Duncan Paterson, Ian McLauchlan, Frank Laidlaw, Sandy Carmichael, Wilson Lauder, Peter Stagg, Gordon Brown, Rodger Arneil, Jim Telfer (capt.).

On the Friday night before the Test some 1,500 protesters marched through the city, and on the match day the police were screening ticket holders. There were no spectators behind the goal posts as those areas had been sealed off. It was feared that not more than 15,000 spectators would show up, but by the time the two teams appeared on the field, there were some 30,000. In the main stand, the President of the South African Rugby Board, Danie Craven, was also present, but captain Dawie de Villiers was watching the match on TV.

About 200 demonstrators started booing when the South African anthem was played, but things became even worse when God Save the Queen was played and the demonstrators stole an opportunity to invade the field as the police stood to attention. Obviously rugby fans were disgusted by this display of disloyalty and disregard for tradition. The police broke formation, got in among the demonstrators and soon removed them from the ground. Some were dragged off, others simply pulled by their long hair, with no sympathy coming from the people who had come to watch the match.

When Welsh referee Meirion Joseph started the match, the Springboks' kicked off with the wind behind them. Lo and behold, Visagie missed two penalty attempts, which could have made a difference to the final score, but on the other hand the Scotland full back Ian Smith also failed with a run of first-half penalty attempts. Just before the interval, the Springboks' fly half succeeded with a 30-yard penalty (his fourth attempt) following a line-out infringement by the Scots. The Springboks' also missed a try when de Vos broke through to feed HO de Villiers, but the strong full back lost the ball on the goal line. At the interval, South Africa was leading by three points to nil.

In the second half, however, they were facing the wind and the question was whether they had done enough to hold the Scots at bay for the next 40 minutes. Scotland were dominating the line-outs, where new Springbok hooker Charlie Cockrell was having trouble throwing in from touch. At one stage Scotland took five line-outs in succession on the Springboks' throw-in. The tall Peter Stagg was causing big problems with his height, with Gordon Brown also impressive, and at the back of the line-outs Telfer, Lauder and Arneil were doing great work.

The Scots controlled through their line-out play, scrummed well and were a bit quicker to the loose ball. Behind the scrum, new cap Paterson had a good game. Soon after half-time Scotland drew level when full back Smith landed at 35-yard penalty goal after Ellis had been adjudged offside at a line-out won by Scotland. Another attempt by Smith from 42 yards went wide, while Visagie also missed with two attempts from 35 and 40 yards.

The Springboks had a good spell midway through the second half, but the Scots held on, and then, after about 34 minutes, they won a set scrum 30 yards out, the ball going from Paterson to Robertson; Rea came dashing in as if to take the pass but left the ball, which went straight to Frame. The big centre crashed through and then passed to full back Smith as he entered the line from the back; with van der Watt standing off to mark Biggar, Smith dived in for a classic try. Shortly beforehand, Springbok wing Gert Muller had left the field with a hamstring injury and van der Watt had been called on to substitute on the left wing. Smith could not convert his own try, but the 6-3 lead was quite handy. The Springboks then had some bad luck when, after having won a maul inside the Scotland 25, de Vos went blindside with players in overlap, but the referee unintentionally blew too early for a scrum and a golden chance had gone. Meirion Joseph admitted the next day that he had been too quick on the whistle.

When Scotland took the lead, there were ten minutes remaining. The Boks tried hard, but the Scots held on until the final whistle. This defeat in the first Test was a big blow, and some players were close to tears back in the dressing room. They nevertheless felt that the Scots deserved the victory on the day. They had lost too much ball at the line-out and in the loose were too slow to the ball. Danie Craven summed it up: 'We were beaten by a better side. It is not that the Springboks' are playing all that badly, but rather they are playing wrongly. The backs are moving the ball away from the forwards instead of playing back to the forwards.' At the N. B. Hotel in Edinburgh after the match, it was a jubilant Jim Telfer and his men who had reason to celebrate, while the dejected

Springboks had to lick their wounds.[9] Years later, Scotland flanker Rodger Arneil still had very pleasant recollections of the match: 'I thought the Springboks were subdued, which surprised me – however, Scotland played well on the day.'[10]

The result in Edinburgh meant that the Scots' captain Jim Telfer had steered his team to back-to-back victories over the Springboks, having captained them in 1965 as well, achieving a 'double' that few international captains could claim. Years later, in 2012, he still recalled those days when the Scots ran out against the Springboks at Murrayfield and beat them fair and square:

> The team we played in 1969 was not the strongest – they never won a Test match on that tour – but when you look down the team-list now there were some big names there. Dawie de Villiers, their inspirational captain, was withdrawn for some reason before the game at Murrayfield [he was down with flu], but they had a good back row of Tommy Bedford, who went to Oxford University, the Namibian Jan Ellis and Piet Greyling, who was a big Afrikaner.
>
> Frik du Preez was an excellent second row and prop Marais a very good ball-playing forward who went on to captain the Springboks, but we did well in the scrum and line-out, stood up to their pack and that set the platform for us. They had good backs too, Piet Visagie at stand-off, Dirk de Vos, a decent scrum half and wings Syd Nomis and Gert Muller, from Stellenbosch, who were quick. But we had a good pack, with guys like Ian McLauchlan, Frank Laidlaw, Sandy Carmichael, Peter Stagg and Gordon Brown, and Rodger Arneil, and backs like John Frame, Chris Rea and Ian Smith.
>
> The thing that made that tour different was the environment that Bok squad found themselves in. The protests over apartheid were in full flow by the time they arrived here and I think the players were a bit spooked. It got really hostile towards them

in Scotland and I remember in Galashiels we were even told by the police that we, the home South team, had to walk the mile or so down to Netherdale because if we got on our bus it might be stoned.

Police were everywhere at the ground. There were thousands of protestors and we were even spat on as we ran down the steps and on to the pitch. The South Africans were quite a young team and were taken aback by the intensity of the hatred and it must have been tough to focus on rugby.

As for the game itself, Telfer recalled that Scotland took advantage of a change in style at line-outs that troubled the Boks, where the hooker took over throwing-in duties from the winger. Visagie opened the scoring with a penalty, but Ian Smith replied with a penalty for Scotland and then finished off a fine break by centre Frame by coming into the back line – then still a novel idea – to score for a 6-3 win.[11]

A student from Dundee University at the time attended two of the Scottish fixtures, at Aberdeen and at Murrayfield, and 32 years later wrote an interesting account from a demonstrator's perspective of the confrontations between students and police, following the release of files from the Scottish Records Office concerning the tour. When the files were being compiled, Nelson Mandela was still hammering away in the stone quarry on Robben Island, with John Vorster as Prime Minister of South Africa.

Apartheid had no shortage of apologists within this country [Scotland]. They were offered a cause to rally round when the rugby unions of the home countries agreed to invite the racially selected rugby team of Vorster's South Africa to tour Britain in the winter of 1969-70. The battle lines were thus drawn for a series of confrontations between those who defended the playing of the games and those of us who opposed them. Inevitably, the former category included the police. There was nothing illegal about the tour taking place since the Government had not banned it. Therefore, it was the police's obligation to ensure that the rugby could proceed without hindrance. Equally, it was the obligation of others to maximise disruption and ensure that apartheid did not achieve the propaganda coup which the tour offered it.

Each police force with a game on its hands devised its own tactics. I was a student at Dundee University at the time and attended two of the three Scottish fixtures. The first was at Linksfield Stadium in Aberdeen, where, as the files confirm, lessons had been learned from earlier tour encounters in England. The chief constable decided that demonstrators should be allowed to enter the field of play and make their point. They were then removed and play proceeded. All very civilised.

I was one of those who intruded upon the playing surface of Linksfield Stadium that day. The seriousness of the cause aside, it was actually a funny experience, and my first encounter with police brutality, albeit of the most benign variety. One of the two big polis who assisted me from the field maintained a constant stream of apology, assuring me that he wanted nothing to do with this, and that he and his colleagues had been brought in from rural Aberdeenshire for the day. Then, just as we approached the gap between the grandstand and the terracing railings, he said to his colleague: 'Oh, well, Jimmy. Better gie his heid a dunt.' And with that, my head was steered firmly in the direction of a concrete stanchion.

A few days later, when the Springboks played Scotland at Murrayfield, the mood was very different. John Insch, the chief constable of Edinburgh, had decided on very different tactics. The terracing was guarded not by police, but by 'stewards' recruited from Scotland's rugby clubs. The police formed the second line of defence. It was a line-up designed for confrontation, and this was duly achieved. There was a huge public outcry about police tactics and the files show that chief constable Insch was unhappy about being called to account by his political master, Willie Ross, the Secretary of State for Scotland.

A memo written by a senior civil servant in St Andrew's House said that Insch 'challenged the right of the secretary of state, or the police authority, to call for reports on specific incidents'. Insch's report did not acknowledge much political diversity within the anti-apartheid movement. There were, he said, about 800 demonstrators inside the ground 'representative of international Marxist groups, the socialist societies of universities, and the Young Communist League'. His men, he said, had been subject to 'abuse in the foulest language' and cries of 'Fascist pigs' predominated. In an effort to pre-empt demands for a public inquiry into police conduct, Insch also argued that the power given to the Secretary of State to hold a public inquiry is likewise restricted to general matters and not to specific incidents.

Much of the controversy centred on the undisputed fact that the Edinburgh police did not wear numbers on their coats. It was also widely claimed that they had refused to identify themselves to the people they were manhandling. Edinburgh was one of only three forces in Scotland in which it was not standard practice to wear numbers on raincoats. The association agreed that the three forces should rectify the position, and it was also agreed that a constable should give his number to a member of the public on a reasonable request.

The aforementioned demonstrator also mentions that after he and his colleagues had been released from their brief incarceration in the Aberdeen police cells, a hundred of them were each fined £15. One of the protestors wrote to John Lennon asking if he would do a concert to raise the £1,500 required, and, incredibly,

Lennon wrote back saying that he didn't have time to do a concert but included a cheque for £1,500![12]

One of the anti-apartheid activists in Edinburgh, then studying at the university, was Gordon Brown, the British politician who became Prime Minister of the United Kingdom and Leader of the Labour Party from 2007 to 2010. Lord Peter Hain recalled, 'He was a local organiser with no special impact on the scale of the protests but an important link for us as an influential student leader and committed anti-apartheid activist in Scotland.'[13]

9

BACK TO WALES

Aberavon/Neath

On Sunday the Springboks left by plane for Rhoose Airport in South Wales, but they almost did not land because of low visibility. From then they went on to the Seabank Hotel in Porthcawl. On the Monday the Springboks trained very hard at the Green Stars Club ground at Port Talbot.

When they announced the team to face the combined Aberavon–Neath XV at Aberavon, it was clear that they had to juggle to finalise the team. No fewer than six members of the squad were down with flu, while André de Wet was played in the hope that his leg would stand up to the strain. Even Don Walton was recalled having cracked a rib only a fortnight prior. Replacement lock Sakkie de Klerk was included for his first official appearance on the tour. His previous match was against the combined side of New Brighton and the North of Ireland, the unofficial fixture arranged to replace the cancelled match against Ulster.

Forward power was the key in the post-war period for the respected Neath Rugby Football Club. They won the Snelling Sevens in 1964 and, led by Brian Thomas, who had been capped

21 times for Wales between 1964 and 1969 and toured South Africa with Wales in 1964, recaptured the Welsh championship as well as the Anglo-Welsh *Sunday Telegraph* pennant in 1966/67. Neath was to become the first senior Welsh club to celebrate its centenary in 1971/72. The last time when the Springboks played Aberavon and Neath, during the 1960/61 tour with Avril Malan as captain, the Boks won 25-5. However, the local side was expected to give them a good run for their money this time around. The fly half for the opposition, David Parker, was only 5 feet 2 inches tall and weighed just 117 pounds. The number eight, Wilson Lauder, only four days earlier had played on the flank for Scotland against the Springboks.

For this match the Springboks had to do well or else their tour would be in difficulty. Fortunately, not many demonstrations were anticipated in the Welsh steel town. It was said that the police outnumbered the demonstrators by seven to one. The senior police officers had prepared their plans well for a peaceful staging of the match. The chief constable of the South Wales Police, Melbourne Thomas, said that they would enforce the law and keep the peace at all times.

When the two teams took the field the weather and the ground were fine and are there was a crowd of some 10,000 people. An English referee, R. F. Johnson, was in charge of the game. The match set off at a lively pace but surprisingly, when the interval arrived, there was still no score for either side. Poor Piet Visagie failed with an early penalty attempt from 35 yards, and although several penalties were awarded, none were within kicking distance. For the Combined side, full back Hodgson fielded and kicked well and made several brave marks to hold out the Boks. The two opposing props, Brian Thomas and Ronnie Potgieter, at one stage engaged in some punching, but after that things settled down.

In the second half, the Combined XV made several attacks through the backs and were ably supported by both forwards, but the Springboks defended well. About 11 minutes after the interval,

Visagie succeeded with a penalty from 30 yards out after an offside infringement by Whitlock. Then followed a scoring spree in which the Springboks scored 19 points in as many minutes to sew up the game, drawing warm applause from the Port Talbot crowd. They scored six tries without reply.

First Visagie got the ball from Eben Olivier on the run, kicked diagonally ahead and then fell on the ball just before it skidded into touch. Visagie converted his own try for the Boks to take an 8-0 lead. Four minutes later Combined wing Fleay was caught with the ball in defence by Olivier, who robbed him and sent Van der Merwe over in the corner for an unconverted try. After another eight minutes the Springboks' heeled from a scrum in their own 25, Visagie kicked over the first line of defence before Olivier booted on. Hall, covering at the back, gathered but was tackled. Grobler gathered the release and ran 20 yards to score at the posts. Visagie converted. Only three minutes later the Springboks won a line-out and the ball went along the back line for Tonie Roux to join in from full back, sending the speedy Van der Watt around full back Hodgson to score the best try of the match. Visagie failed with the conversion but the lead was now 19-0.

In the closing minutes the Springboks' scored two more tries. From a line-out, the Boks worked an overlap to put Olivier in for an unconverted try, and then the final try came after some quick hands, with Olivier again going in for the try. Visagie's conversion made the final score 27-0. It was a happy and content Springboks side that left the field, having displayed some off their best football of the tour. Afterwards, a delighted Danie Craven said, 'They looked like real Springboks today!'[1]

Craven's presence with the team could not be underestimated. After the Test against Scotland, he was to stay on for another five matches. He was requested by the tour management to attend management meetings, to which he agreed, on condition that this would only be in an advisory capacity.[2] 'Doc was one of the most remarkable people I have ever met,' captain Dawie de Villiers says of his former mentor. 'He was an academic, pedagogue, psychologist, rugby historian and many other things, but it was as Mr Rugby that he became the best-known personality in world rugby. His success as coach and administrator was based on his thorough insight into the game, the laws and techniques and innovative approach. He wanted you to learn to think for oneself, as he himself had grown up with the game. He was Mister Rugby because he personified the most noble principles and true spirit of rugby like no-one before or after him. He was strongly opposed to the principle of money in rugby, almost fanatically so. His strength and status was based on his ability to work for long hours, which enabled him to lead South African rugby for so long, be a brilliant coach and still gain three doctors degrees and other academic achievements.'[3]

Following their reception at the Afan Lido, the Springboks party returned to Porthcawl a happy bunch and from there, on the Thursday, returned to the Angel Hotel in Cardiff. Back in Cardiff they enjoyed a civic reception by the Lord Mayor at the Banqueting Hall of Cardiff Castle. Manager Corrie Bornman described the game against the Combined XV as 'one of the best matches of the team to date'. He also reported that 'only two demonstrators had come onto the field and they were jeered by the crowd'.[4]

'The scene at the rugby game between the South Africans and the Combined Aberavon and Neath team at the Port Talbot today was amongst the quietest yet for the Springboks' tour in South Wales,' the *Coventry Evening Telegraph* reported on the day of the match. 'Two demonstrators were on the field after 10 minutes of the second half, but they were quickly removed by police. The match was not held up. Before the match the ground, guarded inside and out by police, was a virtual fortress, but there were no signs of trouble. Anti-apartheid groups had planned to distribute 5 000 pamphlets to spectators on their way in. Police suspected that some demonstrators may have obtained tickets for the all-ticket game.'[5]

In their match report, the *Birmingham Post* suggested that the tourists would have gained confidence from the match against Aberavon and Neath:

> The Springboks, hit by illness and injury, received a welcome boost to their morale at Aberavon yesterday. They won by three goals, one penalty goal and three tries to nil, and will approach the tough match at Cardiff on Saturday with new heart. The combined side must have been optimistic about their chances and gave the 12,000 supporters some heartening moments in a scoreless first half. Winger Ian Hall put in some powerful bursts and diminutive fly half David Parker worried the Springboks defence with some judicious kicking. But these movements were wasted through lack of support.
>
> The Springboks also lacked support after setting up promising attacking positions in the first half and it was not until 10 minutes after half time that they really got on top. As they grew in confidence they really cut loose and produced some irresistible running rugby. Outside half Piet Visagie, who scored 12 of the points, began the scoring spree with a penalty goal and scored a try which he converted after what seemed a forward pass. Reserve scrum half Dirk de Vos had his best game of the tour, so the whole back division prospered.
>
> Grobler, Olivier, Van der Merwe and Van der Watt all ran strongly as the Springboks eradicated the mistakes which had spoilt their chances in the first half. The whole of this three-quarter line scored tries and Olivier's two at the end were real beauties. Visagie converted two of the tries in addition to his own.[6]

Ironically, the tour's biggest opponent, Peter Hain, was to become an ardent follower of the Welsh All Blacks at Neath, where he was of course better known for disrupting rugby than supporting it. Years later, during by-election campaigns, his prospective constituents reminded him of that turbulent afternoon in Swansea: 'I had people coming up to me saying, "I'm a Labour voter but you spoiled my Saturday,"' he recalled.

Swansea proved a particularly fractious confrontation. 'St Helen's is the one protest everyone remembers as it got extremely nasty,' Peter Hain admitted years later. 'I've had at least a dozen constituents tell me they carried me off the pitch that day but the truth is I wasn't even there. There were around 25 matches on that tour throughout the country and as I was organising the campaign I couldn't go to all of them ... There was quite a lot of support but the average rugby fan didn't understand why we were doing it,' Hain explains. 'Sport was considered to be outside politics. It split friends. It split families. Yet since Nelson Mandela was freed, so many rugby supporters have said to me, "I hated you in 1969 but now I understand why you did it." ... I became aware of the relationship between politics and sport when I was a student. It really started because I have always been a sports nut. Even now as a Cabinet Minister I go straight from the front pages to the back pages, look at the rugby and football and work my way back into the paper. So because I'd always been a sports fan and played rugby [at school] I knew how psychologically vital that great fanaticism was to the whole white South African mind set and apartheid. It's very important to Neath that the club are doing well. I'm a season ticket holder and try to catch as many games at the Gnoll as I can.'[7]

Cardiff

The Cardiff vs Springboks matchday programme had a refreshingly entertaining introduction by one 'D. J. H.':

Ever since our own 24th of Foot stopped Cetshwayo's gallop at Rorke's Drift on January 22nd 1879, winning 11 V.C.'s in the process, there has been a strong link between South Africa and

South Wales. There has been an interchange of peoples, ideas and rugby teams to this very day. There has even been an attempt to reproduce in each other's countries certain outstanding features. For this we must thank our Iron and Coal masters, who after going to sink the gold mine shafts on the High Veldt came back with a deep love of South Africa. One of them tried to create a Table Mountain at the top end of the Taff and gave us the old Dowlais slag heap. Another ringed Fochriw with coal tips in an effort to reproduce the effect of the gold tips at Johannesburg. They all decided not to build pithead baths so that the black-faced colliers singing on their way home brought back memories of the Zulus chanting on their way back to the Kraals from the Gold mines.

The sheep farmers of the Great Karroo are in constant touch with the Welsh Hill Farmers. They are hoping to breed a cross between a Merino and a Welsh Ewe and reproduce a hardy sheep with a heavy fleece and succulent meat that doesn't feed in my back garden. Of course there have been failures. For instance, there is no satisfactory translation of 'Sosban Fach' into Afrikaans. We can't copy their climate and they can't make Lava Bread but we are trying to grow our own wine and we wait for a bottle of Chateaux Taibach that equals the products of the Cape.

Wales because of its geography and its two languages can be pretty divided, and this also applies to South Africa [English and Afrikaans]. However, the one thing that brings the separate factions of each country together into a common cause is Rugby Football, and it is Rugby Football that has forged such close links between the two nations. The Cardiff Club and Wales have toured South Africa and no-one who toured will ever forget the magnificence of the country and the hospitality of its people. We have too a healthy respect for their Rugby and I suspect that they don't regard us as pushovers either. We all look forward to a match that is full of what is best in Welsh and South African Rugby and then to an evening when we can attempt to emulate their hospitality.[8]

Decades earlier, on the 1906/07 Springbok tour, with Paul Roos as their captain, the South Africans had beaten Wales 11-0 and only Cardiff had remained to prevent them from achieving a grand slam in Wales. On the day, Cardiff were brilliant in the mud with fast running, accurate handling and controlled dribbling, and won the game 17-0. All this time later, in 1970, that victory was still the best by a British side against a Springbok touring team. On the most recent Springbok tour of 1960/61, Avril Malan's Boks had beaten the Blue and Blacks 13-0. Unfortunately for Cardiff, the great Welsh fly half Barry John could not play and his place was to be taken by B. Davies.

Cardiff prop John O'Shea recalled the general feeling among the Welsh players about the disruptions of the demonstrations. 'Most of us were very upset and very annoyed at the disruptions and demonstrations organised by a Mr Peter Hain who in latter years became a leading politician. The only player that I knew who gave up his place in the Welsh team because of his views on apartheid was John Taylor who toured with the British Lions to South Africa in 1968. My feeling was Rugby was rugby and politics were politics.'[9]

During the tour O'Shea also played against the Boks for Cardiff. Asked if he experienced any antagonism for playing against the Boks, he said, 'The Cardiff game presented me with a very awkward situation. I was a brewery representative in the Cardiff area and I had just organised a major contract for the supply of beer to the Cardiff University. The Students Union wished to present a petition to the Cardiff Rugby Club to ask our players to consider not taking part in the game. The Cardiff Rugby Club refused to accept the petition and would not allow the students on the premises to hand over the petition. The Student's Union then contacted me to make me aware of the situation and hinted that if they were not allowed to present the petition to the players the beer contract at the University could be in jeopardy. I offered them a compromise that I would meet their delegation at the Gwyn Nicholls Gate entrance to the Arms Park approximately one hour before the kick-off. They could then present me with the petition which I would deliver to the players in the dressing room. I advised them that any player who wished to withdraw could do so. The Students Union accepted my arrangement. Cardiff also reluctantly accepted the arrangement as the petition was to be accepted outside the ground.'[10]

The Springboks made several changes for the match against Cardiff. Nomis replaced Grobler and Mike Lawless and Dawie de Villiers' came in for Visagie and De Vos. Hannes Marais replaced Potgieter at prop and Greyling came in for Van Deventer, with Ellis's shoulder not yet ready for hard contact. Albie Bates got another chance on the side of the scrum. HO de Villiers still had trouble with his hamstring, therefore giving Tonie Roux another chance to bid for a test place at full back.

On the Friday night before the match it was announced that Paul Durand had requested to return to South Africa after he was told that he would not be fit in the next four to five weeks. Centre Johan van der Schyff was informed that he would be right to play in another two to three weeks.

Before the match at Cardiff, news was also received of the MCC's decision to invite the South African cricket team to Britain in 1970 in spite of the views of the Stop the Seventy Tour campaign and the Minister of Sport. The question was asked, why should they cancel the tour because of a minority opinion?

The Cardiff side was not regarded as a particularly good one. The team had played indifferently during the first few months of the season; they had difficulty in beating Swansea the previous Saturday. Star fly half Barry John was also absent from the side, but at least Gareth Edwards was there to steer the ship. The main weakness appeared to be the pack's overall lack of mobility, and it was feared that they would not stay the pace once the Springboks started moving the ball.

With the help of the Communist Party and the Church in Wales, the anti-apartheid demonstrators organised a 1,500-strong march through the city of Cardiff, about two hours before the kick-off. Fortunately, these demonstrators were peaceful and presented no problems to the police.

Once again, the weather was fine and the ground good when the Springboks and Cardiff ran out at Cardiff Arms Park in front of 28,000 spectators. There was a good vibe and the crowd rendered a spontaneous national Welsh anthem before referee Lamb blew his whistle for the kick-off. Cardiff won the toss and the Springboks kicked off with Cardiff facing the sun. The Springboks were immediately out of the blocks and before long were awarded a penalty 40 yards out, but Lawless failed to convert it into points. After only 10 minutes of play the signs were ominous that the home side would find it very difficult to conquer the South Africans, who were playing with great spirit and determination.

The Springboks got first points on the board when, following a line-out on the Cardiff 25, the ball went back to Lawless and he coolly dropped a goal from 25 yards out. Before long they went further ahead. From line-out the ball went down the back line some 30 yards out, and Nomis turned in from the right wing and took the ball between his centres to confuse the Cardiff defence. He swerved out towards the right again and, confronted by Gethin, passed to Johan van der Merwe, who went over in the corner for an excellent try. Lawless could not convert, but the Boks were looking good. Just before the half time whistle, Edwards was penalised for not putting the ball in straight, and from 25 yards, near the touchline, Lawless landed the penalty to give the Springboks a nine-point lead.

In the second half Cardiff employed a four-man line-out in an effort to counter de Klerk and de Wet in the middle and the tall Albie Bates jumping at the back. Twenty minutes into the second half Cardiff were awarded a penalty after Lawless had been caught in possession following a desperate scramble in defence. Full back Gethin succeeded with the 30-yard penalty to narrow the score to 9-3. Only five minutes later, and unfortunately for Cardiff, Gethin failed with a second attempt from 25 yards. Five minutes before the final whistle, Lawless had a kick at goal from 40 yards after Cardiff had gone offside at a maul, but it went wide to the right of the posts. Centre Tony Williams gathered, but delayed his clearing kick and it was charged down by Nomis who had come racing up at full speed. The ball rebounded over the Cardiff goal line and Nomis was able to touch down before Ken Jones could get to the ball. Lawless could not convert the gift try, but by now the game was surely safe. Just before the final whistle the Springboks scored a fine try when van der Watt turned in from the left wing and ran straight through before he was stopped; from the quick heel, de Villiers punted to the left corner where another maul developed, and, winning it again, de Villiers put Tonie Roux over on the blindside. De Villiers himself converted, taking the score to a convincing 17-3 victory for the tourists. It was the largest ever gained over Cardiff by any Springbok side in history. The crowd showed its appreciation by warmly applauding the Springboks as they left the field.[11]

At the after-match function, Cardiff's chairman, Brian Mark, told the Springboks in his speech, 'You must be heartily sick of demonstrators and it is a matter of regret that the tour has been full of incidents. Please do not be misled by the minority of militant demonstrators. You are indeed very welcome as our guests. It is a pity that a little more tolerance is not shown by people towards you, for I feel that we should cherish things that unite us, and rugby football is one of these. I congratulate you on your win, which you well deserved, and also the police for ensuring that the match was played in sound and sane surroundings, while the crowd showed their appreciation of your good rugby.'

THE 1969/70 SPRINGBOK TOURING TEAM TO THE UNITED KINGDOM. *Back row, left to right:* Johan van der Schyff, Don Walton, Piet Greyling, Mike Jennings, Gawie Carelse, Martin van Rensburg, André de Wet, Albie Bates, Tiny Neethling, Gert Muller, Eben Olivier. *Middle row:* Johann van der Merwe, Piet Visagie, Renier Grobler, HO de Villiers, Paul Durand, Tonie Roux, Piet van Deventer, Ronnie Potgieter, Gys Pitzer, Andy van der Watt, Mike Lawless, Dirk de Vos. *Seated:* Frik du Preez, Sid Nomis, Tommy Bedford *(vice capt.)*, Corrie Bornman *(manager)*, Dawie de Villiers *(capt.)*, Avril Malan *(coach)*, Hannes Marais, Jan Ellis, Mof Myburgh.

Springboks Andy van der Watt and Johan van der Schyff having a break during the lengthy detour before the match against Oxford University.

Piet Greyling, Dawie de Villiers and another Springbok inside Twickenham Stadium passing the time before kick-off against Oxford University.

Springbok captain Dawie de Villiers feeds his back line in the first tour match against Oxford University. The other Springboks are Mike Jennings and Piet Greyling (no. 13). Note the empty North Stand, closed on police advice.

Anti-apartheid and Stop the Seventy Tour activist Peter Hain (now Lord Hain) is removed from the Twickenham ground by policemen during the Springboks vs Oxford match.

Springboks vs Newport at Rodney Parade. Gys Pitzer about to pass to his captain Dawie de Villiers. The other Springboks are Tiny Neethling, Frik du Preez, Mof Myburgh and Piet Greyling.

Newport centre David Cornwall races away with Barry Llewellyn in support to score one of his side's two tries, with Springboks Paul Durand, Piet Visagie, Sid Nomis and Martin van Rensburg in pursuit.

Policemen forming a human wall against demonstrators at Swansea.

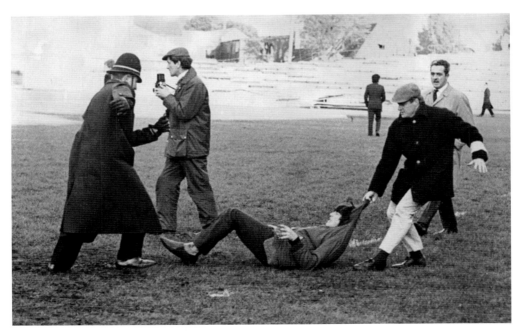

A demonstrator is dragged from the pitch by a steward at Swansea, with a policeman ready to lend a hand.

Above: *The speedy Springbok wing Andy van der Watt goes over on the corner against Swansea at St Helens Ground, with Swansea's Clive Dyer too late to stop him. The Springboks won 12-0.*

Right: *Mike Lawless through a gap against Swansea, with Tiny Neethling, Dawie de Villiers and Gawie Carelse in the background.*

The mobile Springbok prop Hannes Marais breaks away in the match against Gwent with Gawie Carelse and Mof Myburgh in support.

Tommy Bedford scores for the Springboks vs the London Counties at Twickenham. The Springboks finished with a good 22-6 win after a 6-6 score at half-time.

Play interrupted in the London Counties game as demonstrators run onto the field. Piet Visagie (10) and Piet Greyling (13) look on.

The Springboks vs London Counties at Twickenham. A Counties move is stopped by Frik du Preez; the other Springboks are Gawie Carelse, Ronnie Potgieter, Dawie de Villiers (17), Albie Bates and Sid Nomis. No. 8 for Counties is Mervyn Davies.

"T'will be a fight, Paddy—we've even got Paisley and Devlin building barricades!"

A cartoon from the Daily Mirror *of 2 December 1969, depicting Irish labour opposition to the tour.*

The Springbok speedster Gert Muller scores one of his four tries for South Africa against the North of Scotland at Aberdeen.

Scotland full back Ian Smith scores his side's only try with Tommy Bedford (no. 8) too late to stop him.

Above: *Gareth Edwards is confronted by Hannes Marais in the Springboks vs Cardiff match at Cardiff Arms Park. The Boks won 17-3.*

Right: *Tonie Roux scores the Springboks' final try against Cardiff with referee Larry Lamb already well positioned.*

Demonstrators clash with police at Cardiff Arms Park.

Demonstrators at Aldershot before the Springboks' match against the Combined Services.

Springbok lock Frik du Preez easily outjumps his Combined Services opponents, with Tiny Neethling (2), Gawie Carelse (7), Hannes Marais (5) and Piet van Deventer in support, and scrum half Dirk de Vos (18) waiting.

Demonstrators sitting in front of the Springbok team bus at their London hotel to prevent them from leaving for Twickenham.

The man who tried to hijack the Springboks' team bus in London is led away by police. On the extreme left is Springbok prop Ronnie Potgieter, with Gert Muller at far right in the background.

A controversial moment in the South Africa vs England Test. John Pullin is awarded a try after Dawie de Villiers had dotted down first. The Springbok captain looks at referee Dave Kelleher in surprise with Piet Visagie (10) protesting the decision.

England and British Barbarians three-quarter David Duckham was one of the most dangerous backs the Springboks had come up against on the tour.

Demonstrators at Coventry during the Springboks' match against the Midland Counties (West).

Demonstrators at Lansdowne Road in Dublin where the Springboks played against Ireland. Their protests received more press coverage than the match.

More demonstrators at Lansdowne Road.

Piet Greyling scores for the Springboks in the Test against Ireland. With him are Tommy Bedford and Frik du Preez (no. 7).

Dawie de Villiers gets his back line going against Ireland in Dublin. On the ground is Mof Myburgh, with Frik du Preez behind him. On either side of Du Preez are Willie John McBride and Fergus Slattery.

HO de Villiers was one of the stars of the tour, excelling as an attacking as well as defensive full back for the Boks in difficult conditions.

The tour management: Dawie de Villiers, Tommy Bedford, Corrie Bornman and Avril Malan, seen here with Handel C. Rogers of the Welsh Rugby Union (extreme left).

Sid Nomis scores South Africa's only try in the Cardiff mud-bath against Wales.

Jubilation from Gareth Edwards after scoring Wales's equalising try at the death in the Test in Cardiff.

Jan Ellis in full flight against the Barbarians at Twickenham. Ellis was outstanding and scored two fine tries in the Boks' 21-12 victory.

Springbok captain Dawie de Villiers is carried off by Mike Gibson and Gareth Edwards after the final whistle of the Springboks/Barbarians match at Twickenham.

 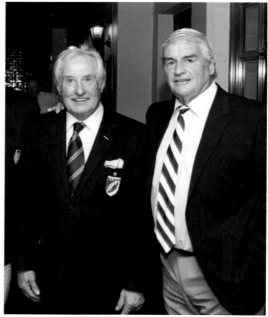

Above left: *Former Springbok captain Dawie de Villiers as South African Ambassador in London in 1979, on his way to deliver his credentials to Queen Elizabeth.*

Above right: *Old foes but forever friends: the legendary Sir Gareth Edwards and HO de Villiers in Cape Town, 2018.*

Below: *Dawie de Villiers and Chris Laidlaw in Auckland in 1998. Both had successful careers in politics after retiring from rugby.*

Corrie Bornman replied that the team had 'got back on the rails in Wales' and that 'it is easy to play good rugby when the atmosphere is right'. He also added, 'The civic reception on Wednesday [at Cardiff Castle] required a lot of courage to stage in these troubled times, but the courage is typical of the people of Wales and we are greatly indebted to them for their kindness.'

Springbok captain Dawie de Villiers had predicted after the defeat to Gwent that the Springboks would be much stronger when they returned to Wales again, and he said, 'We regret leaving Wales after such a happy and successful time. Naturally, we felt downhearted after the Scottish match because we hate losing matches, as do the Welsh. We will remember this week as our Welsh revival. You have made us feel welcome on and off the field, but you also know how to take a defeat like sportsmen, as we feel we did earlier in the tour.'[12]

Sid Nomis must have had a hard day on the field, as he collapsed through physical exhaustion after the function and spent the night in hospital, but the next day he was nevertheless able to travel with the Springboks' party to London.

Cardiff captain John O'Shea said that his recollections 'were both happy and sad, I was proud to captain my great club against the mighty Boks, however, we suffered our greatest defeat in this game to date against any touring side. The game was not particularly rough or dirty, we were able for the first time to match and even pressurise their scrum. The previous Cardiff game in 1960/61 was the game that was very rough. In this game I believe Cardiff took on more than they bargained for and ended up with probably only 12 players that were fit.'

During the match, he came up against the big prop Mof Myburgh. 'I played against Mof first in 1967 for Cardiff against Northern Transvaal, then again in 1968 [for the British Lions] against Northern Transvaal and South Africa. At that time Mof was probably the biggest prop playing international rugby.

The Springbok pack prided itself on being the No. 1 scrummaging side in the world, they scrummed very low and were virtually immovable. Many times they would drive us backwards and Mof played a vital part in their excellent scrum. In the Cardiff game in '69 the Springbok pack were not the scrummaging force that they had been and we had learnt technique from them. We were able to take a couple of tightheads during that game, which to a tighthead prop was like scoring two magnificent tries. Maybe that day Mof felt sorry for me!'[13]

The Combined Services

There was still one match before the Test against the Roses. This match took place on 16 December against the Combined Services at Aldershot Military Stadium. The team travelled from Cardiff by train to London to book in at the Park Lane Hotel, and the Monday before the match they travelled to a hotel near Aldershot where they could sleep, in order not to have to do the fairly long bus trip on the day of the match.[14]

Back in London on the Sunday afternoon, the Springbok team to play the Combined Services was announced with 10 changes from the side that defeated Cardiff convincingly. Nine of the players in the Test against Scotland were included with an eye on the forthcoming test against England on the weekend. HO de Villiers returned at full back, Renier Grobler on the wing, De Vos and Visagie were paired at halfback, and Mike Jennings was included at no. 8 for his third match of the tour.

On the side of the Combined Services, two players had faced the Springboks before: Ian Smith, the full back, played in the Test for Scotland at Murrayfield; and Doug Boyle, the centre from Oxford, had already tasted victory against the Springboks in the first match of the tour.

With the team's arrival at the field everything seemed neatly organised. There was even a small camp for demonstrators with a clear sign board that read 'Demonstrators Arena'. Here the demonstrators stood shouting at the top of their voices as much as they liked, but it seemed that there were many soldiers who would have liked to get among them to shut them up.

The programme for the match against the Combined Services was not impressive, consisting of only two pages, but it did contain the following words:

> As this was written, the South African touring party were battling with a start to their venture bedevilled by circumstances beyond their control in the shape of injuries and public demonstrations against them. The majority of people think that whatever the rights or wrongs of the political implications, and while conceding that anybody is perfectly entitled to voice his opinions peaceably as loud as he likes and for as long as he likes, as soon as demonstrations physically threatened law and order they lose the strength of reason.
>
> Whether rightly or wrongly, we invited the Springboks, and while they are here, they are our guests. But the early demonstrations could hardly fail to have a damaging psychological effect on the youngsters of the party, here for the first time. This was probably a true explanation of the Springboks' shaky start than the loudly ventilated opinion that they were weaker than any predecessors.[15]

Conditions were good for the match at the Military Stadium, which was attended by 6,000 spectators. No large demonstrations were anticipated, but in order for any such events to be dealt with by the civil authorities, it was agreed that the Hampshire Police patrol the ground and not the Military Police.

There was a general feeling that the Springboks would win comfortably, but the men from the Combined Services were a determined bunch and not prepared to just roll over. They took the lead after only five minutes of play. They won two mauls in quick succession and the big lock Hanna led the charge before the Combined Services won another maul, scrum half Spawforth put right wing Jeffray over in the corner. Full back Smith failed with the conversion, but the Combined Services were in front by three points to nil. Both Carelse and Visagie failed with penalty attempts, but after 18 minutes the Springboks drew even when Van der Merwe made a good break, and with HO de Villiers joining the line Van der Watt got away on the overlap and scored in the corner with Smith unable to stop him. Visagie failed to convert, and soon after Frik du Preez failed with a 52-yarder and then Visagie again with the Boks' fifth attempt.

The Combined Services then took the game to the Springboks; first Campbell and then Spawforth failed with drop goal attempts, but in the 34th minute the Combined scored their second try through no. 8 Hoon, who collected from a ruck and charged over. Smith was again wide with his conversion kick. Soon after de Villiers failed with yet another Springbok penalty attempt, and as half time arrived, the Combined Services were leading 6-3.

The Springbok forwards were not playing as a unit and lacked drive in the tight and loose. In addition, Cockrell still had problems throwing in at the line-out. About 10 minutes into the second half, De Vos made a fine break off some 60 yards, but unfortunately Grobler missed a pass that could have led to a try. Smith then missed a penalty from 45 yards out, to the dismay of the Combined Services supporters. Then, when the Services failed to clear from their own 25, De Vos started a move on the open side of a maul, with Visagie, Olivier and Van der Merwe handling before the latter dived over in the left corner. HO de Villiers' conversion was wide. Fortunately for the Springboks, Spawforth failed to gather a tap from a line-out and Hannes Marais pounced on the ball before crashing over for a try. This time de Villiers converted. But the Springboks were not done yet, and in the last minute of injury time

Grobler ran in for a try after a rapid backline move from a line-out. De Villiers' conversion was again wide, but the Springboks could breathe a sigh of relief with a 14-6 win.

The general consensus was that the Springboks had a lucky escape and that the scoreline flattered them.[16] But as they say, a win is a win, and the Springboks really needed that.

In the meantime, the Somerset and Bath police chiefs had discussed the venue for the game against the Southern Counties, which was being transferred from Bournemouth because of its open ground. It was eventually decided to take the match to Gloucester, where the Kingsholm ground was better suited for a big match in the prevailing conditions.

The Springboks returned to London from Aldershot and on the Wednesday had a hard practice. The police preparations for Twickenham were building up; it was the third match to be played there and it was therefore expected that things would be a lot less difficult for the players. It was an all-ticket match, and many more rugby fans were expected to attend than demonstrators.

The Springbok team to face England was announced on the Thursday morning. It was expected that changes would be made in the second row and that Lawless would come in at fly half at the expense of Piet Visagie. The latter had been only a shadow of his true self, with even his renowned place-kicking failing to provide points. Lawless was perceived as being better on attack and it was felt that the backline would be more potent with him at stand-off.

During the week it was announced that two of the Springboks, full back Paul Durand and centre Johan van der Schyff, were to return home to South Africa after the England Test. Durand had picked up minor injuries; he could perhaps have played before the end of the tour, but he was apparently not a happy tourist and felt homesick. It was also announced that the experienced Springbok three-quarter Mannetjies Roux, from Griqualand West, would be joining the team. He had not been available for the whole tour because of his commitments as a sheep farmer near Victoria West in the Great Karoo, but when the call came from Britain he was ready to come to the aid of the national team. Roux had toured Great Britain with the Springboks of Avril Malan in 1960/61, so the conditions – apart from the demonstrators – would not be unfamiliar.

The Test against England awaited. The tour was now about halfway, and there was still a lot of rugby to be played – and plenty of troubles off the field to be overcome.

10

ENGLAND & COUNTIES GALORE

England

Peter Hain and the Stop the Seventy Tour campaign were still exploring all avenues to stop the tour. One was to send letters to the members of the England rugby team due to play South Africa at Twickenham via their clubs, asking them not to play against the Springboks. One of these players was Bob Hiller, a Harlequin and the new England captain, who received the following letter:

To allow the Springboks to play in Great Britain shows the hypocrisy of making these representatives of apartheid welcome. As a member of the England team, you are obviously deeply involved in this matter and we appeal to your conscience to refuse to play in this match.

We fully realize the great personal sacrifice this would entail for you, especially as this would be your first captaincy, but a courageous refusal on your part and by the team as a whole would have a tremendous effect in the fight against racialism in sport.

In response to the letter, Hiller said that it would not change his intention to play in the game. He said, 'I will be at Twickenham to play rugby. I do not feel that politics are part of sport.'

The Right Revd David Sheppard, Bishop of Woolwich and former England cricket Test captain, said he would take part in a demonstration against the Springboks at Twickenham. 'I felt I wanted to take a genuine part in a protest against racial discrimination in sport. I believe in non-violent protest. The organizers of the demonstration also believe in this and I wanted to associate myself with them.'[1]

The clash was eagerly awaited by both England fans and the Springbok supporters back home. On the day of the Test, the *Birmingham Post* carried a lengthy but insightful preview, written by British rugby writer Michael Blair, in which the England side's ability to conquer the Springboks was questioned:

England have never beaten SA in a test and on the face of it they may never have a better chance than at Twickenham this afternoon. The Springboks, as has been proved four times already, are far from invincible. What Oxford University, Newport, Gwent and Scotland have achieved, the best prepared England side of all time should be capable of repeating. So says logic. But reasoning tends to flounder at the point where we start to assess the calibre of the side England have in the field. They represent the first venture of the new selection regime and no one can tell how they will shake down. As a trial side they were pretty dreadful and I can sense no great conviction behind their chances of making a significant improvement. They have been picked for courage and bulk and this at the expense of class. The pack is large, but is it able? The halfbacks are brave and they are steady, but are they clever enough to use a brilliant three-quarter line? These are the key questions. In theory, the best way to beat the Springboks is to make them run about, to disorganize their forward drive and split their collective power. But England have sunk their capital in a side who will stand and fight.

Strength, of course, must be met with strength otherwise England would have no starting point. But supremacy or even parity up front should be the means of attack elsewhere and there must be doubts about Nigel Starmer-Smith and Ian Shackleton, both of them playing in their first international at halfback. A breakdown here would be ruinous for England, for in Tommy Bedford the Springboks have one of the world's great loose forwards, a predator and a builder, and if he and De Villiers get the South African pack moving forward then I would not fancy England's chances.

Shackleton does not appear today as the people's choice. He has never, in his short career looked like an England fly half and one hopes he has not been unnerved by his two flops at Twickenham in the second trial and in the University match. The selectors obviously have great faith in him and perhaps they have seen more to his game than the rest of us. He's certainly an aggressive player and does not shirk his defence but these are scarcely the credentials that stamp a first-class player. My belief is that Shackleton is in this side on the strength of his defence and the danger is that England have bent too far backwards in their search for a contrast to John Finlan, whose defence they plainly mistrust.

Given that Shackleton turns out to be at least an adequate link, then England should be the better side behind a scrum. I say this because there is another element that threatens to undermine their effectiveness. That is the presence of Bob Hiller as full back and skipper. I do not think any man should lead a side from behind and it seemed to me that Hiller was trying too hard to justify the honour in the final trial. His entry into the three-quarter line was too frequent and too badly judged and he gave the impression of getting in the way. And his defence suffered. This England three-quarter line is big enough, quick enough and clever enough to look after itself and Hiller should join them for surprise value rather than as a standard ploy... For the South Africans this match is vital. The air of invincibility they have carried over here for 64 years has long since blown away and they are now fighting to salvage their tour. The best friends, and a host of apologists who saw them lose three of their first five matches, said they would be a different proposition when the Tests started. Scotland shattered that one.[2]

Prior to the Test against England, a nasty incident occurred at the Springboks' hotel in London, to become known as the 'bus incident'. The Test team had unobtrusively moved to the Excelsior Hotel near Heathrow Airport the night before the Test to avoid the Christmas weekend traffic through London as well as any noisy demonstrators. The rest of the squad would travel to the same hotel by bus on the Saturday morning, have lunch together and then travel to Twickenham with the Test players.

Springbok centre Johan van der Merwe was one of the players who experienced the bus incident first-hand:

The non-playing members left our hotel [Park Lane] to get onto the bus that would take us to Twickenham for the Test. Some of us got on board while others still waited between the hotel and the bus. A small group of demonstrators plonked down in front of the bus, but the bus driver assured us that they would move their asses quickly once he started the bus and took off. While the bus driver was talking to the Boks still standing outside, a demonstrator must have got on and made himself at home behind the steering wheel. I was sitting towards the back chatting to Dr Craven [President of the SA Rugby Board]. We only realised something was wrong when the bus took off with some of the Springboks still standing in front of the hotel. Gawie Carelse [Springbok lock] with a sore ankle was still standing upright in the passage and when it accelerated, he stumbled in our direction. Doc Craven immediately sensed trouble. We saw that the demonstrator had handcuffed himself to the steering wheel and obviously finding it difficult to drive hit another parked vehicle. The players in the bus charged onto him and I think Ronnie Potgieter [the burly South African prop] got to him first. Some of the Boks layed into him and brought the bus to a standstill. The real bus driver then came running along the sidewalk, mad as a snake. When he saw the guy handcuffed to the steering wheel, he grabbed a cutter from his toolbox and threatened to cut off the 'hijacker's' hands, never mind the handcuffs! The police then took the guy away and we could then all get on board again and we were off to Twickenham.[3]

Veteran Frik du Preez, dropped for André de Wet for the Test, recalled that at the moment that the bus took off with the 'hijacker' behind the wheel Mr Bill Saunderson, an official of the Transvaal Rugby Union, was still getting on board and his coat got caught in the automatic doors. Fortunately Frik, who was close at hand, pulled him free from the doors. Who knows what injury Saunderson could have sustained if he hadn't. Just outside, Jan Ellis, who was still recovering from an injury, was running next to the bus with his coat tails flying. 'I thought the bus was leaving without me,' an out-of-breath Jan explained, 'and I didn't want to miss the game.'[4]

The team bus returned to the hotel to pick up the rest of the tour party, but before it could depart another group of demonstrators went to sit on the ground in front of the bus and also behind it. They had to be removed by the police and then the trip could be continued to Twickenham.[5]

Just one block away from the hotel where the team was staying was a house that had been occupied by people opposed to the tour. On one of the walls they painted the message to the Boks, 'We are the writing on your wall.' Flyers were distributed by the

Anti-Apartheid Movement, part of which read, 'By welcoming them [the Springboks], playing against them, going to their matches, we are accepting their evil politics.' It also said, 'Join those, like John Taylor, Welsh international, who rejects apartheid in sport.'[6] The irony was that Taylor (not to be confused with England no. 8 Robert or Bob Taylor) had no problem touring South Africa with the British Lions only the year before.

Some 4,000 to 5,000 protestors gathered on a vacant piece of land near Twickenham. Among them were religious leaders like Revd David Sheppard, a former England cricketer, and Bishop Trevor Huddleston, who had done missionary work in South Africa during the 1940s and had been a well-known anti-apartheid activist before returning to England in 1956. At some stage about half of this crowd broke away and tried to dodge the police to get access to the rugby ground, but to no avail. One demonstrator did manage to shackle himself to the goalposts, but the handcuffs were quickly cut through by the police and the culprit led away from the pitch.

It was a cold and grey day when the Springboks started preparing for the second Test of the tour against England. One could feel the tension and there was a certain determination among the Springboks. The English had appointed their captain a few weeks before the Test, namely Bob Hiller, the full back. Their preparation was intensive, and they were convinced that they could beat South Africa. A lot had been said and written about the new England approach, about their group coaching and the thorough manner in which they had been preparing for the match for months. The England coach, Don White, said after the Test that they had made a study of the game of each Springbok by watching film recordings of previous Springbok Tests. They even went as far as asking for the assistance of Fred Allen, the famous All Black coach, to learn more about forward play and especially the All Blacks' second-phase play.[7]

When England named their team, most people were talking about their dangerous backline, where the big, fast and dangerous centres John Spencer and David Duckham featured, but felt that their forwards were not too great. However, after the match that perception would be just the other way around. Five of the English players would play for their country for the first time: Peter Hale, Ian Shackleton, Nigel Starmer-Smith, Bryan Stevens and Tony Bucknall. The first time these two countries played against each other, in 1906, the result was even.

On the South African side, two South Africans would be playing for their country for the first time. The first was Transvaal lock Sakkie de Klerk, who had come over from South Africa as a replacement and had joined the squad before the unofficial match against New Brighton at Leasowe. The other was the tall loose forward Albie Bates, who was perceived as being very useful at the tail of the line-out. There were seven changes to the team that had played against Scotland in Edinburgh, but on paper these changes were not that radical. Don Walton returned to the side in the place of Charlie Cockrell, who had been the only available hooker against Scotland. The solid Mof Myburgh replaced the more mobile Tiny Neethling, and one of the major surprises was that the veteran Frik du Preez was left out and replaced by André de Wet. De Wet had a good game against the Cardiff but it was nevertheless a surprise that the physical and mobile lock made way for de Wet. Springbok captain Dawie de Villiers was returning at scrum half in the place of De Vos, but Piet Visagie was retained at fly half against expectations. The other change in the backline was Andy van der Watt coming in for Gert Muller, who was still carrying a hamstring injury. The team was: HO de Villiers, Andy van der Watt, Eben Olivier, Tonie Roux, Sid Nomis, Piet Visagie, Dawie de Villiers (capt.), Hannes Marais, Don Walton, Mof Myburgh, Albie Bates, Sakkie de Klerk, André de Wet, Piet Greyling, Tommy Bedford.

On the England side, there were five debutants: wing Peter Hale, fly half Ian Shackleton, scrum half Nigel Starmer-Smith, Brian Stevens (the Cornwall prop affectionately known as Stack Stevens) and flanker Tony Bucknall. The side contained three of the tight forwards in the pack that had struggled against Wales in Cardiff in April 1968. The side in its entirety was: Bob Hiller (capt.), Peter Hale, David Duckham, John Spencer, Keith Fielding, Ian Shackleton, Nigel Starmer-Smith, Keith Fairbrother, John Pullin, Brian Stevens, Tony Bucknall, Peter Larter, Mike Davis, Brian West, Robert Taylor.

The match was to be handled by Irish referee Dave Kelleher. It was a special occasion for England, who had never before managed to beat the Springboks; the best they had managed was a draw at the old Crystal Palace during the Springboks' tour of 1906/07.

The weather for the match was a bit misty, but conditions were reasonably good. Before the kick-off there was a big march of anti-apartheid demonstrators led by bishops and Members of Parliament; some 300 militant demonstrators had acquired tickets for the southern enclosure through a ticket agency, apparently buying four at a time. They were posted at the front of the enclosure while at the back National Front supporters with large banners containing the words 'Welcome to the Springboks' were positioned. As soon as the teams took the field the militants started their slogans and the Nazi salute. But the teams were greeted with a loud roar from the crowd of some 60,000.

The Test was to be one of the best matches of the tour, with mistakes but also some thrilling football. Probably the highlight was the magnificent fightback by England after being eight points down 35 minutes into the game. It turned out to be a hard-fought but clean match. Throughout the match only six penalties were awarded, and there was only one attempt at goal.

The Springboks took the lead after only six minutes when they were awarded a penalty from a line-out. It was not a difficult kick – 30 yards out and 15 yards in from touch – and Visagie, surely to his relief, made no mistake. After another 12 minutes Visagie attempted a dropped goal in front of the posts, but it was charged down by Starmer-Smith. After 35 minutes the Springboks' went further ahead when Dawie de Villiers, from a line-out inside the England half, kicked into the box, chased after it along with his forwards, and as Hiller failed to cover it Andy van der Watt gathered it and sped away before passing to Piet Greyling who ran in for a well-worked try. Visagie added the conversion to put the Springboks into the lead by eight points to nil, and they must have fancied their chances to go on and win the match.

England soon rallied, and hardly four minutes later they scored a good try of their own. From a line-out, Shackleton at fly half passed back inside to Starmer-Smith who exchanged passes with Bucknall, West and Larter. It was the big lock Larter who crashed over for the try. The conversion attempt by Hiller was just wide, but England were back in the game. At the interval, South Africa was leading by eight points to three.

England came out after the break with some of the forwards putting in a strong effort and the backs running the ball, Starmer-Smith orchestrating matters very well from behind the pack. After 15 minutes, the Springboks' centre Eben Olivier badly pulled a hamstring and had to be replaced by Lawless. With 21 minutes of the second half played, the Springboks were blown for offside at the line-out and Hiller made no mistake with a kick from 35 yards out, reducing the deficit to only two points. Greatly encouraged, the English launched a series of attacks which stretched the Springboks' defence to the limit. At one point Hiller intercepted and raced clear, with Tonie Roux scrambling to save. Then came a full three-quarter movement which saw left-wing Hale only stopped at the corner flag.

Before the ball could be thrown in, a demonstrator ran onto the field. What went through his head is a mystery, but he tried to

argue with Roux, who refused to respond. The line-out resumed
and the Springboks won possession; the ball came down into a
maul and popped out of the side and rolled over the Springboks'
goal line. Both England hooker John Pullin and Dawie de Villiers
dived on it, but to everybody's surprise the referee, Kevin Kelleher
of Ireland, awarded a try to Pullin. De Villiers, a minister of religion
and as honest a man as one can get, was thoroughly convinced that
he had dotted down a few seconds before Pullin. Photographs
in the newspapers afterwards also showed the disbelief on the
players' faces.[8]

Hiller converted with a fine kick to take England into an
11-8 lead. Another 10 minutes plus injury time remained and the
Springboks rallied to try and regain the lead. Visagie attempted
a drop goal from a scrum outside the England 25, but the ball
went wide of the left-hand post. As play went into injury time,
Sid Nomis still had two dangerous swerving runs. England lost
their captain when Hiller injured his hip and had to leave the field,
to be replaced by Chris Wardlow, winning his first cap for England.

During the last few minutes, the Springboks had another
chance to score a try. From a scrum in front of the English
posts at the death, De Villiers sensed an opportunity and kicked
towards the corner for the speedy wing Andy van der Watt to
follow up. As the ball jumped up, Van der Watt tried to catch it,
touching it with his fingertips. As it came down, Mike Lawless,
who had replaced Eben Olivier, grabbed it and dotted it down
to the joy of the Springboks and their supporters. But the joy
was short-lived when the referee ruled that the ball had gone
forward. However, the famous Welsh fly half Cliff Morgan,
commentating for TV at the time, believed that the ball had not
gone forward and that it was therefore a try.[9] De Villiers later
said, 'One does not always want to blame referees for certain
things. We should have been good enough to beat the English,
irrespective of Pullin's try.'[10]

One of the England players that day at Twickenham was Robert Taylor. 'I think most of us players were well aware of the protesters whose views were clearly against the apartheid system in South Africa,' he recalls. 'The disruptions were mostly on the periphery on match days causing a nuisance before play and sometimes during play which the authorities, in most cases the police, dealt with efficiently. I did not receive any antagonism or personal attack of any sort during the tour because I was going to play, or had played, against the Springboks.' As for the match itself, he recalled, 'For the Test match at Twickenham the England team came together extremely well whereas the Springbok team did not play with quite the same togetherness. I felt at the time that this was the main difference between the teams and we coped more readily with the demonstrations both before and during the match.'[11]

England lock Peter Larter recalled that 'as players we weren't aware of the extent of the demonstrations before the Test, and only heard much later that the Springboks' travel to the match had been disrupted'. As for the game, 'It was as always against South Africa a very physical match, and I think we went eight points behind before I scored shortly before half time. I remember it pretty well because I didn't score many! I think that Nigel Starmer-Smith was involved with the build-up to the try, and Keith Fairbrother, the tight-head prop gave me an overhead scoring pass; I only had to run a couple of yards to score.'[12]

It was a memorable moment for England rugby; they had beaten South Africa for the very first time in their history. It was a close finish that either side could have won, and it was a pity that one side had to leave the field as the loser. Obviously the Springboks were disappointed, but they did not publicly complain about lost chances. After the match, Springbok captain Dawie de Villiers said, 'We are going to get lynched when we get to South Africa, but it is not a disgrace to lose to such a fine England team. At halftime, I thought the game was ours.'[13]

The authorities did well to prevent any disturbances inside the ground, and the game itself was trouble free. On the Sunday after the match, however, Corrie Bornman expressed concern about the bus incident at the team's hotel. 'If this new intensity of violence in the demonstrations against us continues and we are not assured of our safety, then the position must be subject to review. The future of the tour depends on whether we are convinced by the police and the rugby football union that the new intensity of the demonstrations against us are not putting us in danger of injury and even death. The attempt to kidnap our coach in Park Lane on Saturday morning could have ended in both. The demonstrators seem now to have lost their peaceful intentions. I cannot reconcile peaceful intentions with the attempt to kidnap us.'

On the Monday after the England test, Bornman again referred to the situation: 'I see no reason why the tour should be called off for one isolated incident, but if this trend of violence continues there may be cause for reconsideration. The decision to call off the tour would have to come from South Africa although I am sure the South African Board will act on my recommendations as the man on the spot.' He also went on to praise the police: 'I am sure the police will come up with something. They have been marvellous in the past.'[14]

Danie Craven had left for South Africa on the Sunday, and when he arrived at Jan Smuts Airport in Johannesburg on Monday he was met by several press reporters. The big question was whether the tour was to continue under the circumstances. 'The Springboks will try to see out their tour of Britain for the sake of the Springbok cricket tour next year,' he replied. 'There is a real possibility that the rugby tour could be called off unless there is an improvement in the security arrangements for the players, as these had left much to be desired. The players have been under great stress as a result of the recurring incidents. I believe that this has affected their performances.'[15]

Two days before Christmas, there was more concern for the touring party. The *Coventry Evening Telegraph* reported that demonstrations would no longer be confined to the Springboks' tour matches, according to a warning by Peter Hain, after a threat by Corrie Bornman that the tour could be called off. The Springboks could expect direct action protests to follow their every movement: 'Demonstrations will no longer be confined to the matches,' said Hain. 'The physical safety of members of the Springboks touring team has never been in question, and it must therefore be obvious that concern for their safety is not the true reasons for the Messrs Craven and Bornman's threat to cancel the tour. The current campaign against a racialist sport in general, and the present rugby tour and the 1970 cricket tour in particular, has proved that opposition to sports apartheid is both widespread and massive, and certainly not confined to "long-haired students" as the supporters of racialism claim. We welcome the suggestion that the tour be stopped and suggest to Dr Craven that he make every endeavour to have his boys home, safe and sound, by Christmas.' Mr. Bornman said he wanted assurances that the players would be safe, both on and off the pitch, or the tour could be curtailed. His comments came after weekend incidents involving demonstrators.[16]

Christmas 1969 was a pleasant yet also sad day for the Springboks. Their captain, Dawie de Villiers, formerly a minister of religion, led a simple but touching religious service. The players' thoughts were obviously with their loved ones back in South Africa. 'I won't forget the day easily,' said Frik du Preez. 'It's the time of year that you long for people in South Africa that you don't even know!' One of the fathers in the side, big, burly Mof Myburgh, could not hold back the tears when he spoke to the little daughter of South African radio commentator Gerhard Viviers. Mof played the role of Father Christmas, wearing a red gown and white whiskers, and doing a good job of it.[17]

The next day they were on their way to the south-west of England, travelling by train from Paddington to Exeter, where they were to oppose the South West Counties. They endured a cold run and no food was served on the train. Hopefully the big Christmas dinner the previous day kept them from starving of hunger! In Exeter they were booked in at the Rougemont Hotel, according to the team manager perhaps the worst hotel the tour party stayed in. They had now passed the halfway mark of the tour. The period ahead would see another arrow added to the quiver of the anti-apartheid campaign against the Springboks – late night phone calls, warnings of bombs that were going to explode, and a deafening racket in front of the team's hotels, sometimes in the late, late hours of the night to prevent them from getting some sleep. There were also protestors' slogans painted against the walls of the public toilets of the hotel. As a result, Bornman arranged that at subsequent tour stops only long-distance calls would be transferred through to the players after 10.00 p.m. More policemen were required, even detectives in the hotel lobbies, on every floor, among the rugby crowds and on the team buses.[18]

South West Counties

The South West Counties XV was chosen from the players of Devon and Cornwall. One of the notable inclusions was the legendary Penzance and Cornwall prop Stack Stevens, who only eight days before had packed in the front row for England at Twickenham. On a heavy, muddy field in Exeter, the Springboks delivered one of their best performances, although the 9-6 scoreline may suggest that they made hard work of it. Conditions made place-kicking difficult, and the Boks had to settle for two tries by Mike Lawless and Mike Jennings and a penalty by HO de Villiers. The referee was one G. A. Jamieson from Ulster.

It was a cold day in Exeter, with 15,000 spectators watching, when the two teams ran on to the field at the County Ground.

Conditions were the worst the Springboks had faced all tour. Shortly after kick-off, the Counties no. 8, W. R. George, pulled a penalty attempt wide, and then HO de Villiers was short with an attempt from a wide angle for the Springboks. After 12 minutes the Springboks took the lead when skipper Dawie de Villiers sped away from a maul, and Tonie Roux kicked through before regathering and sending Lawless over for a try. HO de Villiers failed with the conversion, and soon afterwards also missed a penalty.

The Counties drew level when the Springboks were penalised at a line-out and full back Bate succeeded with a penalty from 30 yards. But the Springboks hit back with a try when Dawie de Villiers again broke down the blind side supported by Piet Greyling, who sent Mike Jennings in for the score. HO de Villiers again missed the conversion. Bate levelled the score once more with an easy penalty from 20 yards, and at half-time the score was 6-6.

The bigger and heavier Springbok forwards found it harder to move around in the muddy conditions, which suited the Counties players better. Only 12 minutes into the game, prop Ronnie Potgieter had to go off with a knee ligament injury. At the time it was thought that he would be out of action for three weeks, but his leg was later put in plaster and he returned home before the end of the tour. It was a pity, because Potgieter had been playing good rugby and was a definite candidate for a place in the Test line-up. Mof Myburgh, who had his fair share of games on the tour, came on to replace him.

Early in the second half the Springboks took the lead when they were awarded a penalty at a maul, and from 30 yards out HO de Villiers made no mistake to take the score to 9-6. This was the last score in the match. The Counties only once came close to a further score, when flanker George touched down after the forward rush, but the referee called them back for a scrum. There was an added 10 minutes of injury time, but neither side could add any more points to their score. The Springboks therefore ran out winners by nine points to six in a close but deserved win. While the loss of Potgieter was a blow, Martin van Rensburg at least made a welcome return to the side.

On the Counties side, full back Bate was arguably the best player, while for the Springboks Frik du Preez, Mike Jennings and Piet Greyling were most prominent. After having been dropped for the Test against England, du Preez surely staked a claim for inclusion in the match against Ireland in two weeks.[19]

The Springboks left Exeter on the Sunday for Bristol, where they would take on the Western Counties on the last day of the year. The Springboks line-up for the match included 12 Test players and was captained by Tommy Bedford. The Counties, meanwhile, included 13 players from Gloucestershire, the western area champions in the English County Championship. They were led by the international flank Dave Rollitt from Bristol. Another familiar face was the hooker John Pullin, also from Bristol.

At this stage the experienced Mannetjies Roux joined the Springboks. The Karoo farmer was sporting a great suntan in contrast to the rest of the team. His first appearance would be on the first weekend of 1970, against the North East Counties in Gosforth.[20]

Western Counties

In Bristol the day before the match against Western Counties there had been talk of a huge demonstration, but in the end there were more policemen than protestors, the latter mainly made up of school pupils. The demonstrators focused their actions on the team at the Unicorn Hotel. At about two o'clock the night before the match, someone set off a fire alarm after a smoke bomb hadn't drawn the necessary attention on the fourth floor. He was signed in as an ordinary guest. Detectives in the hotel apprehended the culprit – a professor from the London School of Economics – who refused to divulge the name of his sponsors in the capital. Because of this disturbance, and because of demonstrators carrying placards and shouting abuse in front of the hotel, the players had very little sleep when they really needed it. Following the bus debacle on the morning of the England Test, the hotel had a special police guard to keep an eye on anything suspicious, which made for an uncomfortable atmosphere.[21]

The match was played in bitter cold, according to the players the coldest day of the tour, but the ground was firm. The two sides ran out in front of 18,000 spectators, and when referee R. S. Waddell from Scotland blew for onside, the Springboks' kicked off with an icy, biting wind behind them. Visagie had two penalty attempts from 45 and 30 yards, but could not nail either of them. Perhaps he could be forgiven, as it was bitterly cold and demonstrators were shouting, 'Sharpeville! Sharpeville!' This, of course, was a reference to the so-called 'Sharpeville Massacre' of 1960, when 69 black protestors against the pass laws were shot dead when thousands threatened the police station.

The Counties took the lead when John Morris kicked an easy goal in front of the Springbok posts, and when the interval arrived they were still ahead by three points to nil. Before the interval the Springboks failed with two more penalty attempts, one by Visagie and one by de Villiers. The Counties forwards were playing well, and behind them the halfbacks launched some high kicks to really test the Springbok defence.

Then, during the interval, for the first time a new threat reared its ugly head when a demonstrator dodged the police, ran onto the pitch and strew upholstery tin tacks around on the playing field. While he was apprehended by the police, players from both sides and stewards had to pick up the tacks before the game could resume after about five minutes. The 45-year-old man was later identified as Peter Edward Jordan, a schoolteacher, who was charged with possessing 'an offensive weapon'. The fact that the Counties players could also have suffered probably made him an unpopular man among the local rugby fans.

Six minutes into the second half the Springboks equalised when scrum half De Vos went through the infield side of a line-out and put a grubber through; captain Tommy Bedford chased after the ball, got a foot to it, pushing it towards the Counties goal line, and fell on it as it crossed the line. Unfortunately for the Springboks, Gawie Carelse failed with the conversion. A successful kick was all the Springboks needed to secure the win, but it was not to be. They launched several more attacks, but the Counties defence was solid, with full back Waterman standing out. On the Springboks side, full back HO de Villiers was equally brave to draw the admiration of the crowd.

The Springboks had to settle for a draw because their placekicking was below standard. Piet Visagie, HO de Villiers and Gawie Carelse all had a go, but without success. If they had only succeeded with one of their seven kicks at goal, they would have clinched the match. The match was marred by too many penalties – 29 in total – but it was nevertheless a hard and clean match.[22]

Years later, Peter Hain, who himself had been opposed to the use of violence while still living in South Africa, said that throwing thumb tacks and nails on the playing field and the use of bombs by protestors during the tour were incidents inspired by individuals. 'I vigorously opposed tacks and nails which were only used on one occasion by someone I had never met in Bristol in January 1970,' he insists. '"Bombs" were never used unless you are referring to smoke bombs.'[23]

North East Counties

The Springboks left Bristol on the Thursday by train for Newcastle, a six-hour journey, and settled in at the Five Bridges Hotel at Gateshead. As this was soccer country, and the students of Newcastle University were on vacation, little trouble was expected in terms of demonstrations. Because of the smoke bomb incident at the Springboks' hotel in Bristol, police protection was ramped up even more. The night before the match a call came through to the police from some demonstrators to warn that they had left a bomb in a player's room. Assisted by the hotel manager, the police then searched a few of the rooms for a bomb, which obviously upset the players quite a lot, and the hotel manager then felt that he should consult Connie Bornman. From his experience of previous warnings, Bornman asked the police to stop the search as it only upset the players and he was by now convinced that it had just been meant as a big distraction to the Boks.[24]

For the match against the North East Counties at Gosforth, the Springbok selectors included Mannetjies Roux in the side. He had very recently joined the squad in Bristol as a replacement for the injured Johan van der Schyff. The North East Counties had to make a few changes at the last minute, but it was nevertheless a strong side that included several international players, among them Rodger Arneil of Leicester and Scotland. Another name that would become familiar in South Africa during the British Lions tour in 1974 was that of Roger Uttley from Gosforth. At no. 10 they had selected Alan Old, regarded as more of a running fly half.

The Springboks were hoping to do well in this encounter as it was important for their build-up to the test against Ireland. Injuries complicated selections, and an important decision had to be made regarding the position of fly half. As Piet Visagie was playing well below his normal standard, many observers thought that the time had come to give Mike Lawless a chance to stake a claim for the team to face Ireland.

On the day of the match the weather was cold – in fact, the Springboks said that the wind had been even colder than in Bristol – but the ground was firm. A crowd of about 6,000 turned up to watch the Springboks take on the Counties. This time, there was little interference from demonstrators.

For the Counties, Arneil and Uttley worked tirelessly, with full back Sheard having a fine game for his side. At fly half, Alan Old sparked some good attacks. After McKenzie had failed with two penalty attempts, centre and captain Carter landed a good one for the Counties to take the lead. The Springboks now replied with a try by Mannetjies Roux, following a fine break by captain Dawie de Villiers from a ruck. His namesake HO de Villiers converted. Before the interval, the Counties scored again when the Springboks failed to control an awkward bouncing ball and flanker Parker pounced on it. Carter's conversion took the score to 8-5 in favour of the Counties at the interval.

In the second half the Springboks had the wind behind them and had good territorial advantage. After 10 minutes, Andy van der Watt ran diagonally from his wing, took a pass and raced over for a good try. HO de Villiers could not convert, but compensated soon after when he worked an overlap and cut inside to score. His conversion was good and the Springboks were leading by 13 points to eight. But the Counties came back strongly, before wing Littlechild collected a miskick by the Springbok captain and ran down the left touchline to score in the corner. The conversion was missed and the Springboks were still in the lead by 13 points to 11. With 10 minutes remaining, prop Keen was blown for off-side, and HO de Villiers made no mistake with the penalty kick. Flanker Piet van Deventer touched down for the Springboks straight after, and then skipper Dawie de Villiers followed up his own punt and gathered again to score. HO de Villiers' conversion took the final score to 24-11.

After the match there was general agreement among the pressmen that newcomer Mannetjies Roux had brought some spark to the backs, and that wing Sid Nomis had another consistent performance. The Springboks would have been pleased at scoring a quick 11 points in the last few minutes.[25]

The *Daily Mirror* had a lot of praise for the Counties' fly half Alan Old and suggested that he would be a good choice for the England side.

The slim and adventurous 24-year-old fly half Alan Old from Middlesbrough made a very good impression for his side against the Springboks at Gosforth, and surely staked a claim for inclusion in the England side to face the Boks at Twickenham. He showed perfect balance and a devastating sidestep off either foot, and ran the ball with uninhibited freedom, something that lacked the game of Roger Shackleton, the current incumbent in the England side.

He once shot clear off a ruck ten yards inside his own half, drew three Springbok defenders to his right, then jinked inside and switched the point of attack; teammates Ron Tennick and Dave Murray supported well and finally left wing Ted Little went over in the corner. Unfortunately for Counties, he failed to ground the ball as he was tackled by Springbok full back HO de Villiers. The heavier Springbok forwards gradually gained more and more possession, but the Boks failed to capitalise until the last ten minutes when they ran in 11 points to close out the Counties completely.[26]

Midland Counties West

On the Sunday, the Springboks travelled from Gateshead to Coventry and settled in at the Leofric Hotel. The evening before the match there was a large torch march through the streets of the city, and during the morning of the match another mass march at the hotel. But there was also a counter-demonstration by a single person on a small truck, who made his message clear through a megaphone and placards.[27]

Some sections of the British press were sceptical about the Springboks' chances and suggested that they would be in for a hard time against the experienced XV of the Midland Counties West. The *Coventry Evening Telegraph* reported:

The Springboks come to Coundon Road on Tuesday for this 17th match of a tour which can already go down in rugby union history as the least successful which any South African side has made to these shores. Demonstrations and defeats have marked the Springboks' route since the opening match against Oxford University almost exactly two months ago. England's victory at Twickenham on December 20 took the visitors' total of losses to five, and no previous Springbok side since the first in 1906 had lost more than three games on British soil.

In the international matches South Africa had been beaten only once by Scotland back in November 1906, but within the last month they have succumbed to both Scotland and England, and their prospects against Ireland next Saturday and against Wales on January 24 look no brighter. The reasons for their downfall can be fully examined only after the tour is over. But on the evidence so far it looks very much as if it may be the case of British sides catching up as much as South Africans slowing down. Never have clubs and representative teams prepared so thoroughly, and never has the influence of top level coaching been felt so profoundly.

The Springboks' game on Tuesday against Midlands Counties (West) at Coundon Road will give the tourists no respite. The home side is full of experience and talent, and includes three of England's current back division and two of their forwards. It is in fact almost as strong as any the Springboks will have met on the entire tour.

Forward power, the springboard for so much of South Africa's success in international rugby union in the past, has crumbled and no longer are home sides faced with the inevitable fate of being outplayed in the tight and loose. The Midland Counties front row of Keith Fairbrother, Don Lane and Jim Broderick go into Tuesday's game with every confidence of holding their own in the battle for physical supremacy.

Fairbrother and Coventry club mate David Duckham were among those who first gave indication that the South Africans might no longer be the power they once were. Their visit to the Republic last summer with the Barbarians gave them the opportunity to see the Springboks at close quarters and they returned home happy in the knowledge that the tide was at long last beginning to turn.

It will not need a convincing win on Tuesday to confirm that. But a resounding success will at least dispel any doubts as to the strength of the game in the West Midlands this season. The County championship matches in the Midland group produced little of note, though title-winners Staffordshire, who provide six members of Tuesday's side, may yet redeem past deficiencies in the semi-final at Burton-on-Trent on 7 January.[28]

It was another very cold day at Coventry as 15,000 people gathered at the rugby ground to see the Springboks take on the Midland Counties. Unfortunately for the Counties they lost two key players on the eve of the match: full back Sam Doble and lock Mike Davis. For the Springboks, the two Rouxs, Mannetjies and Tonie, were combining in the midfield for the first time. On this day, Mannetjies was to make the headlines for the wrong reasons – but more about that later.

Only 10 minutes into the game, hooker Don Walton was badly injured. He suffered a depressed fracture of the skull and was rushed to hospital immediately. Replacement hooker Charlie Cockrell then came on to take his place. Walton was operated on the next day but could take no further part in the tour, although he did re-join his teammates at Peebles before the South of Scotland match on 17 January.

Probably the most talked-about incident of the match concerned Mannetjies Roux, who experienced his first real taste of the demonstrators on this occasion. During the match, a protestor ran on to the field in front of him, and, acting instinctively, he picked up the ball and chucked it against the head of the invader. Roux also had something to say to him and was cheered by the crowd as the police dragged the demonstrator off the field.

In one of the most convincing displays of the tour, the Springboks ran in five tries in a matter of 23 minutes to bury the Midland Counties. It was Mannetjies who initiated the first try, by Jan Ellis, before one of the highlights of the game when Springbok lock Frik du Preez peeled away from a line-out and galloped some 40 yards in an arcing run to score a magnificent try that was reminiscent of the astonishing try he had scored against the British Lions in 1968 at Loftus Versfeld, Pretoria. Both tries were converted by Piet Visagie, and at the interval the Springboks were leading by 10 points to nil.

In the second half, scrum half De Vos stole away on the blind side with HO de Villiers in support for the strong-running full back to run in for the try. Then, from a tighthead scrum, Mannetjies Roux scooted past his opposite number Griffiths to score, and Visagie converted. The Springboks' final try came when scrum half Webster fumbled in the midfield and Tommy Bedford gathered the loose ball, fed Cockrell and Roux, and the latter sent the speedy Van der Watt in for a try in the corner. Three of the Springboks' tries were converted by Visagie. For the Counties, full back Rossborough landed a penalty goal and a long drop goal to account for all the Counties' points. The final score: 21 to the Springboks, six to the Counties. The win provided a good boost to the tourists. It was only Jan Ellis's fourth game of the tour, but he had an outstanding match for the Springboks.[29]

A substitute hooker was sent for immediately after the match and the choice fell on Robbie Barnard of Transvaal, brother of the mercurial fly half Jannie Barnard, whom many considered unlucky not to have made the touring team. Jannie Barnard had last played for the Springboks when he toured Australia and New Zealand with the squad in 1965. But the tour management also had to address the incident involving Mannetjies Roux. In South Africa the popular and likable but no-nonsense player was regarded as a hero for his action, and in many sections of the press he was presented as such.

Some of the players on tour started asking if that was not the way they should react towards the demonstrators. Another important consequence was that a high-ranking police officer went to discuss the incident with the team's management. He made it clear to them that should another such incident occur the police would have no defence to protect the Springboks, and it could mean the end of the tour. The protesters' goal was in fact to get the players to start reacting, and for the sake of rugby and a continuation of the tour it was vitally important that there should not be a repeat of the incident. The tour management discussed the matter with Mannetjies, who realised the implications of his actions. That the whole issue affected him was evident from the fact that afterwards he was only a shadow of his former self on the field.[30]

For the police to try and maintain law and order at Coventry during the demonstrations was a costly exercise. The *Coventry Evening Telegraph* ran a report that estimated the expenses and the damage to the cathedral walls through anti-apartheid daubings. The Provost of Coventry also gave birth to the expression 'sewer rats' to describe the vandals.

The cost of the police 'beat the demonstrators' operation at the Springboks' game in Coventry was about £9000,' the report read. 'Ratepayers in Coventry and Warwickshire, however, would only pay about £1500 of the bill. Most of the total was made up of routine wages for the 1100 policemen from six forces on duty for the match. A senior police officer explained today that this would not have to be paid separately. Men from other forces are provided without charge on a mutual aid arrangement. The £1500 covered extra expenses for the day including transport and food for policemen on duty.

Praise for the efforts of the men on duty outside the ground came today from Mr R B Matthews, chief constable of the Warwickshire and Coventry Force. He made special mention of the Birmingham men who made up most of the frontline against the demonstrators. 'They were magnificent,' he said. A number of policemen are said today to be suffering from minor injuries, none was seriously hurt. An officer said that eight demonstrators had been ejected from the ground after incidents. Five had run onto the pitch but only one had been charged. Outside the grounds only two demonstrators had been arrested.

The Bishop of Coventry, Dr Cuthbert Bardsley, who has voiced his support for the anti-apartheid protests, today condemned the violent action of demonstrators at the ground. 'It is sad that a genuine pronouncement against an evil thing should be so misused by some that the evil methods of protest cloud the real issues. They prevent people from reaching the same assessment of that problem.'

The Provost of Coventry, Dr H C N Williams, who was born in South Africa, has spoken out against people responsible for anti-apartheid daubings on the stonework of the Cathedral.

He said: 'Every city has its sewer rats.' He pointed out, however, that he thought those responsible may not be from Coventry, but from outside the city.

Stonemasons were called in by the Cathedral authorities to remove the daubings, all in red paint. One said: 'The paint managed to get well into the soft stone. We had to take quite a thick layer away to get it off.' Similar daubings were found on other buildings in the city centre, including the High Street branch of Lloyds Bank, where England international rugby player David Duckham is employed.[31]

The same paper also ran an article in which the police expressed their gratitude to the public for looking after them with refreshments while they were countering the vandalism of public property:

A senior Coventry police officer was out today thanking the wonderful women who helped the 1100 police. Superintendent

R Coleman from police headquarters walked around with thanks from the policemen who had been given tea by local people. He said: 'It was wonderful. It reminded me of the old war time days when everyone came out to help. We had tea laid on, but long before it arrived these people we're giving cups of tea to police. They were doing it all afternoon and many of them who ran out of sugar and milk went to buy more.'

During the two-hour confrontation between police and demonstrators a few garden fences were damaged, a 'No Waiting' sign was bent and a high fence surrounding playing fields at Moseley Avenue Primary School was broken by protestors climbing over it. Local residents had nothing but praise for the police. Many had prepared to protect their gardens with hose pipes, garden forks, coshes and other 'weapons' but none was needed. Mrs. Violet Clarke said that she was just behind the police lines and for a time she had been worried about the garden. 'But the police forces were absolutely wonderful. They gave us a wonderful sense of security.'[32]

It appears as if there had even been criticism of the Coventry City Football Club for allowing medical staff to treat injured Springboks. 'The Bishop of Coventry, Dr Cuthbert Bardsley, cannot see any harm in Coventry City Football Club staff treating injured Springbok players,' a report in the *Coventry Evening Telegraph* read,

The South Africans left two of the team behind in Coventry when they flew off to Dublin for today's game with Ireland. They went to the City's Ryton training headquarters for treatment from Mr. Norman Pilgrim, the club's physiotherapist.

Earlier this week the Bishop supported protests against the Springboks. Apartheid, he said was basically evil and ran counter to the teaching of Christ. The Bishop is president of Coventry City

Football Club. But he has no objection to the club offering facilities to the two injured South Africans, Gert Muller and Tiny Neethling.

He said: 'I cannot see any harm in this. I think it is unfortunate that they have chosen the team from whites only. But they are here and they must be looked after and cared for. I am sorry that they are injured and am glad they have gone to the experts at Ryton for help.'[33]

On the Wednesday after the match at Coventry, the touring party had to fly from Birmingham Airport to Dublin. Their flight was delayed because the airport authorities had received a message that a bomb had been planted in the players' luggage, and the plane bound for Dublin and their luggage had to be thoroughly searched. Obviously the players as well as the airport staff were very uncomfortable about this, but finally after a close inspection of the aircraft and no sign of explosives, the plane was cleared to take off.

But their troubles had only started. On arrival at the Dublin International Airport a large number of aggressive demonstrators were awaiting them in the airport itself, anti-apartheid activists headed by Abdul Kader Asmal of the Irish Anti-Apartheid Movement, clutching tricolours and the flag of the African National Congress. The IAAM had been founded in 1964, and by the early 1970s had branches in almost all parts of Ireland. It's a strange world indeed, as some two decades later the Springbok captain and Asmal were serving in the same government cabinet. But more about Asmal in the next chapter. As the Springboks' team bus was about to depart, it was pelted with eggs and cupcakes. A large group went to squat in front of the bus and had to be removed by the police. It was clear that the demonstrators in Ireland were more aggressive and vicious.[34]

They did not stay in Dublin itself, but at the Royal Starlight Hotel in Bray, some 10 miles outside Dublin, where there was very strict police protection. As they approached the hotel, a large group of protestors – led by Seamus Costello, a Sinn Féin member of Wicklow County Council – tried to prevent the bus from entering the premises. Then Gawie Carelse and Hannes Marais noticed a man who tried to ignite a bomb to throw it under or inside the bus. But he failed to light it and he was pointed out to the police by the two players, who arrested him with the device still in his possession. The police later confirmed that the device contained explosives but that it was not really dangerous. On top of everything, local rugby clubs denied the team the use of their facilities out of fear that their property and equipment may be damaged by malicious people. Obviously this incident upset the already nervous players even more. Apart from these demonstrators, there were over 100 children, young rugby fans, lined up and shouting support for the rugby heroes.[35]

DUBLIN DEMOS

Ireland

In 2017, in an effort to revive Ireland's flagging bid to host the 2023 Rugby World Cup, the Irish Rugby Football Union (IRFU) wrote to World Rugby challenging the evaluation report by the World Cup Technical Review Group, which rated South Africa first and Ireland last. The IRFU alluded to the South African crime rate and the country's sovereign 'junk' credit rating. In an absorbing article in the *Irish Times*, historian Mark Duncan then pointed out how hard it was to reconcile the hard-edged attitude taken by the IRFU to the passivity it displayed during the decades when South Africa did deserve 'the jabbing of judgmental fingers':

> Over the course of three decades – from the early 1960s to the mid-1980s – the IRFU maintained and encouraged sporting contacts with South Africa at a time when it was a focus of angry public protests ... The Irish Anti-Apartheid Movement founded earlier that decade was in fact an impressive coalition of academic activists, politicians, trade unionists and others

who did much to raise public consciousness of the obscenities of the apartheid regime and challenge any attempts to normalise it. Sport did just that, though the Irish rugby authorities were frequently at pains to deny it. Whenever the spotlight turned on their sporting links with the Springboks, they clung to a progressively threadbare line that sport and politics were wholly separate spheres.

For a time, too, Irish governments indulged a similar fiction. In principle, of course, the official government policy was unambiguously opposed to apartheid but sport presented the point at which they were unwilling to press that principle. Speaking to the Dáil in 1965, shortly before the South Africans arrived to suffer their first international defeat to Ireland, then Taoiseach Seán Lemass expressed the view that the 'refusal of all contacts with citizens of a country whose government practises discrimination' was not the best way to end it. That view would change, but only gradually and over time. Even into the 1970s, the Irish government was abstaining on a United Nations resolution urging member states to take all necessary actions to sever links, including sporting, with South Africa...

And yet, the government's position hardened all the same – and at the expense of its good relations with the IRFU ... they never again hosted an apartheid-era South African team on Irish home soil. Instead, the traffic flowed in the opposite direction. The Lions toured South Africa with IRFU backing in 1980 and the following year, Ireland returned for a tour of its own. On both occasions, the IRFU defied the wishes of a government all too aware of the wider reputational fallout ... and yet, it was not the sport's governing body but the small number of rugby dissenters – the clubs who refused their grounds for training to visiting Springbok teams and the players who turned their backs on opportunities to travel on Irish and Lions tours – who would ultimately find themselves on the right side of history.[1]

It appeared at one stage, before the South Africans put foot on Irish soil, that almost every trade union in the country would hinder the touring party in some way or other. Aer Lingus workers threatened not to handle the team's baggage at Dublin Airport, and the General Workers' Union asked their members at the Royal Starlight Hotel in Bray, the Springboks' base for their visit, not to prepare food for the team, and even the postal unions got in on the act by telling members not to assist with phone calls from the team hotel. The most bizarre threat came from the IRA. The organisation issued a statement three days before the game, promising to 'take action' against the IRFU president and his committee if any protestors were hurt on the day of the game.

As it was, few of the unions felt it necessary to carry through the threats and the IRA definitely didn't implement theirs, but things were tense, as Irish prop Phil O'Callaghan remembers. 'There was an awful lot going on,' recalls the Cork native. 'People were on the streets on a daily basis in the build-up and there was an awful lot of ill-feeling towards the Springboks. People are entitled to protest, to put across the dissatisfaction, but it didn't have an effect on me at all. I got a few letters from various organizations and individuals asking me not to play, but personally there was no decision to be made. I'm not into politics, I never have been and never will be. I just wanted to play rugby.'[2]

On the day of the game 6,000 anti-apartheid protesters marched from O'Connell Street to Lansdowne Road, with 1,000 Gardai for company. There were fears that a certain section of the march would try to gain entry to the ground but nothing untoward occurred. Despite this, all the controversy during the week leading up to game meant the attendance dipped to below 30,000. The trip was worth the money for those who went to the bother of turning up, though. The Springboks were coming to the end of a very dominant era and actually deserved to walk off the Lansdowne turf as victors. A try from flank Piet Greyling and a penalty and conversion from full back HO de Villiers gave them their eight points, while an Alan Duggan try, converted by Tom Kiernan, meant that Ireland only trailed by three points as the game moved into eight minutes of injury time. Almost inevitably, in the seventh minute of additional time the French referee saw fit to award Ireland a penalty in front of the posts and Kiernan did the necessary to earn the draw. 'We got the draw, but I should have won the game,' claims O'Callaghan. 'Before Tom's penalty in injury time I caught a stray South African kick and charged for the line. I only had the full back to beat but he caught me just before I could touch down.'

Before the arrival of the team in Ireland, it was clear they would face organised opposition from the Labour movement. An official from the Post Office Officials' Association said, 'If the Springboks' headquarters hotel was known, all telephone and mail services to it would be withdrawn ... When we find out the hotel, we will give the telephone number to all exchanges and see that it is not serviced ... Similarly no mail will be delivered to the hotel. All other guests will be affected. The ban will last for the Springboks' stay.' In addition, trade unionists at state broadcaster RTE were eager that the match was not screened, and were adamant they would not work on any transmission of the Irish Test.[3]

The issue of the Springboks' visit was discussed inside of the Dáil during heated debates, and Fine Gael TD Patrick Donegan made his views clear: 'We have heard a great deal about the Springboks' tour. We all deplore the fact that there is discrimination in South Africa, but I have come to the conclusion that 15 men on one side and 15 men on the other, all young, rolling around in the mud, have nothing on their minds but where they are going to get the prettiest girl and take her out for a meal as soon as the match is over, and I am afraid that is not political. If I am not at the Springboks match I shall be out hunting and anyone who wants to protest about either can protest away.'[4]

The game at Lansdowne Road was played behind barbed wire, erected to prevent protesters from disturbing the game. There were demonstrations in the city, with a crowd of between 8,000 and 10,000 marching through the streets. Among those who marched was Charlie Byrne, later a successful broadcaster with RTE: 'I got involved in the Labour Party and with the Young Socialists. These were exciting times ... In January 1970, the all-white South African rugby team arrived in Dublin. The Springboks were touring Britain and Ireland and the opening match of the tour was scheduled for Lansdowne Road. I was one of those on the picket outside the Royal Starlight Hotel in Bray where the Springboks were staying. There was a huge march outside the stadium on the afternoon of the match: 10,000 protestors marched from the city centre to Lansdowne Road. I helped to carry a Labour Party banner. Despite the size of the crowd, the demonstration passed off without any serious incidents.'[5]

While Byrne's account suggests a lack of confrontation between protestors and police, the fact is that the Gardaí baton-charged protestors at Lansdowne Road.

At the time of the Springbok tour, a man called Abdul Kader Asmal was the deputy chairman of the Irish Anti-Apartheid Movement (IAAM), which was founded in 1964 with the aim to isolate South Africa economically and culturally, and in sport and diplomatic relations.[6] Asmal was an Indian South African, the son of a small-town Natal shopkeeper, and had left the country in 1959 with his wife, Louise, for London and then Dublin to escape the claws of the apartheid regime.

In his autobiography, written decades later, Asmal recalled that in the 1960s Ireland was a country of large-scale unemployment and social division, while Northern Ireland was under the shadow of looming political violence. Ironically, although he had a decent job at Trinity College, Asmal and his wife were confronted with Ireland's own race and class issues. In trying to find a flat they were turned away every time, having looked at dozens of places. As Asmal remarked, 'Of course, the name Asmal was hardly Irish.'

Few Irish people had ever heard of apartheid, but the Rivonia trial of Nelson Mandela and his comrades made the Irish aware of the system and the oppression. 'The real passion came from the ordinary people of Ireland,' Asmal wrote. 'The strongest support we got in Ireland came from the Irish trade union movement … It was the unions who got the boycott campaign in Ireland up and running, it was the unions who gave firepower to the application of the academic, sporting and cultural boycotts by threatening to withdraw their labour. At every turn, the unions were there to support us. They formed the backbone of the Anti-Apartheid Movement in Ireland and their material, financial and ideological support added enormous value to our struggle.'[7]

It has to be mentioned here that after his return to South Africa in 1990, Asmal became Minister of Water Affairs and later Minister of Education. Ironically, the Springbok captain he protested against in 1970 was to serve in the same ministerial cabinet in South Africa many years later under President Nelson Mandela. Dawie de Villiers' comment on this coincidence was, 'We never spoke about it. Perhaps we deliberately wanted to avoid the subject.'[8]

One man who usually watched Ireland play at Lansdowne Road, though, was absent that day – Eamon de Valera, the Irish president. Educated at Rockwell College and a former Munster triallist, he had been taking his place in the crowd at the Dublin ground throughout his life. By 1969, however, he was already 88 years old so his absence may not necessarily have been politically motivated.

Soon after their stormy arrival at their hotel in Bray, the team to take on Ireland at Lansdowne Road was announced. It showed five changes from the Test side that had lost to England at Twickenham. Because of injuries, Eben Olivier and Don Walton were not available for selection and they were replaced by Mannetjies Roux and Charlie Cockrell. Fly half Piet Visagie was replaced by Mike Lawless, André de Wet by the in-form Frik du Preez and Albie Bates by Jan Ellis, who had recovered well enough from his shoulder injury. Lawless had last played for South Africa as far back as 1964, against France in Springs in a match that Michel Crauste's Frenchmen won 8-6. It was the first time in 18 matches that Visagie would miss a test, but it had been clear that he was going nowhere and something had to be done. Replacement hooker Robbie Barnard also arrived in London on the Thursday before joining the team in Bray. The Springbok side was: HO de Villiers, Andy van der Watt, Mannetjies Roux, Tonie Roux, Sid Nomis, Mike Lawless, Dawie de Villiers (capt.), Hannes Marais, Charlie Cockrell, Mof Myburgh, Piet Greyling, Sakkie de Klerk, Frik du Preez, Jan Ellis, Tommy Bedford.

On the Ireland side there was a new cap in Eric Campbell, who replaced Mick Molloy at lock. A notable inclusion was 20-year-old University College flanker Fergus Slattery, who was to become a legend in Irish and British Lions history. Then there were the well-known Ulstermen Willie John McBride, Sid Millar, Roger Young and Mike Gibson. The full team was: Tom Kiernan (capt.), Alan Duggan, Bresnihan, Mike Gibson, Barry McGann, Roger Young, Sid Millar, Ken Kennedy, Peter O'Callaghan, Willie John McBride, E. Campbell, Ronnie Lamont, Fergus Slattery, Ken Goodall. The referee, T. F. Grierson of Scotland, was handling his first international.

On the morning of the Test, the bus had to take a detour to Dublin, as the straight road went across a bridge where the police suspected the demonstrators were going to erect a barricade to prevent the team from getting to the stadium. Again demonstrators squatted in the road in front of the bus, while others pelted the bus with eggs and cupcakes.[9]

The weather was fine and the ground was good when the Springboks and the Irish ran out in front of 30,000 spectators to tremendous cheering for both sides. Considering the heavy rain on the Friday, the conditions were excellent. The turf looked green and firm when the straw had been removed and the players were reassured that they would be playing on one of the best pitches in the international rugby world. The Ireland team appeared in unfamiliar white jerseys and shorts and green stockings so as not to clash with the colours of the Springboks. In contrast to the unruly and disgraceful demonstrations at Murrayfield, there were no demonstrations and there was silence when the national anthem of Ireland was played. It was clear that the Irish Rugby Union and the Garda had properly planned to counter any possible disruptions of the match.

The toss was won by Ireland, and HO de Villiers kicked off for South Africa. There were some up-and-unders but HO de Villiers was solid on defence all afternoon and fielded Irish fly half Barry McGann's diagonal kicks very well; Tom Kiernan, on the other hand, appeared a bit shaky, and he revealed later that he had been taking antibiotics for a couple of weeks. Frik du Preez had a strong run but Andy van der Watt was stopped before he could get a score, and on the Ireland side Duggan could not hold on to the ball after being put in the clear. The first Irish score came some 12 minutes later when they capitalised on a handling error by the Springbok backs. Tonie Roux threw a high pass to Van der Watt, who had turned inside from his wing, but the latter only got a hand to it and Mike Gibson intercepted and raced off with Duggan in support on the right wing. As he was lined up by HO de Villiers, Gibson passed to the unmarked Duggan who then sprinted 45 yards to score at the posts, evading a desperate effort from Sid Nomis to cut him off. It was really a gift try, but no Irish player or supporter would have complained about the score. Kiernan easily converted and suddenly the Irish were leading by five points to nil, against the run of play.

Three minutes later, Sid Millar was penalised for falling on the wrong side of a maul, and from 40 yards out HO de Villiers landed a fine penalty kick. Frik du Preez also had a long shot at goal from another penalty but was off target. At one point, Tonie Roux got away from the defence and threw a high pass to Sid Nomis, who only had to cover 10 yards to score, but it was ruled forward. Then young Fergus Slattery was penalised at the tail of a line out for holding back Tommy Bedford by the jersey, but HO de Villiers narrowly missed from 35 yards. At half-time the score was 5-3 to Ireland, but the locals had an uneasy feeling that the Springboks would gather momentum in the second half and go on to win the match.

Both Kiernan and McGann failed with penalty attempts, while the Springboks still could not convert possession into any further points. Two players were injured and required attention, adding to the extra stoppage time at the end, which went into a full nine minutes. Half an hour into the second half, the Springboks had the put-in from a 5-yard scrum, wheeled to the open side and Piet Greyling dived over to score, with Irish scrum half Roger Young powerless to stop him. The try was well converted by HO de Villiers, and the Springboks found themselves in the lead by eight points to five.

At this stage a bottle was thrown from the enclosure below the press box and struck Irish hooker Ken Kennedy in the back. This action delayed the match for another half minute. Thereafter Kiernan failed it with the 50-yard penalty attempt and then with an easier one from 30 yards. Following this second attempt, the match went into injury time. During this period there was still a lot of excitement; Hannes Marais came close to scoring at the head of a Springbok rush, and then in the ninth minute of injury time, in the Irish half of the field, Mannetjies Roux threw a pass to Andy van der Watt that was intercepted by Duggan. Duggan kicked ahead into the Springboks' 25, where Jan Ellis tried to save, got hold of the ball and fell to the ground with other players on top of him. Referee Grierson quickly blew his whistle for a penalty against the Springboks and as soon as Kiernan had kicked the easy penalty, he immediately blew again for no-side. Grierson explained afterwards that he had blown up a Springbok for not releasing and preventing Ireland from regaining possession. It was 8-8, and it was a bitterly disappointed Springbok team that walked of the field at Lansdowne Road.[10]

Even Irish captain Tom Kiernan said afterwards that 'Ireland had her slice of luck'. A heading in the *Daily Mirror* read, 'Boks robbed by luck of the Irish.' The report said that 'Irish luck excelled itself in permitting skipper and full back Tom Kiernan to snatch a draw with the last kick of the match, from beneath the very shadow of the goalposts in the eighth minute of injury time … So South Africa let slip a victory they should have clinched by a mile … There could have been two, three, or maybe four, more Springbok tries, such was the lavish possession their heavyweight forwards extracted. What they didn't have was luck, and in Ireland you need all you can get.'[11]

The Ireland scrum half on the day was Roger Young, who was continuing his contest with the South African scrum halves from the 1968 British Lions tour to South Africa. He recalled, 'We didn't really experience or witness any antagonism beforehand, even at my university – Queens University, Belfast. Remember, also at that time, the Ulster players were experiencing many of their own problems with the troubles in Northern Ireland. However, I was advised on selection for the game against the Springboks to never go out alone for fear of kidnapping!'

Taking the field with some of the greatest rugby legends of all time – Willie John McBride, Sid Millar, Fergus Slattery, Mike Gibson – he knew it was going to be one hell of a contest. 'It was a test match against one of the more formidable teams in the world. Our team's job was to go out to beat the Boks – end of story. We were advised not to get involved in politics as our selection could be in jeopardy. The build-up to the test affected both teams as it was a most strange situation. However, once the opening whistle blew, it was after all a game of rugby.'

The demonstrators were no bother during the match, he recalled, although, because of their presence, getting to the stadium and to the changing room was a new experience: 'The game was played like any other International – hard, physical, no quarter asked or given. My recollection is that we were completely focused on the match and to try to be successful. I didn't really feel any negative impact from the demonstrators, but, then, in any rugby international, one never really notices the crowd. It was rather exciting, and also tense or disconcerting, before the game, with our team bus having a police escort and a phalanx of Irish police to escort us to the changing room.'[12]

The dinner in honour of both teams was held at the Hibernian Hotel, and the Springboks set off to walk from the Shelbourne to attend the dinner, but as there were some 60 to 80 demonstrators with banners in the area between the hotels, they were advised to take a bus. When the teams arrived at the Hibernian Hotel, eggs, tomatoes, cupcakes and even bottles – one that broke a bus window – were thrown at the bus, and there was a lot of shouting and taunting. The well-known Irish activist Bernadette Devlin was also present and managed to get an interview with Springbok captain Dawie de Villiers. 'Ms Devlin also requested to have a meeting with me, to which I agreed,' de Villiers recalls. 'The conversation, however, was more or less just a repeat of the questions with which Mr Corrie Bornman and myself had been confronted at the first press conference in London at the start of the tour. My recollection was that she had a very sharp tongue and that she was brimming with hatred. Again I maintained that we would answer the questions of the media on rugby, but not the questions on the demonstrators and politics in the streets.'[13]

To ensure that players could safely reach the bus, the Gardai, out in force to keep an eye on any troublemakers, had to resort to baton charges to keep the demonstrators at bay. After the dinner, the tour party went back to the Shelbourne Hotel.[14]

That evening in Dublin, an opportunity fell into the lap of three of the Boks to take 'revenge' on a couple of demonstrators. The story goes that they were walking the streets of Dublin along with their fiery Irish opponent Ken Kennedy when they became aware of two men following them. They had just been telling Kennedy how fed up they were with the demonstrators. Kennedy said, 'Wait a minute, let me do it for all the players in Ireland,' and they quickly moved around the corner where Kennedy started to take off his jacket to teach their followers a lesson. He was still busy getting rid of his jacket when the two shadows appeared around the corner; one was abruptly knocked over by a burly Bok forward while the other got the fright of his life and ran away as fast as he could. A disappointed Kennedy had to put on his jacket again before he could 'do it for all the players in Ireland'!

The Springboks had to leave for Limerick for their match against Munster, but early on the Sunday morning there was another rumour about a bomb outside their hotel. The police and army were called in to investigate and they did find a device, but it contained only a timing mechanism and no explosives. When they had to board their train to Limerick, there was another bomb scare and they were delayed until the train had been searched. Nothing was found and they could finally sit back and enjoy the train journey to the west of Ireland.

Attention soon turned to what was likely to happen at the Wednesday match in Limerick. An unnamed Limerick rugby official expressed the fear that there could be serious trouble in the town, as the nature of Limerick's rugby support, 'dockers and bank clerks, like in Swansea or Cardiff, made them more likely to respond to protest aggressively'. The *Irish Times* too suggested that the local reaction in Limerick, a city unique in Ireland, where rugby cuts across all social barriers, would be very different to that of Dublin. The *Limerick Leader* also predicted widespread disorder with reports that thousands of outsiders, many of them extreme left-wingers, would descend on Limerick intent on trouble. The *Limerick Leader* editorial gave its blessing to a tough approach considering that since 'dangerous thugs' had been in evidence at Lansdowne Road the Gardai were entitled to defend themselves however they saw fit: 'We are sick of the modern kid glove methods of toleration and we are fed up of the fanatics featured on RTE.' The *Leader* also urged trade unionists in the city to make up their own minds about the issue and not be influenced by unrepresentative agitators.[15]

When the Springboks arrived by train to Colbert Station, they received what the *Leader* described as a 'heart-warming reception'. About 200 people greeted the team with banners and flags and there was an official greeting party of officials from Bohemians, Young Munster, Shannon and Crescent. Fewer than 20 people, including Jim Kemmy, took part in an anti-apartheid picket and the Springbok players blew kisses at the protestors as the bus took them to the Shannon Shamrock Hotel. Later that night there was a banquet for the team at Bunratty Castle, and Corrie Bornman thanked Limerick for giving them 'one of the best welcomes of the tour'. The *Limerick Leader* suggested that not one of the demonstrators had kicked a ball in their lives.

Despite rain and near gale-force winds, about 25 supporters of a group called the National Movement marched from the city to the hotel and handed a letter of welcome to the Springbok team. Members of this group had placards proclaiming: 'We Support White Christian South Africa' and 'Boks Yes, Reds No'. The group's spokesman, John Buckley, exchanged insults with a small group of anti-apartheid pickets. In the days leading up to the game, posters had been placed around the city and workplaces leafleted by the National Movement called on people to welcome the Springboks in order to show their opposition to communism in Limerick.

Munster

On Wednesday, 10,000 attended the match itself – according to the *Irish Times* this was the biggest attendance ever to watch a rugby game in the province. Only about 350 people, of whom only 30 were thought to be local, including three Jesuit priests, took part in the anti-apartheid protest. Later that evening, however, Gardai baton-charged some demonstrators in O'Connell Street, with anti-apartheid protesters claiming Gardai had overreacted to some minor scuffles. The *Limerick Leader* was pleased to report that the workers of Limerick had defied their union leadership and gone to the game. Indeed, there had almost been a walkout at the Ranks flour mill in support of the Springboks, and only the intervention of a union official had stopped it. Corrie Bornman described Limerick as certainly the nicest place they had visited, where the 'intense rugby atmosphere was like a balm on your nerves' after Dublin and Bray. Dawie de Villiers agreed that their time in Limerick was the happiest part of the tour and hoped that 'this city is more representative of Irish opinion than Dublin'.

In Limerick, the Springboks stayed at the Cruises Hotel. Of the team that drew with Ireland in Dublin, only seven players were selected for the match against Munster, namely HO de Villiers, Sid Nomis, Mike Lawless (at centre), Tonie Roux, Dawie de Villiers, Hannes Marais, Mof Myburgh and Jan Ellis. Johan van der Merwe, Eben Olivier and Tiny Neethling were not available for selection. The side also included the Transvaal hooker Robbie Barnard, who had only joined the team in Dublin the previous Thursday, and it would be his first match in a Springbok jersey. On the Munster side, the Irishmen unfortunately lost their captain, Tom Kiernan, and the Ireland fly half Barry McGann took over as skipper. Their side also included Irish internationals Bresnihan at centre and O'Callaghan at prop from the Dublin clash, as well as the other internationals Tydings (wing), Moroney (wing), Waldron (lock) and Moore (no. 8).

There was good weather as the Springboks, led by Dawie de Villiers for the twelfth time on tour, ran on to the field at Limerick. The match was refereed by E. W. Lewis of Abertillery. With so many internationals in the side, Munster was obviously a strong opponent and the visitors expected a really tough encounter, but they had the match won by the interval. Along with his forwards, De Villiers put in an outstanding performance, and there was a sense of freedom in their play, now in the friendly territory of Limerick and far away from the troubles of Dublin. Their 25-9 victory, which included four tries, two by backs and two by forwards, suggested that they dominated the game, even though they slacked off somewhat in the second half when the game was all but sewn up.

Munster's kick-and-charge approach came to nothing, and they only had three penalties by John Moroney to show for their effort. Munster took the lead early on when Moroney kicked the first of his three penalties, but the Springboks immediately replied with a try by big Mof Myburgh, the likeable prop's first try of the tour and his third in a Springbok jersey. This came after a break by Dawie de Villiers and good support play from Nomis, Van Deventer and Ellis. HO de Villiers missed the conversion, but soon after succeeded with a penalty goal to put the Boks 6-3 in the lead. Then came a neat little grubber from Tonie Roux that was gathered by Van Deventer to score; his try was converted by HO de Villiers. Soon after Dawie de Villiers broke free again from a ruck and sent Nomis over in the corner for the Springboks' third try, which was beautifully converted by HO de Villiers. When the interval arrived, the Springboks were already leading 16-3. In the second half, Munster were first to score when Moroney kicked his second penalty, reducing the deficit to ten points, but soon wing Renier Grobler scored an unconverted try for the Boks. As Moroney landed his third penalty attempt, Munster sneaked closer again, but a penalty apiece by Piet Visagie and HO de Villiers saw the visitors pull away for a final score of 25-9.[16]

The next day, the *Daily Mirror* had high praise for the Springbok skipper in a piece entitled 'Springboks skipper dazzles the Irish':

London Irish man John Moroney kicked three splendid penalties for Munster and that was the end of the happy story from Thormond Park, Limerick, yesterday. Physical education instructor Moroney put the Irish province ahead with a penalty after 6 minutes. But from then on the massive South Africans did exactly as they pleased and swept to victory by two goals, three penalties and two tries to three penalty goals.

South African captain Dawie de Villiers had a great game. He was everywhere, initiating attacking movements. His handling was perfect, he kept his backs moving smartly and his tactical kicking was immaculate. The other De Villiers, full back HO, also gave an excellent performance...[17]

With a good win under their belts, the Springboks travelled from Limerick to Dublin and then flew to Edinburgh before settling in at Peebles, one of their favourite places of the tour. Their next fixture was against the South of Scotland at Galashiels. The South of Scotland fielded a strong team full of internationals led by Jim Telfer, so unsurprisingly the Springboks put out a strong side to oppose them. Mannetjies Roux returned to the side to partner Eben Olivier in the centre while Lawless had another chance at fly half, this time partnered with Dirk de Vos at scrum half. Tiny Neethling and Martin van Rensburg had recovered from injuries and were to play their first games in a while. Gawie Carelse would partner Van Rensburg and Albie Bates and Piet van Deventer packed at the side of the scrum, with Tommy Bedford at no. 8, also the captain.

After the troubles in Dublin there was a big decision to be made: should the tour continue under the circumstances? Was it still worth it? Corrie Bornman said that he had received letters from players' wives, fiancés and girlfriends expressing concern about the players' welfare and safety, which also added to the pressure of continuing the tour. 'Following our experience with the demonstrators in Dublin, the management felt that we should telephonically inform the President of the [SA Rugby] Board about the situation and enquire what the judgement of the Board would be to what extent the tour should continue,' Bornman wrote in his after-tour report to the Board. 'After I had spoken to Dr Craven and I had spoken to the team the next day, we unanimously decided to continue under these difficult circumstances.'[18] Dawie de Villiers recalls:

After the Irish part of the tour where we had been badly plagued by demonstrators, some of the guys wanted to go home. There were players who became depressed and just did not want to go on. They told me they played the game for fun and that it was no longer pleasant to play under these circumstances, and asked my permission to return home as soon as they can. I felt sorry for them because we had endured so much on and off the field. But my view was that no-one should complain somewhere in the background where management could not be aware, but that we had to speak openly and honestly. Some of the senior players on the tour helped me a lot to determine the feelings amongst the team members, someone like the experienced and popular Frik du Preez, who had already toured through the United Kingdom way back in 1960/61.

The tour management called the players together to talk about the issue, after we had consulted the rugby bosses in South Africa beforehand. They, however, left the final decision with us. I said to the players that the tour was almost finished, we only have to hang in there for another few matches. We can then go home in the knowledge that we did not throw in the towel. Consequently, we tackled that last part of the tour with a vengeance and finished the tour with a great game against the British Barbarians.

If I have to choose between the two types of demonstrations, I would say I'll take the demonstrations on the field and it would not really matter that much. But surely not the cold, calculated psychological war that was focussed directly on our places of abode. Even before we had to go to Ireland some of the hard, experienced men came to me and asked me, do we really have to go there, can't we just stop the tour. My answer was that we are going to Ireland as a team. If it had not been for our country, we could have returned to South Africa, but at the stage where this was fully realised and became part of the team's psyche, we never looked back.[19]

Springbok coach and assistant manager Avril Malan said, 'Obviously every one of us, on occasion, asked ourselves if it was worth it to continue with the tour. The British rugby representatives, however, were convinced that the tour should not be called off and that created confidence with the team.'

Veteran Springbok lock Frik du Preez was the most senior player in the squad. He had toured the UK and France ten years before, Australasia and Ireland and Scotland in 1965, and France in 1968. If there was one player whom one would have bet on to ignore all the disruption going on around the team, it would have been Frik. But even he said, 'Later during the tour I doubted whether it was worth it continuing with the tour. We were bothered when we wanted to sleep, we felt unwelcome and everywhere we were insulted – even though the rugby people went out of their way to make us feel welcome and at home – but I thought about it again and decided we should see it through.'

Asked if he at any stage thought that the tour should be cancelled in view of the disruptions and even possible danger to the members of the touring team, Eben Olivier replied, 'The only time that I really felt danger was when a guy ran next to the team bus and wanted to throw something into the bus that appeared to be a smoke bomb. Then there was also the incident where some protestor got access to the team bus and chained himself to the steering wheel and drove off with some team members and officials inside. But personally, I never thought that it would stop the tour. We were once approached in a team meeting and we were asked if we wanted to continue with the tour, or not. I'm not sure if anyone thought that the tour should be stopped ... I was young and inexperienced. I did not even have a girlfriend, let alone being married. I never really felt that my life was in danger. Perhaps I would have thought differently now when I see how violent it could become. The police were our friends. If we could have won right from the start the tour may have developed differently. We played poorly in the beginning and lost our first match to Oxford that we were expected to beat. The psychological mindshift we had to make was that the players against whom we play, are actually our friends and not our 'enemies' as it should be in sport. We could not comprehend how a group of about 200 can disrupt matches, because at that stage we had come from a country where law and order were a high priority.'[20]

One of the players who, judging by his fine on-field performances, did not seem to be too troubled by the disruptions was full back HO de Villiers. About calling off the tour he said, 'The impression I gained as one of the South African players (and I believe that the majority of the Springbok team felt the same), was that the British Rugby representatives did NOT want the tour to be terminated – personally, I was loving the tour, I was enjoying the rugby, and was meeting and able to mix with tons of rugby supporters and opponents. There were a few negatives but not sufficient enough for me to want the tour to end prematurely!' De Villiers also said that he could not really recall any incidents where his or his teammates felt that their lives were being threatened. 'I cannot recall any experience, or any event or incident, that I would have considered to be life-threatening to ourselves. I do believe that such an event may possibly have been reported, but I am/was not aware thereof. Demonstrators did, however, regularly lie directly in front of our team bus to avoid/delay our departure.'[21]

The experienced Springbok prop Hannes Marais recalled that 'we would rather have died than admit that the demonstrators affected us in any way. Our challenge was to press on regardless and after a while we learned how to cope. In Swansea, we were walking around the field before the game when someone threw a brass tap that landed on the grass at my feet. It could have killed one of us, but nobody panicked. We just decided we would not walk around any field before matches again.'[22]

Another fairly experienced player, flanker Piet Greyling, in his third season for the Springboks, was totally taken aback by an incident on the field. 'We were playing one match and early in the first half three long-haired guys ran on to the field,' he recalls. 'I just stood still but one of them ran up to me and spat in my face. I was astonished. As Springboks, we thought we were quite important. We were heroes at home, and we thought we were doing a great job. Now this guy was spitting in my face and I just could not imagine why. It seemed so strange. I was more amazed than angry.'[23]

With the threat of demonstrators, the Springboks were obliged to spend a lot of time indoors and seek each other's company, more so than on previous tours. Consequently, the players spent a lot more time talking; they learnt to know each other better and understand each other better. The jokers had their fun and no one took any exception. New caps in the side were immediately accepted as full members of the team, and the younger players did not hesitate to seek advice from the more senior players. These things went a long way to strengthening friendships and maintaining a very good team spirit throughout. They played bridge for hours at a time. The really good ones were Tommy Bedford, Gawie Carelse, Piet Visagie and Albie Bates; the keen players being Piet Greyling, Avril Malan,

Dirk de Vos, Sakkie de Klerk, Renier Grobler and Tiny Neethling; and the now-and-then players were Dawie de Villiers, Corrie Bornman and Mof Myburgh. There was also singing – sometimes dissonant, but singing nevertheless.[24]

In Limerick, a few of the Springboks even had the chance for donkey-riding. It all started when Frik du Preez, always one for fun, noticed three donkeys in a small paddock behind the hotel building: a grey one named Peggy, a black one and a quite dirty brown one. Soon the players were daring each other to go for a donkey ride, and finally it was Frik, Sakkie de Klerk and radio commentator Gerhard Viviers who strode out to the paddock, with Mof Myburgh carrying a bottle of Cape red wine as a prize for the winner – if anybody won. Frik was wearing a tie to honour the tradition of fox hunting, looking strange in his shorts and without a jacket. At first the farmer and owner of the donkeys was worried about the strange procession approaching, but, learning what it was all about, he was very amicable. But the donkeys were obstinate, and needless to say there were no 'winners' in the rodeo, with all three jockeys regularly ploughing head-first into the mud. The next evening saw celebrations at the popular Bunratty Castle.[25]

South of Scotland

Two days after the Munster game, it was announced that Springbok wing Renier Grobler would not play on the tour again after fracturing a bone at the base of his left thumb against Munster. The injury would normally take six weeks to heal, and with the Springboks' last game scheduled for 31 January he had no chance to play again. It was also announced that prop forward Tiny Neethling and centre Eben Olivier, who missed the game against Munster through injury, were included in the side to play against South of Scotland at Galashiels. Neethling had recovered from his knee injury and Olivier from his hamstring injury.

The Springboks chose a strong back division for this, their final game in Scotland, and full back HO de Villiers was to play his ninth game in succession. Only three of the forwards who had played against Ireland the previous Saturday were included: hooker Charlie Cockrell, prop Hannes Marais and Tommy Bedford, who captained the side.

It was further reported that by virtue of a good game for the Navy against Southern Counties, the Portsmouth no. 8, Tony Hallett, had won a place in the Southern Counties side to play the Springboks at Gloucester on 28 January. This was one of three changes the selectors had made to a side that was not very convincing in beating a young Navy XV. Phil Hall, a Bath flank forward, replaced Lewis, and Army scrum half David Spawforth replaced Derek Bagnell. Hall was described as a tearaway-type loose forward whom the Counties could do with when facing the tourists.[26]

The match against the South of Scotland was one of the toughest the Springboks experienced during their tour. Their opponents included ten international players, with the legendary Scot and British Lion Jim Telfer at the helm of the side. If that was not enough, the weather was awful, cold and wet and before and after the match it was snowing. In comparison to the preceding matches, the match conditions – the muddy surface and icy weather excluded – at Galashiels were ideal, with no interruptions by demonstrators due to the large contingent of police present at the venue. Some 8,000 spectators were in attendance to witness an epic battle, especially up front, which ended in a 3-3 draw.

Prop Tiny Neethling and lock Martin van Rensburg had just recovered from niggling injuries. A highlight was the Springboks' deadly defence, with no. 8 and captain Tommy Bedford leading the way. At full back, the courageous HO de Villiers was magnificent; it would be fitting to call him the man of the match. The mobile Springbok prop Hannes Marais scored for the South Africans from a pass from Mike Lawless, while left wing Gordon Tweedie scored for the Borderers following a fine break by centre Frame. The try scored by Marais was the Boks' fiftieth of the tour. Both sides fluffed important kicks at goal, with HO de Villiers, Gawie Carelse and Martin van Rensburg failing for South Africa while Peter Brown, brother of Scotland lock Gordon Brown, missed five for the Scots. For once big old Mof Myburgh could watch the match in peace from the stand, being neither a starter nor a reserve. He would finish the tour with no fewer than 19 out of 24 official matches behind his name, the most of all tourists along with centre Tonie Roux.

On the day of the match it was cold, with snow showers, and the ground heavy like that in Bristol, which did not suit the Springboks at all. The Scottish pack took on the Springboks and the two flankers, Lyall and Elliot, were quick to the breakdown. The Springboks later conceded that the South of Scotland forwards had given the best display of rucking during the entire tour. The Bok forwards had a slight advantage in the line-outs, but their opponents put a lot of pressure on De Vos under those poor playing conditions. The South of Scotland suffered a setback when scrum half Paterson had to leave the field with a rib injury, and he was replaced by Davidson.

The teams went in at the interval with no points on the board. The Scots were first to register after half-time when Frame came bursting through from a line-out and put Tweedy over for a try in the corner. The difficult conversion was missed, but the South of Scotland had taken a precious 3-0 lead. Sensing another defeat, the Springboks fought back hard and their chance came when Frame tried to clear and sliced the kick; Tweedie gathered but was smothered by HO de Villiers. Lawless then collected and passed to the hardworking Hannes Marais, who went over for the Springboks' fiftieth try on tour. Unfortunately for them, the conversion failed and the match ended in a 3-3 draw. While they would have been disappointed with the draw, the Springboks at least gained some preparation in muddy conditions with a view to the Llanelli match and the Wales Test that still lay ahead.

After Scotland's win over the Springboks earlier in the tour, their skipper, Jim Telfer, had achieved a 'double', having skippered the Scots to victory in 1965 as well. With this draw, Telfer gained the rare accolade of having gone three matches against the Springboks without a loss.

With the match done, it was goodbye Scotland and hello again Wales. But the Boks had made many friends in Scotland. Johan van der Merwe recalled, 'I would say that our best support we experienced in Wales, where club officials did their best to protect us from interference from the protestors, but having said that, we have also enjoyed wonderful support and hospitality from the English, Scottish and Irish public. In Scotland, for instance, before Christmas we were placed with Scottish families for a delightful dinner. I still remember going to say goodbye to the kids of the family that hosted me, before we had to leave again.'[27]

12

WALES & 'WAIT FOR LLANELLI'

Llanelli

'Of all areas in the British Isles, I believe Llanelli to be the most intense in its interest in, and devotion to, the game of football,' wrote the respected Welsh rugby writer Bryn Thomas. 'Per head of population it has the best following and is in every way a successful and hospitable club. It prepared well for its special day of the year and the Springboks were guaranteed a great welcome.'[1]

The Llanelli Rugby Football Club was established in 1875, and by 1884 had settled in at the famous Stradey Park and adopted the scarlet-coloured jerseys behind the nickname 'The Scarlets'. The club is also nicknamed 'Sosban Fach', after a Welsh song meaning 'Little Saucepan', which is sometimes sung by the club's fans during matches as an anthem. The club's members were originally drawn from the local steel industry, as were many of the supporters. During the time of the Springbok tour, the steel industry provided perhaps the best-paid work in Wales, with Port Talbot and Llanelli's steelworks in particular being large employers.

The club was then coached by the well-known Carwyn James, a former Welsh player who had played 150 games over seven seasons for Llanelli. But he was also a nationalist and stood as the Plaid Cymru candidate in Llanelli in the 1970 general election. He was a strong opponent of apartheid and during this controversial 1969/70 tour he prepared the Llanelli team for the match but stayed in the dressing room as a protest. At the time he was regarded as probably the best coach in the world.

In 1969, James – a lecturer at Trinity College, Carmarthen – had gone to Stradey Park to simplify the game and to prove that his philosophy of moving the ball swiftly from one touchline to the other to create space for the wings could be very effective. The pinnacle of his coaching career outside Wales would undoubtedly come with the 1971 British Lions, who achieved a series victory in New Zealand. A year later, Llanelli would beat the touring All Blacks 9-3, a feat that would become part of Welsh folklore. This was the man who stood at the helm of Llanelli's effort to topple the Springboks at Stradey Park on 20 January 1970. Many years before, on the 1912/13 Springbok tour of the UK, Billy Millar's Springboks had a very close shave against Llanelli, winning only 8-7, and James would have been determined to push on and get the win.

The Springboks flew from Edinburgh to Cardiff and travelled by bus to Swansea, where they settled in at the Dragon Hotel. Here, on the Sunday and Monday evenings, a small group of demonstrators took up position.[2]

In the week before Llanelli's clash with the Springboks, the Welsh selectors announced three new caps, while handing a full cap to the Llanelli player Phil Bennett, who had previously come on as a substitute for Wales against France for some four minutes. The Llanelli club was affected by the 'sixth day' rule concerning Test matches, which meant that their two leading players, Phil Bennett and Delme Thomas, who were due to play for Wales, would be unable to play against the South Africans in the club fixture. Llanelli flankers Clive and Alan John were the brothers of Welsh fly half Barry John.

The Springbok selectors chose 12 players who were to play in the Test against Wales, which showed the high regard in which they held the Sosban Fach men. The three who did not run out in Cardiff were Andy van der Watt, Piet Visagie and Robbie Barnard. On the weekend, Llanelli had drawn with Cardiff, chiefly because they did not use their chances in midfield as they could have.

The day before the match, several groups of malicious people damaged a number of the major county cricket grounds, digging a hole in the Sophia Gardens ground at Cardiff and then vandalising a car belonging to secretary of the Glamorgan County Club with paint. Such actions did not help the cause of the anti-apartheid movement, causing annoyance and anger rather than fostering sympathy.

By the time the match arrived, the Springboks were without experienced wing Sid Nomis, who had to withdraw because of a cold. On the field, both teams stood in silence in honour of the club's late chairman, Alderman W. J. Thomas, who had sadly passed away a few weeks before the match.

From the start, the Llanelli players' handling of the muddy ball was something to behold. The Springbok forwards were involved in a very tough match, with tough forward play required, and at times they were outstanding, with the back row of Jan Ellis, Piet Greyling and Mike Jennings, the second row of Frik du Preez and Sakkie de Klerk and the front row of Hannes Marais, Robbie Barnard and Mof Myburgh giving it their all. At full back, HO de Villiers was again a tower of strength. From the first minutes the game was alive and had fire, hardness and physicality. After five minutes, Dawie de Villiers was penalised for a crooked put-in at the scrum and Llanelli's young full back Hamilton Jones from Birmingham University landed a straight 35-yard penalty that brought cheers that could be heard well beyond Llanelli.

Llanelli captain Stuart Gallacher was penalised after the restart, but the penalty attempt was hooked by HO de Villiers. Play went on with ferocity, and after 15 minutes English referee Lovis had a word with the fiery lock forward Derek Quinnell as the forwards charged into the Boks with all their might. The referee later commented, 'There was no danger of my having to send a player or players off. They just needed spells to cool off and I lectured them to this end. However, I found difficulty in getting hold of Gallacher to chat quietly to him, and his short addresses in Welsh were most amusing.'[3]

Because of the intensity of the clash, stoppages occurred frequently, but the South Africans kept their heads and after 28 minutes went into the lead. Dawie de Villiers broke close to a scrum with Greyling in support, and from the ensuing ruck Lawless took it on; when he was stopped, Jan Ellis gathered from the next ruck and dived over. HO de Villiers converted and the Springboks led 5-3. Unfortunately for his side, he pulled a penalty attempt wide later. The referee spoke to the two captains again just before the interval. After the resumption came one of the most exciting halves of the tour.

The Springboks attacked from the kick-off, and like in the first half, rucks and mauls were fierce; at one stage there was a big struggle but with no one playing the ball! Llanelli scrum half Gareth Thomas had to leave the field with a hamstring injury, but his replacement, Selwyn Williams, introduced more of a running approach. Thirteen minutes into the second half, Llanelli scored a great try, displaying their speed and skill. Clive John started a move up the left touchline, and with some ten Llanelli boys taking part in the following moves – Selwyn Williams and John Thomas among them – Gallacher finally passed to Hamilton Jones, who sent wing Alan Richards over in the corner. The mobile Hannes Marais got to him but could not prevent his dive. The conversion attempt was wide but the Scarlets had gone into the lead 6-5.

After this, both HO de Villiers and Piet Visagie failed with penalty attempts, and then Gert Muller was stopped in the right corner while the Boks kept the pressure on the Llanelli line. With 32 minutes played of the second half, the Springboks wheeled a scrum to the open side where Mike Jennings gathered and set up Jan Ellis, who ran across the defence and scored at the posts. Visagie took the easy conversion and the tourists led 10-6. But Llanelli still had some fuel in the tank and Clive John went on a weaving run from halfway and near the left-hand corner lifted an outside pass to prop Brian Butler, who went over in the corner. The conversion kick was a difficult one and unfortunately for the Scarlets it was wide, and the Boks could breathe a sigh of relief, albeit just briefly. Llanelli kept on attacking but the Boks held on until Lovis's final whistle. As in 1912, the Boks had scraped home by a single point. Flanker Clive John had been outstanding for the Scarlets, while on the Springboks' side both flankers – Jan Ellis and Piet Greyling – had great performances.[4]

After the match, all went to the Stepney Hotel in the town for dinner. The Llanelli captain, Stuart Gallacher, had praise for both his side and his opponents. 'The Springboks are a credit to South Africa and they must have thought today that they were not playing 15 players but the whole town! I thank my own players who worked so hard but we just couldn't grasp it in the end. Again, I admire the Springboks for the way they have held themselves back on tour amidst difficulties. They are a credit to their country and themselves, and their manager. I hope they will come again to Britain and to Wales where there will always be a welcome.'[5]

Dawie de Villiers remembers those tough games in Wales very well. 'Matches were generally clean but in rugby mad Wales our match against Neath & Aberavon was very hot and the match against Llanelli – just before the Test against Wales – probably the hardest of the tour,' he says. 'Just a few days before the match Phil Bennett, who was to become a Welsh legend, was selected to play for Wales in his first full Test against the Springboks, so we wouldn't be facing him. All along we have been reminded by the Welshmen, "Wait for Llanelli". Before this robust match against Llanelli the referee came to see me and told me that he wanted to see a calm flow of rugby and that we shouldn't be aggressive. I tried to answer him in a friendly way. If I remember correctly, I said to him, "Mister Ref, rugby is not a game of chess where you can move the pawns around. Rugby is a hard, physical game and we will play it according to the laws of the game." He still wanted to argue further but I said we wanted to win the next day's game and said goodbye to him. We narrowly beat Llanelli 10-9 but the important thing was we won.'[6]

Wales

Prior to the Test at Cardiff, two totally opposing groups with regard to the tour resumed their campaigns in the press. It was noteworthy that both were looking for publicity in the same newspaper, as the advertisements below show.

WELSH SPORTSMEN
Support the
WELCOME THE SPRINGBOKS MARCH
Saturday next, 24th January
Starting from Queen Street Station, Cardiff
At 1.15 p.m. (assemble 12.45 p.m.)
The march will be of approximately
half hour duration only.
Please turn out on this, the Springboks'
last match in Wales and ensure that
these Great Sportsmen are given a
TRUE WELSH WELCOME.

WALES REJECTS APARTHEID
Assemble 12 noon Saturday, 24 January

At Museum Avenue, Cardiff, for a
MASS MARCH through the city to
PICKETT CARDIFF ARMS PARK
Followed by a
RALLY in CORY HALL at 3.45
Speakers:
Lawrence Daly, N.U.M., Abdul Minty, A.A.
Tennyson Mariwane, A.N.C.
Jack Straw, N.U.S., Hugh Anderson
Vincent Kane.[7]

The Test was to be Wales' seventh meeting with the Springboks, and over all these decades of rugby they had never managed anything better than restricting South Africa's margin of victory to three points. The first ever meeting between the sides came in 1906 during Welsh rugby's original golden age when Wales collected three Grand Slams and six Triple Crowns. Their success was enhanced by a victory over New Zealand in 1905 and a win against the Wallabies in 1908. But South Africa proved too much for Wales and the Springboks ran out comfortable 11-0 winners in the 1906 meeting at St Helen's, Swansea. Now, 64 years later, they were meeting again but at the Cardiff Arms Park. The most recent scores were 6-3 in 1951, 3-0 in 1960 and, on the Wales tour of South Africa in 1964, 24-3.

This Test in 1970 was also the Test in which Phil Bennett, who was to become a legend in world rugby at standoff, made his full debut for Wales – but on the wing, with Barry John in the no. 10 jersey. Only the previous year Bennett had made history by becoming the first replacement player to appear on the field for Wales. Bennett had very little time to get accustomed to the role of throwing the ball in at the line-out, and it was a struggle. After a few practice sessions, one of his forward teammates simply advised, 'Phil, throw it in on the day and let's hope for the best!'

Another teammate tried to prepare the 21-year old Bennett for the prospect of facing the big, rugged Springboks – men like Frik du Preez, Mof Myburgh, Hannes Marais and Jan Ellis. 'Phil, don't worry,' he said, 'when the Welsh fans sing the anthem, think of your family, your wife, your children, your mother and believe it or not, you'll open your eyes and look at the opposition and they won't look so big – they'll shrink a little bit.' But to Bennett it didn't work that way. 'The anthem was magnificent and I felt so proud,' he said afterwards. 'But I opened my eyes and had a look at the South African lot and believe me they weren't getting any smaller!'[8]

Frik du Preez, playing in his 29th match (a lot for those days), reached a special milestone when he passed Johan Claassen's South African record for the most Tests for a Springbok forward.

The weather was good on the Friday before the Test, but on the Saturday of the match heavy rain showers that would have broken the worst South African drought started falling, and by the time the match had to start, it was still raining non-stop. The conditions were undoubtedly the worst of the tour and the field was similar to the mud bath the Springboks encountered in the second Test at Carisbrook, Dunedin, during their tour in 1965. Captain Dawie de Villiers believes that the conditions at Cardiff Arms Park had been the worst he had ever played in, apart from those in Dunedin. 'While we were standing at attention while the anthems of South Africa and Wales were played, the rain was hitting you so badly in the face that you had to actually lean forward to make it more bearable, he says. 'Before the kick-off, your boots were already covered under the mud. The pitch that at the start still had a green appearance, was just a slushy mass after ten minutes. At the time the Arms Park was also poorly drained, and that day it was a proper clay pot.'[9]

Speaking of conditions, the Springbok coach Avril Malan was a man who would know about British playing conditions better than anyone in the touring party – with the exception of the veterans Frik du Preez, Mof Myburgh and Mannetjies Roux, who had been members of his team in 1960/61 – and he was asked to compare the conditions a decade apart. From his experience as captain on the 1960/61 tour, would he say that climate conditions were worse during the 1969/70 tour? 'In my view there was not really a great difference in the conditions between the two tours of 1960/61 and 1969/70,' he says. 'Perhaps during the 1960/61 tour there were more wet matches than in 1969/70. But in both these tours I cannot recall that we had to cancel or postpone a practice because of weather conditions. But on both tours you needed a warm coat!'[10] So here, in 1970 in Cardiff, the Springboks had an additional foe to contend with as they took on Wales.

In wet weather and on a very muddy surface, the Welsh and South Africans ran onto the field in front of 42,000 spectators for the last Test of the tour. Not long afterwards, of course, it would be difficult to distinguish between the red and green jerseys of the two sides, which made life hard for the TV and radio commentators. The match opened quietly after Air Commodore Larry Lamb had blown for kick-off, but Wales were awarded a penalty after five minutes. Phil Bennett was asked to take it, but his kick went wide. The Bok forwards were playing well, and the Welsh had to clear on several occasions. On the Welsh side, Barry John opted for some rolling touches in the terrible conditions. But he was the culprit when he gave away a penalty to the Springboks for going offside after 20 minutes of play. HO de Villiers stepped up and from about 25 yards landed a good kick for the Springboks to lead 3-0.

However, HO de Villiers was penalised a few minutes later, and from about 50 yards out Gareth Edwards attempted an ambitious place-kick, considering that it was a long distance in the conditions with a heavy ball. But it was a good effort, the ball going just wide. Ten minutes before the interval, however, Edwards succeeded with a diagonal penalty kick to level the scores. The sides went in at 3-3.

Soon after the resumption of the second half, the Springboks took the lead with a well-worked try. From the back of a scrum, Tommy Bedford fed Jan Ellis, who broke away on the open side and ran diagonally to draw in the Welsh midfield defenders for a ruck to develop. From the ruck the ball came back to Dawie de Villiers, who slipped around the blindside, creating a classic three-on-two situation, and from him the ball went to Lawless and then to Sid Nomis, who went over in the corner. HO de Villiers' conversion was a very good attempt but it just missed the target. Nonetheless, the Springboks were leading 6-3 in awful conditions, and with their forwards going really well, the Welsh struggled to get out of their own half. For some 15 minutes the match stood delicately poised, and then Edwards narrowly missed a penalty attempt after the Boks had been penalised for obstruction.

In the first minute of injury time, Barry John punted diagonally to the left, where Nomis had to gather, but Hall was on to him quickly, followed by Dawes and Llewellyn, and from the ruck Llewellyn passed to Edwards who raced down the blindside for the corner with Hannes Marais chasing. Marais was clinging to his legs as Edwards went over the line, but it was all too late. Wales were now tied and a crucial conversion would have seen them win the match, but unfortunately for the Dragons – and fortunately for the Boks – the difficult kick failed. Two minutes later, the final whistle sounded with the scores tied at 6-6. It was a hard battle in poor conditions, and there were several stoppages for players to wipe the mud from their eyes.[11] The only 'consolation' for the Springboks was that they remained unbeaten against the Welshmen after 64 years.

Under the heading 'Injury time try denies Springboks', the match review of the *Birmingham Post* reported:

The Springboks forwards should be exempted from most of the blame for their side's dismal record. Despite ankle deep mud and continuous rain, they quickly established control up front. Cockrell's quick striking demonstrated their dominance in the tight. De Klerk, Du Preez and Ellis won most of the decisive line-outs and their rucking was superior to that of the Welsh. At their heels, Dawie de Villiers turned in another sound display but yet again the poor handling and lack of thrust by Lawless at stand-off and the centres wasted position. Man of the match was undoubtedly Edwards.[12]

It was not a matter of all work and no play as the Springboks and the Welshmen could enjoy a dance at the Angel Hotel in Cardiff following the official dinner, and on the Sunday they left for Cheltenham, where they stayed at the Queens Hotel. Here they were to get ready for their penultimate match of the tour against the Southern Counties. The match was originally scheduled for Bournemouth, but in the interest of crowd control and safety it was moved to Gloucester. The Southern Counties group of the County Championship, from which the team to face the Springboks was chosen, contained Dorset and Wilts, Hertfordshire, Oxfordshire, Buckinghamshire and Berkshire.

The Boks did not have many days left in England, and in Cheltenham they did a lot of shopping, buying presents for their loved ones back home, whom they were to see again in about a week's time. There was a very pleasant atmosphere in the market town, and for the first time some of the players could also participate in a demonstration: farmers were moving through the streets with their tractors, trailers and trucks demanding higher prices for their products. They greeted the Boks in such a friendly manner and were so keen on chatting that the tourists rode along with them for some distance.[13]

13

A GRAND FINALE

Southern Counties

The Springbok management gave most of those players who would not be playing in the Barbarians match a run against the Southern Counties at Kingsholm, Gloucester, the well-known West Country ground. Looking at the team, it was fairly obvious who would be running out against the Barbarians four days later. Tonie Roux would start at full back, his namesake Mannetjies Roux in the centre with Eben Olivier, and Visagie and de Vos as the halfbacks. The two fastest players in the squad, Gert Muller and Andy van der Watt, were posted on the wings, and in the forwards, the tall lock Gawie Carelse had to shift to prop, with Tommy Bedford captaining the side from the flank and Mike Jennings at no. 8. Flankers Piet Greyling and Jan Ellis were rested to be ready for the big finale against the Barbarians.

While the Southern Counties included several experienced players, with some present and past Oxbridge 'blues' among them, there were no international players in the side. Scrum half Spawforth made his second appearance against the Boks, having faced them for the Combined Services at Aldershot, and so did hooker D. M. Barry from Oxford.

A crowd of some 15,000 watched as the Llanelli referee Ken Jones blew his whistle for the kick-off in good weather. The Boks struggled in the scrum with the unbalanced front row of Carelse, Barnard and Neethling, and lost two tightheads in the first two scrums. Visagie missed two penalty attempts and Van Rensburg another during the first half, while Moffatt also missed one for the Counties. At the interval there was still no score. The Counties pack played hard and had a few moves in the Boks' half, but they didn't really look like scoring. The Springboks also struggled to get going and their finishing was not up to standard.

Just two minutes into the second half, the Springboks took the lead. They won two rucks in quick succession, and then De Vos darted away on the blindside and fed the strong-running Gert Muller, who ran in for a powerful try with Moffatt desperately trying to stop him. Van Rensburg failed with the conversion attempt, so the Boks led 3-0. The next move came from two demonstrators who ran on to the field, but they were quickly 'bundled into touch' by the police with press photographers on their tails as usual. The Counties boys defended well, but were tiring against the superior weight of the visitors, and about ten minutes from the end they finally gave way. Full back Moffatt was harassed by Bedford and Jennings, and when he failed to clear, the alert De Vos was ready to gather and run some 20 yards before scoring at the posts. Van Rensburg's conversion took the score to 8-0. Then in injury time hooker Robbie Barnard went over the final try when a Counties move broke down on their own '25, for Van Rensburg to convert. The final score 13-0 to the South Africans. Unfortunately for the Springboks, their inspirational skipper Tommy Bedford suffered a bone fracture in his leg, but he stayed on the field until the very end. It ruled him out of the Barbarians game so for him the tour in terms of match play was over.[1]

British Barbarians

From Cheltenham the Springboks went back to London and settled in at the Park Lane Hotel to prepare for their last match of the tour, versus the British Barbarians, and which could be considered as a kind of 'fifth Test', considering all the top international players the club fielded. On the day of the match, the *Birmingham Post* carried a preview which emphasised the flair of the British backs against the power of the Springbok pack of forwards as the crucial elements in the game:

> David Duckham and John Spencer, two of the most exciting attacking backs in the world, will play behind a world-class fly half Barry John for the first time today. This is what makes the Barbarians match against the South Africans at Twickenham such a splendid prospect and why the game is being billed as the fifth Test.
>
> If the Barbarians were to find themselves an impresario, superlatives would be thick in the air. Besides these three there are Gareth Edwards, possibly the best and certainly the most aggressive scrum half, Mike Gibson, the complete rugby player, and John Williams, a full back on his own in attack. As a point of argument this back division might be called potentially the best assembled in this country since the war.
>
> The important word is potentially for when we come to consider the pack the prospect pales a little. Are the Barbarians forwards big enough to get them the ball? This is a scratch pack and they will be working in that area where the Springboks are strongest. The chances of regular line-out ball look a bit dim. Mike Davis is a front of the line specialist and Stuart Gallacher does not look big enough to jump at number five. And now that Ken Goodall has dropped out of the side, back of the line effectiveness could be lessened as well. Form, as read in the matches the Springboks have played on this tour, suggests that the Barbarians would have been

well advised to have selected the England pack ... It could be a famous occasion, the classic contrast – the best of British back play against the best of South African forward play.[2]

It was suggested that the Welsh loose forward John Taylor's refusal to face the South Africans for Wales in 1970 – although he did tour South Africa with the British Lions in 1968 – cost him a place with the Barbarians. The story goes that after Mervyn Davies fell ill before the classic 1973 Barbarians encounter against the All Blacks, Taylor's name was suggested as a replacement. But the club secretary for the Barbarians, Brigadier Glyn Hughes, responded negatively to the idea with the response, 'He's not playing. The man's a Communist!'[3]

The match marked a big milestone in the career of Frik du Preez. When he ran on, he passed Johan Claassen's record of 71 matches in the Springbok jersey – his total in test and tour appearances.

The game could be divided in two quite distinct halves. The Barbarians started off like a house on fire, overcoming the lack of cohesion typical in scratch sides to really make the Springboks scramble to stop the gaps. It took them only 7 minutes to score their first try, which came after a strike against the head. It set up Gareth Edwards for a blindside break, who passed inside to Rodger Arneil to go over for the try. Scarcely three minutes later it was that man Edwards again, making the initial gap after a ruck before passing to David Duckham, who raced some 60 yards down the left touchline before stepping inside Springbok full back HO de Villiers to score. The Springboks suddenly found themselves 6-0 down.

But the Springboks kept their composure and slowly found their rhythm to play themselves back into the game, with Frik du Preez, Mof Myburgh, Hannes Marais and Jan Ellis, in one of the best games of his great career, at the forefront. De Villiers combined excellently with his forwards to put heavy pressure on the Baa-Baas. During this period HO De Villiers unfortunately failed with four penalties. It was no coincidence that Ellis was the first to score for the Springboks. Following some excellent handling between the Springbok forwards and backs, in which Dawie de Villiers, Sid Nomis and Mike Jennings featured prominently, the man from South West Africa took the final pass from his captain and crossed in the corner. Springbok captain de Villiers now took over the kicking and converted excellently from far out to reduce the deficit to 6-5. However, the Barbarians soon struck back when John Spencer found a gap in the Springboks' defence and fed Duggan on the wing for a fine try. Just before half time, Dawie de Villiers succeeded with a penalty to bring to the Springboks to within one point of the home side's total (9-8).

The second half saw some of the greatest rugby produced by the Springboks on tour. Their forwards were dominant in the tight and loose play, with Dawie de Villiers in great form behind them. Before long fly half Mike Lawless dropped a goal for the Springboks to take the lead, and this was followed by a try by Andy van der Watt after Piet Greyling had gathered before sending the speedy wing in to score in the corner. Again De Villiers made no mistake from the touchline, and the question was asked why the Springbok captain had not kicked for posts much earlier on tour. The Springboks now looked well in control.

Then, with some 12 minutes to go, the visitors' best moment of the match came when the ubiquitous Jan Ellis got the ball from a move that was started by Johann van der Merwe and Lawless. For a 16-stone flanker Ellis could really move, and now he ran some 40 yards, dummying twice before beating Mike Gibson with a marvellous jink that left the Irishman helpless before dotting down. This was Ellis at his best. As a South African radio commentator said, by the time he could shout, 'Jannie, Jannie, Jannie!' Ellis had scored in the corner. De Villiers converted superbly to take the Springboks' score to 21-9. In the dying minutes prop Keith Fairbrother crossed for an unconverted try for the Barbarians, taking the final score to 21-12 in favour of the South Africans.[4]

The Barbarians flanker Rodger Arneil, who scored his side's first try, still has fond memories of the final game of the tour, which actually took him back to the 1968 British Lions in South Africa, when, playing with big names like Gareth Edwards and Barry John, he was testing himself against some of the best back-row forwards in the world. 'The Springboks had Tommy Bedford, Piet Greyling and Jan Ellis. I wasn't daunted; it was a great challenge to be competing with them. I loved everything about that tour. It was easy to play with the Lions because they had such good vision of the game.' Now, in the Barbarians game, he faced Greyling and Ellis again, and of course his best recollection was 'scoring a try and enjoying the game against some of my erstwhile heroes'![5]

The protesters' behaviour on this day was probably the worst and ugliest of the whole tour. They were continuously throwing smoke bombs, flour bombs and oranges onto the field. The yellow and white smoke were hanging thick over the ground. At the same time, they never stopped shouting for a moment. They also spread thumb tacks on the field, which had to be removed by way of a big magnet.[6]

Springbok captain Dawie de Villiers recalled the match:

While as a team we played good rugby, the match will probably always be remembered as Jan Ellis's match. At times Jan had been somewhat of a loner, but he was extremely fit and I have seldom seen a forward who could run and swerve like him. Jan scored two tries in our victory of 21-12 against the cream of the British Isles.

There is a well-known photograph taken at the end of the match, showing Gareth Edwards and Mike Gibson carrying me on their shoulders off the field. At the time I waved at the crowd to thank the packed stadium for their hospitality and support. One cannot see it on the photograph, but in those moments I cried – proud and grateful tears flowed until we got back to the change room. It was one of the most memorable experiences of my whole life.[7]

The *Birmingham Post* reviewed the historic clash:

The Barbarians did not lose this match at Twickenham on Saturday; the Home Unions lost it. By their apparent indifference, by their insensitivity to the needs of British rugby morale, they allowed the Barbarians, a rather nice, but archaic institution, to send out the cream of our players without ammunition against the might of the Springbok pack ... In the first half we saw rugby the like of which we have not seen for years, majestic running rugby from the best set of backs in the world. British rugby. In the end, it was not enough because the Barbarians sent out a scratch pack of forwards, without the drills and, basically, without the strength to hold the whole thing together...It could not last. With Ellis a man among boys in the loose, and Dawie de Villiers' using a wealth of possession to keep his back row on the move, the game changed dramatically.[8]

After the match, the Barbarians Rugby Club president, Major Glyn Hughes, was full of praise for the Springboks' thrilling rugby and impeccable conduct throughout the tour:

I must, of course, start by congratulating the Springboks on the wonderful game they played today. It was just like old times; we have always known that you are capable of it and now you have shown us. We all enjoyed it immensely and do not grudge you one iota of your victory; it was a happy result and now you can go home much more contented.

In these words of farewell to you and your chaps it is I'm afraid impossible not to make reference to the incidents which have occurred on this tour and made it different to any other.

May I straightaway congratulate you and your team on your tolerance, on your impeccable behaviour in the face of every indignity and your refusal to make excuses although we are all conscious of the effect on you that must have resulted. You have had the most devastating spate of injuries and also the cruellest of bad luck in several of your games; but not a word of complaint or extenuation has passed your lips. You have all much to be proud of and deserve the highest praise for your calmness and courtesy.

On the other side of the picture I think your hearts must have been warmed by the reception you have received from the vast majority of spectators at every game. I feel that in the interest of sport now and in the future, there are some things that should be said, particularly in our anxiety to cement our sporting relations with South Africa. I will be brief, but if by anything I say I could bring home to this vociferous and ignorant minority of agitators the error of their ways [most of them are young and I hope impressionable] I would feel rewarded for what may be regarded as out of place at a dinner such as this. Perhaps it is easier for me as president of an ordinary club to make these remarks than the president of a national side. As I said, it is disgraceful that these ignorant agitators should interfere with the peaceful enjoyment of an overwhelming majority. I think it is sad too that certain individual members of the church have joined them in actions and demonstrations, many communist planned: that can only lead to strife, chaos and eventually anarchy, surely quite contrary to the tenets of their religion. I would have restricted them very much more if they had protested against the expulsion of Rhodesia from the Armistice Day Service of remembrance and thanksgiving.

Some of these churchmen are in high places and openly admit that they have never been to any part of Africa; as I am sure is the case with the majority of these agitators. What do they know? If they had they would have seen the fantastic improvements that have been made in the last 10 years to upgrade the conditions and the education of the coloured people ... Nation can help nation very much more by not interfering. Surely, stopping of a Springbok tour is only a minor issue. Remember that rugger is the greatest freemasonry in the world – it is against all our traditions of fair play that attempts with violence have been made to disrupt it. It is senseless and cruel to take it out on a team which came to play friendly football and by their behaviour has earned the respect of us all. It is mainly the work of a lunatic and militant fringe, much of it communist inspired. We must never let violence and vandalism succeed, it would be fatal.[9]

Two days after the match, the *Coventry Evening Telegraph* said in a review of the match that the Springboks 'finally salvaged some pride and prestige at Twickenham on Saturday with a highly disciplined performance against the star-studded Barbarians'. The report also added: 'This from every point of view was an outstanding game of a chequered tour. Beaten in five of their first 13 games, the Springboks can at least claim to have survived the last 11 without defeat, and many memories of earlier failures were erased as they saved the best until last ... The standing ovation they received as skipper De Villiers was carried off shoulder-high must have helped the Springboks to forget so many of the tour's troubles. A pall of orange smoke from a demonstrator's bomb came down like a curtain on a long-running musical which never quite repaid its backers' investment.'[10]

Life as a Springbok on the Demo Tour

About two-thirds of the way through the tour, an insightful article on life in the Springbok camp appeared in the British *Farmer and Stockbreeder* magazine, roughly the equivalent of

South Africa's *Farmer's Weekly*. It is not the kind of feature that would appear regularly in an agricultural magazine, but one can only assume that with all the hype generated around the controversial Springbok tour in the UK, the editor probably thought it wise to get in on all the publicity. Two of the headers stand out, and go a long way to capture the essence of the team's strange circumstances on tour:

There is something unnatural about a group of robust, healthy young men stealing back silently to their hotel after a night out, but this is how they are living.

The police surveillance of Springbok hotels, which operated discreetly in the early part of the tour, has now become almost the basis of the road show.

The author profiles captain Dawie de Villiers:

He is exceptional, a captain's captain, with the ability to inspire other men simply by being with them. He's also one of the very few men I could listen to for hours simply talking rugby. It is sheer poetry when he talks about the game. Early in the tour when the Springboks fortunes looked like reviving after their defeat of London Counties at Twickenham, he said: 'We are going to try to win every game, but apart from the internationals in which you must do everything to win, it is as important to play with imagination and play well as it is to win.' Now he says: 'We have got to try to win every match, but we must still play well.'

He tries to keep everyone's spirits up by stressing the positive things, even if it is only so many days and we are home. Whatever has happened to us, it has been a maturing experience for all of us, and I think we are all coming out of it more balanced people.

Moving on to manager Corrie Bornman, the writer observes that 'Bornman does not look that much like Lee Marvin. But snoozing under his hat on a slow train going like one in the old steam days across England on a sleepy Sunday morning, he takes on a likeness to him. He has a superbly battered face, worthy not only of the very battering job he has just now but of a tired voice singing "This guy's in love with you." But then the gentle eyes and a soft voice belie it all and he doesn't seem quite the tough guy he looks. You really wonder what he does in his spare time, apart from endless rounds of bridge which everyone seems to take part in. He talks constantly and paternally of "Ma Boys".'

The author also had a long discussion with vice captain Tommy Bedford.

The person most badly hurt by the demonstrations and the whole climate of the tour is probably Tommy Bedford, the vice captain and nephew of the writer Lawrence van der Post. As an Oxford undergraduate, he enjoyed all that England so generously gives to intelligent and privileged young men who are top rugby players and was captain for a season. Possibly the most thinking and sensitive member of the team, he has desperately tried to understand the reason why and work out his own moral and political position in it. When he talks about his experience on the tour, you listen to a man crying somewhere in his heart about the country he loves deeply and can no longer understand. 'I come from a very small town and until the age of 11 I spoke only Afrikaans, despite my English name,' he says. 'It was a strict community and you grow up accepting their values. Then I went to New Zealand on a rugby tour and I saw Maoris, and I thought maybe there is another way of doing it. It was just a thought.'

'Then I came to Oxford, and I saw what happened here. Again I thought about it. I had a very good life. I loved it. I enjoyed everything this society offered.' After three years at Oxford he returned to South Africa to practice as an architect 18 months ago. 'I came back to play rugby this time as I have always done,' he says. 'But I had no idea there would be anything like the demonstrations we have had. We knew there might be something. People keep telling us demonstrators are a vociferous minority, but whatever they say the demonstrations have affected us. We cannot behave like a rugby touring team. We cannot go out on the town and enjoy ourselves and roll home. We always have to be on our guard. If people are against the South African system and want things changed, they had a wonderful opportunity to try to influence our minds if only we could have been free to go out and mix with people and behave like people among them. People in rugby in South Africa are very powerful. If we had the chance to get to know people as they really are here, we might have started thinking about things and maybe we could start changing things slowly. Maybe we are not necessarily right. But the opportunity has been lost, we have been forced back in on ourselves. We have become more committed to our system. When we were in Swansea we couldn't open our hotel windows. There were demonstrators outside, but the central heating was so hot that half a dozen of us just had to go out and get some fresh air.

'I wanted to talk to the demonstrators. I tried to argue with them but you cannot. They are well informed on the superficial stuff. They can quote all the statistics on the number of schools and hospitals for white people and the number for black people. But when you try to take it logically with them one stage further and explain the separate development system they change the subject.

'They say: but YOU voted for Vorster. You wouldn't be here if you hadn't voted for him. But it isn't so. I know what the students are thinking. I know how they feel. I felt a lot of things as a student. But what can you do? You try to forget it but you cannot. It is on television and in the newspapers all the time. And there are police on every floor of the hotels and you can't help seeing them. So how can you forget? I write home depressing letters to my wife. She's getting the worst of it (he has been married barely six months). They must be terrible letters. I wonder what I will feel when I reread them?'

One senses that as he wrestles with his conscience and the questions of right and wrong the deepening of his relationship with Dawie de Villiers on this tour has become important to Bedford. 'Before we came here I had a good relationship on the field with Dawie. I always respected him. But he's a minister and I am a guy who likes a good night out. I could never have asked him to join me on a night out. But everyone needs someone to talk to and I have talked to him. I feel now that I could ask him along on the town and he would understand the person I am and the way I like to enjoy myself and neither of us would be embarrassed. I went to see the musical *Hair* when I was in London and I cannot understand why it is so held up in this country. People did wrong in the past, but they knew it was wrong. Why is the wrong made the right in England today? I am constantly thinking England, oh my England, I love you. You are one of the finest countries in the world. But what is happening to you. And why?

The author goes on:

The irony and the tragedy of the demonstrations is that they have defeated the purpose. If the Springboks had not been forced into such isolation on this tour and could have lived freely among us, they could not help seeing the best in our system. And they are all intelligent enough to think. As it is, their young minds must surely now be closed…

When you consider that the Springboks come from a country where rugby stars are treated like versions of George Best and the Rolling Stones made into one, it is pretty awful for them. They almost seem stunned and disbelieving when someone asks for their autographs, grateful as it were, to find a friend. To meet, they are charming and well-mannered and puzzled why all this is happening to them when they have not actually done anything.

For one of the things the team have to cope with is the whole maleness of British rugby with its endless after-match dinners in contrast to the dances and buffet suppers which follow South African games. This is made even harder to bear when even at a dance (and there are some) the players tend to be monopolised by local rugby men. 'I love rugby and I love talking to men about it, but at two in the morning at a dance, it would just be nice to talk to a girl for a change,' said one. But apart from a mild criticism like this, the players say little about what they feel about what they do see of British life.

Sid Nomis is one of the mainstays in getting a bit of humour going when spirits sag. He certainly does a lot to entertain the world in general. Every time we met he gladly told me an entirely different story of his life just in case I was short of information![11]

A very long tour – three months and eight days to be precise – had come to an end. On the last day, their bags were packed and handed over to their friendly English baggage master, Graham Short, and the players went into town to do some last-minute shopping before their departure. London appeared different to them now that the tension was gone.

On the Sunday evening, Corrie Bornman, Avril Malan and Dawie de Villiers met with the Rugby Laws Committee of the Four Home Unions on the interpretation of the laws. The discussions took place in a very good spirit. The Four Home Unions Tours Committee also arranged an official farewell function for the tour party on the Sunday evening. It was very well attended, and for the first time in the history of such events all four presidents of the Home Unions as well as the president of the French

Rugby Federation were present. Bornman stressed the excellent cooperation that the tour party had received from all the rugby officials of the four Home Unions.[12]

In his team manager's report, Bornman pointed out that there could be no criticism of the number of matches played and the venues at which they had been held. However, the South African Rugby Board should on future tours thoroughly study the place of the Barbarians match in the tour programme. With the tour just completed, the Barbarians team was nothing less than a choice 'British Lions' side and therefore had to be approached as a fifth Test. Bornman felt that having such a match take place within a week of the last Test – that against Wales – was asking a lot from a team.[13]

Bornman also concludes his report with praise for the team, the coach and captain and vice captain:

I would like to express my congratulations and admiration to the team for the wonderful team spirit, courage and determination to achieve still achieve such success in spite of difficult circumstances. Their behaviour was impeccable throughout and there was never any reason or occurrence where I felt it necessary to reprimand a player about his behaviour or actions. In particular I just want to expand on the following persons:

Coach: Avril Malan should be congratulated with the success he had with the team. I have become convinced that he has made an in-depth study of the game. He also captured my admiration for the way in which he elicited discussions from the players, where it concerned techniques and game patterns.

Captain: Dawie de Villiers proved throughout that he had the respect and admiration of the players and I want to congratulate him on the way that he acted as captain of the team. Whether it was as leader amongst the players or as speaker at events one cannot but admire him for his fine and strong performance. I also want to express my thanks for his help and support during the tour.

Vice-captain: Where the vice-captain normally plays a less important role I have to express my thanks and appreciation to Tommy Bedford for his active help and support on the tour. He assisted Dawie loyally at all times.[14]

In summing up the results of the Sixth Springboks, Bornman said, 'The results of a Springbok team are necessarily measured by the number of matches, and especially Tests, won or lost. However, the rugby man who is in touch with the game knows that if one just blindly stares at the final score without looking at the game of the day, one can easily come to the wrong conclusions. The difference between winning and losing is in rugby often very small. All things considered, the 1969/70 touring team had built up a good tour record. In the first few matches up and until the Scottish Test the team did struggle to find its feet, but thereafter it only got better. With regard to the Test matches, we came up with poor play against Scotland. Against England, Ireland and Wales we may well have walked off the field victorious.'[15]

Bornman finally had something to say about the referees. 'A player will never be 100% satisfied with a referee, even more so if he loses,' he wrote. 'We have accepted the decisions of referees on tour, but with regard to the application of certain laws in the British Isles we have objected strongly to the British Home Unions.' A copy of the letter to the Home Unions was sent separately to the South African Rugby Board.[16]

Like Corrie Bornman, assistant manager and team coach Avril Malan had only praise for the captain and vice captain, Dawie de Villiers and Tommy Bedford, on tour:

They were ideal personalities. They were both calm and throughout they suggested possible improvements in our game and preparation. I remember after one match, after we had got dressed and had gathered in the lounge, Dawie asked me to say a few words to the team. I had already gone a fair way with my speech when he interrupted and told me: 'I asked you to say a few words, not have a team talk!' We all had a good laugh!

The tour management were happy with the assistance they had received from the various Home Unions, even though it had been difficult for them to give their best to accommodate the tour party under the difficult circumstances. We had throughout enjoyed only the best support from the Home Unions, and at the same time we also felt really sorry for the police who had to contain the demonstrators.[17]

Results in Perspective: The British View

The Sixth Springboks returned to South Africa with a record of 24 matches played, 15 won, four drawn and five lost – which is not good reading by Springbok standards of that era. But there is consensus that they were a better team than their tour record suggests. Former Wales and Cardiff prop John O'Shea, who captained Cardiff at the Arms Park against the Springboks, recalls: 'The management and players were continually under pressure and facing demonstrators wherever they were. I believe at times they would not wear their South African blazers in public to avoid any confrontation. Probably the only time they really felt welcome was amongst the true Rugby fraternity. I believe the whole atmosphere of this tour made it virtually impossible for them to play to their full ability, as the strain on them mentally would have been immense, therefore this would have affected their overall performance.'[18]

One of the England players who faced up to the Springboks at Twickenham, lock Peter Larter, believes that they were a better team than results suggest and that the political disruptions must have had an effect.

Many of the Springbok players on this tour were those I had played against on the 1968 Lions Tour to South Africa, when the Lions lost the series, so on paper they were a very good side. Undoubtedly the anti-apartheid demonstrations took their toll on the players and gave us a little advantage. I wasn't aware until recently that it was the first time England had beaten South Africa. So it is with great pride that I can claim to have played in three Tests against the Springboks and never lost: two wins with England [1969 and 1972] and a draw in the second Test in 1968 [with the British Lions in Port Elizabeth].

South Africa is a great nation and a great rugby nation and, in other circumstances, I would love to have played all of my rugby in South Africa. I came to Cape Town last June 2018 on the 1968 Lions 50th Anniversary Reunion Trip, and it was great to see how things are progressing. Good fortune for the future.[19]

Scotland and Barbarians loose forward Rodger Arneil said, 'Yes, I think that the Springboks did underperform on that tour and the home sides happened to perform well to achieve the result, however, that is sport for you and the less that politics are involved the better!' Former Ireland scrum half Roger Young has no doubts about underperformance because of unusual circumstances: 'Yes – definitely,' he says. 'A one-off situation that I experienced had no effect, but I could imagine that for the South African players the psychological effects, practice and match disruptions, always heavily guarded at their hotels, the inevitable fear of being in danger, living in a cocoon and unable to move around freely must have negatively impacted on the Springbok squad, including the management and the press. Having said that, Ireland played well to earn an 8-8 draw that, given the status of the Springboks, was considered to be quite an achievement.'[20]

Former England player Bob Taylor, who opposed Dawie de Villiers' men at Twickenham, is sure that events influenced the

Springboks' tour record: 'I believe that the Springbok party were affected by all the protests and demonstrations which continued throughout the tour. So, yes, I think the Springbok team was better than their tour record suggests.'[21]

Home at Last

The time had come for the Springboks to go to Heathrow Airport. Even on their last trip the police were there, and the bus left the hotel under police protection that remained all the way to the airport. There were still some demonstrators waiting for them at the airport, but these were sidestepped by entering the building through the arrivals hall. It was a surprised and disappointed group of demonstrators who could only look at them through the thick glass windows.

There was the wonderful prospect of arriving home after such a long time, and very few of the players managed to get to sleep on the flight. Even Avril Malan's sleeping tablets did not help much. Quite a few of them sat on the floor in the back of the Viscount, in the aisle and even in the kitchen to talk about everything from their kids to biltong and braais.

When they arrived at Jan Smuts Airport in Johannesburg, they were taken aback by the huge and hearty welcome of thousands of fans in and outside the airport. 'We returned with heavy hearts because Springboks hate to lose,' Dawie de Villiers recalled. 'But when we arrived in a Johannesburg, we were overwhelmed. Thousands of supporters had come to the Airport to welcome us. They understood how we must have felt and had come to cheer us up. It was wonderful.'[22]

The Springboks did get some reward when on 20 February 1970 they received the State President's Award for 1969 in the historic Cape Town Castle from the state president Jim Fouché. At the time, it was the most esteemed sports award in the country. In his presentation speech, Fouché said, 'Mr. Bornman,

Mr Malan and Mr De Villiers, you and your team did not only earn admiration through your strength of character, but you have also set a praiseworthy standard for the South African sportsmen of the future. I once laid a wreath on the graves of our South African soldiers up there in the mountains of Italy and when the mayor of the town made his speech, he said: "Sir, they were not only soldiers but gentlemen." Today I myself have the opportunity to put the crown on the very lively rugby Springbok team with these words: they were not only rugby players in the true sense of the word, but they were tradition builders; they were character builders. They were gentlemen.'[23]

14

LOOKING BACK

A Divided Britain

In their dealings with the British public and through the numerous reports on the tour and its accompanying demonstrations, the Springboks grew increasingly aware of how their presence was dividing Britain, even dividing families on the issue of demonstrations or support for the Boks and the rugby fraternity. The late South African radio commentator Gerhard Viviers, for instance, recalled having drinks with a British couple at the bar while their son was demonstrating against the Boks outside. The lady remarked, 'Isn't this a strange world? Here we are enjoying a drink with you while our son is demonstrating outside against you.' She also added that she thinks 'the demonstrations were madness, but the kid was young and it was one way of earning a few pennies'.[1] When the Springboks toured New Zealand a decade later, they found the same issue – a rugby tour splitting a rugby-mad nation, families against families, brothers against brothers, friends against friends. And as one of the Springbok heroes of that tour, Ray Mordt, says, 'What did we know, we were young, we just wanted to play rugby, in New Zealand of all places, which for our guys was the ultimate.'[2]

Tommy Bedford, who knew Britain better than anybody else in the tour party, has no doubts that the Springbok tour divided Britain:

Yes, families, communities, etc., were split and divided. Take for example the very first match against Oxford University. We were secreted away to the middle of a golf course with its hotel miles south of London while the Rugby Football Union (England) debated whether the match against Oxford should take place. The Dons of the University had so much pressure put on them by the student body and academia that they decided that the University's rugby ground at Iffley Road would no longer be made available for the match to be held on that first Wednesday of the tour. But the University's rugby team captained by the New Zealander Chris Laidlaw, who wrote the book on the All Black tour to SA in 1970, *Mud in Your Eye*, held a poll amongst his XV and they, contrary to the University's wishes, bravely decided they would honour their rugby commitment to play the Springboks. That is why at the 11th hour the game was changed and took place at Twickenham, in front of virtually no spectators (except policemen). Given the circumstances, with the University split and thus the thousands of rugby followers of Cambridge and Oxford denied the chance of seeing Oxford winning, and the Boks losing, that is how the tour started.[3]

Bedford was asked about the extent of the touring side's support, and in which part of the UK it had been the greatest:

It is difficult to tell in view of the fact that there was so much controversy about the tour. The rugby people over there were obviously most supportive towards us. But as there were demonstrators and demonstrations everywhere we went, which thereby had us confined to hotels and under police protection constantly, meaning the people we did meet were always rugby people and not the general public at large. We really did not have those freedoms to wander about and see the best Wales, Ireland, Scotland or England could offer and present us with – one of the great frustrations for me in that the experiences I had in broadening my outlook to the extent I had been fortunate enough to experience which was being denied the rest of the team and our management. I felt that had Hain and the demonstrators allowed the Springboks to broaden their outlooks and not deny them the richness of multi-cultural society with its ethnically divergent people living in a true democracy with its Mother of all Parliamentary systems, this team of important South Africans in the context of the South African situation, the predominant Afrikaners making up the team, could take back so much that was influential to bring about necessary change within their communities. This is what I had hoped the tour would possibly help to foster beyond the mere business of playing rugby across all of the Four Home Unions. But instead, given that the demonstrations were all consuming and that we were isolated from experiencing much that was good and important and relevant and different to life in societies living without the apartheid ideology, which had made us such worldly pariahs. The demonstrations drove us collectively into a naturally protective laager seeing that it often felt you are being on the television as 'the news' night after night and making the front pages of the papers day after day along with the sports pages that almost everyone was against you as white apartheid South Africans, rather than rugby players.

And so yes, in that sense I hated what Peter Hain, Bernadette Devlin, and the rest of the anti-apartheid movements were doing through their incessant demonstrations by denying the 32 of us on the tour the best of what Britain and Ireland had to offer as communities living without the hang-ups of South Africa. For by then the 21 years of National Party machinations via its Afrikaner Broederbond was getting us further and further isolated from the real world which existed beyond the southern tip of Africa including, as was becoming absolutely obvious to me as the tour progressed along its three month duration, that rugby tours like this one happening as it was would not be feasible in future. No sane country would in future be prepared to put up happily with what Britain and Ireland felt they had to in view of respecting the rights of the rugby fraternity to invite Springboks and the right of the people to demonstrate against rugby's officialdom for having done so.

Of course, my added frustration on the tour was that the team's management consistently refused to speak, discuss or debate the issues with the news media, only the sports media. This made the tour take place under so much more pressure, because in addition, the British and Irish rugby officials and their presidents also backed away from taking on the demonstration leaders and putting the case for rugby, for sport and thus the tour. This was no different from our people sitting comfortably at home in their armchairs who organised the tour thousands of miles from where we took the negative flack day by day being in the trenches at the front. It meant that the likes of Peter Hain and the rest of the anti-apartheid campaigners had carte blanche publicity for their cause for three months while we had none. Hardly anyone was sticking up, or daring to stick up, for us, defending our role as a rugby team on tour and not as the front per se of the South African Government's apartheid policies (although one accepted it would have been difficult for the management to have shied away from their support of National Party and the Government's policies if they believed in it themselves and were supporters of Government, as seemed likely given the silence).

This non-defending of the team on tour by anyone in the official position to do so undoubtedly added yet another string to the bow of the Peter Hains and the Anti-Apartheid Movement, and thus in turn to the constant strategy of harassment by demonstrations and demonstrators. Police presence was thus always required and, in the longer term, it meant that the further campaigns against the Springbok rugby teams on tour in Australia in 1971 and New Zealand in 1981 would be as telling finally to kibosh completely international rugby for (white) South Africa.[4]

The Springbok coach Avril Malan recalls that 'at rugby receptions people were talking throughout about the rugby of the day, and then there was also the familiar question, "So, are you enjoying the tour?" What we did find, however, was that rugby people apologised all the time for the behaviour of the demonstrators, but that there was also another side, who were not happy with us, was quite obvious. Looking at the extent of the support for the touring team, and where it had been the greatest, we had support throughout the British Isles, wherever we went, and of course it varied from one area to another, looking at the events for instance in Dublin as opposed to Limerick, both cities in Ireland. If I have to guess where the support for the Springboks had been greatest, I would say Wales. Like us they really love their rugby and it is their national sport.'[5]

Eben Olivier said, 'I felt sorry for the British rugby public because they wanted to compensate at all costs for the chaos at the grounds where there was barbed wire to keep the demonstrators away. I think for the rugby public it was also something strange because demonstrators were more part of the soccer scene and not of rugby. We never went onto the streets in our Springbok colours, but always in private dress so as not to draw attention upon us. As a result the team spent a lot of time in the lobbies of hotels. At the end of the day I would say that it had after all been worth it because the rugby people had been very good to us.'[6]

HO de Villiers also offered his thoughts:

It was probably far easier for those Springboks who were predominantly English speaking (as a home language) to mix with the British public, and to mix with our opponents for that matter. Most of these people tended to show appreciation for the Springboks touring the U.K., but then again, it should be considered that we would mostly mingle after games, amongst rugby-loving people. I found that most of these folk were almost apologetic for the behaviour of some of their countrymen. However, some of the U.K. players did make themselves unavailable for selection to compete against the Springboks. It is difficult to say where in the U.K. we were best received or supported.

I seem to think that 'rugby lovers' simply love the game of rugby, and then again every country as such has its loyal and unwavering supporters. I could not choose one of those countries over anyone of the others and standing on the field and listening to the respective anthem of that country that you were about to play against always sent shivers down my spine, be it Wales, Ireland, Scotland or England – what a privilege, and what an experience!

Lord Peter Hain, just a student at the time of the tour, said that he did run into former British players, who had played against the Springboks, at functions and otherwise subsequent to the tour. Asked about their reaction when met him, whether there were any signs of hostility or whether they understand where he was coming from, he said: Yes, I have. Welsh players – I was a Welsh MP for 24 years and the Cabinet Minister for Wales for seven of those years – were for the most part friendly though some were not![7]

Lord Hain has said that he has frequently met Springbok vice captain Tommy Bedford in the years since the tour. 'I have met him frequently and he told me that in retrospect he supported our campaign, though that is not what he felt at the time,' recalls Lord Hain. 'Within a year he publicly stated I should be listened to, not vilified, and praised STST's objectives. Although his response was a relatively isolated one in South Africa, it signalled the huge and destabilising impact of the Stop the Seventy Tour campaign.'[8]

To this Tommy Bedford replied, 'Peter Hain is correct but not quite correct. I have responded to his role at the time and how it differed from what I had hoped would rub off on the team on tour in the way my own views as a South African were broadened on the rugby tours I went on and by the time I spent in England as a student. Instead we ended up seeing none of the best that living in Britain or Ireland could offer because we really saw only hotels and stadia and, not being allowed to experience British and Irish life and living and interaction, we understandably drew defensively into the protective laager we felt necessary, seeing that management for the officials back home nor in the four home unions were prepared to stick up for us properly as rugby players on an *invited* tour. That was for me the pits since, as I mentioned, it allowed Peter Hain and all the anti-apartheid people to get off scot-free on the band wagon and have carte blanche access and time on TV, radio and in their newspaper interviews complete with photos, while we sat holed up in hotel rooms or unusually long in changing rooms before matches.'[9]

The British Police

During the Springbok tour, the British police had almost constantly been in the spotlight, either being praised for their efforts to contain violent demonstrations or criticised for being too 'firm' with demonstrators. It was a thankless job, with police physically attacked, sworn at, spat on and taunted. To remain calm under such circumstances was admirable. In the last week of the Springbok tour, the demonstrations and the police were again a subject of discussion in the House of Commons. Wallace Lawler, Liberal MP for Birmingham Ladywood, spoke about the circumstances and challenges of being a policeman in the face of such provocation and brought up the issue of decent pay for the police.

'We expect and we get high standards generally from our police,' he said. 'However militant the demonstration – whether one against the Springboks' tour or a revolt by students – the police are expected to be there safeguarding the right to demonstrate within the framework of law and order, and sometimes with risk to life and limb. One spectacle which the House and the country would not like to see would be police holding back police at a demonstration by police. The very nature of the duties of a policeman prohibits him from taking part in a demonstration of any kind. I believe we have one of the best police forces in the world, but it continues to lose some of its best men day by day.'

Lawler said further that it reflects little credit on the government that they do not respond by ensuring the best rates of pay, conditions and allowances for the police who serve the public so well. He stated that the net pay of a policeman was about 10s a week less than it was before their previous pay rise, due to increased superannuation and graduated pension payments. It was a plain fact of which the House could hardly be proud and underlies the seething discontent within the police force, at a time when the responsibility, dangers and risk of injury for a serving policeman – with obvious reference to the political demonstrations – were never more pronounced.

He said that the House would no doubt have taken special note of the unusually strong, but totally justified, warning from the chairman of the Joint Control Commission of the 100,000-strong Police Federation, backed by 1,400 police delegates at their conference at Brighton the previous week. Lawler warned, 'The police are seething. Constables of many years' service are leaving to drive dust carts and buses.' He went on to warn that the British public, 'some of whom would not sleep so soundly if they knew how thin the blue lines are, may discover to its dismay the true costs of false economy'.[10]

Changing Rugby and Political Perspectives

To the Springboks, the tour had been an eye-opener – not just in terms of the intensity of political demonstrations but also in terms of the improved strength and more professional approach by the four Home Unions. Springbok captain Dawie de Villiers said later, 'What we also found over in the UK was that a country like Wales already had been using a so-called "squad system" and national coach/manager [Ray Williams] who was paid by the Welsh Rugby Union and the British Government. In Wales and England the coaches assembled a group of 30 players over weekends so they could practise together, and that bore fruit. We learnt in a hard way that South Africa did not know everything about rugby and that in this regard we could learn from the British. Hardly a year after the tour, the British Lions beat the All Blacks in New Zealand in a Test series. We may as well follow their example, I thought.'

Also, on a personal level the tour was an experience that had a profound personal influence on De Villiers' life.

Our team left our shores with no idea of the difficult, disruptive and frustrating experience awaiting us. The continuous stress and pressure the demonstrators had placed on us for more than three months were exhausting. But I used the opportunity to talk to many people about South Africa – politicians, academics, students, journalists, sportsmen. I tried to answer their questions to the best of my ability, but realised every time how my best explanations did not convince these people. I did not have answers anymore.

Later, as South Africa's Ambassador in London, I had the same experience – notwithstanding the fact that Mrs Margaret Thatcher had shown our country a lot of goodwill. My term in London coincided with the Lancaster House negotiations on Rhodesia [now Zimbabwe]. I often met Mrs Thatcher, Lord Carrington, the British Minister of Foreign Affairs, and Mr. Ian Smith and some of his Ministers. South Africa was not officially part of the negotiations, but our country had so much interest in the events that I continuously had to act as intermediary. Lancaster House convinced me that eventually we would have to walk the road to freedom like we later did. I gained a lot from this experience.

When our team returned from the UK in 1970 I was convinced that there will never be a normal Springbok tour unless South Africa had not addressed the political issues in the country and had found solutions for that. I was also determined to be outspoken and consistently promote the necessity of political change in future.

One of the consequences of the tour was that I was summoned to London at the beginning of 1972 to give evidence in a court case in the Old Bailey against Peter Hain, a main leader in the demonstrations against the Springboks.[11]

It was clear that the experiences of the tour in the longer term had an influence on the players' lives, in the sense of changing political perspectives. Back home, some of them were asked if the events of the tour had in any way changed their views on the political situation in the country. One answer came from star full back HO de Villiers:

I have always been a fair-minded person, but I was, as such, never really 'into politics' – in spite of the fact that my father-in-law happened to be a Member of Parliament representing the United Party in those days! However, I have since 1970 often thought about that tour, and about the antics of the demonstrators, but I am still not sure whether or not they, the so-called organisers, chose the correct event, the time, the place, the methods, etc., to attract attention.

For me as a boy from King William's Town in the Eastern Cape, to be plunged into all of that turmoil was a challenge. The proper preparation for the matches was lacking, because they just hid us away. Our hotel in Peebles, for instance, the night before we had to face Scotland, was surrounded by demonstrators and they caused a racket all night, and we received abusive phone calls in the middle of the night.

Back then, we asked ourselves, do these people know what they were demonstrating about? Now, of course, you look back and think how could we have ever agreed with the apartheid system? My kids have asked me why I didn't question it all and admittedly I found it hard to answer their questions. But I did not know any better, we all grew up under that system and you went to school where everybody in your class was white, and you assumed black kids went to black schools.

As you got older, you thought about what was going on around you, and when you look back you realise what a tragedy it had been for the country because of the lack of proper education amongst the other population groups and the brain power that had been wasted. We were born into that society, but it was still a tragedy.[12]

Springbok centre Johann van der Merwe, also from the Eastern Cape, and just a lad of 22 years at the time, said that the tour did change his perspective of things in his home country. 'Not immediately, but indeed later,' he says. 'As Stellenbosch players under Doc Craven we have done coaching early on at a Coloured rugby club outside Stellenbosch (Blakes Bricks) and there were some wonderful players amongst them. We enjoyed that very much and they really went out of their way to make us feel at home amongst them. We then already started asking questions, why can we not play against each other and along with each other?'

But in spite of the disruptions, the whole tour had been a worthwhile experience for van der Merwe. 'My most outstanding memory of the tour was to have become a Springbok, it was a dream since my primary school days that had come true, and to represent South Africa in a Test against Wales at Cardiff Arms Park.

Other memories were to see snow for the first time, to see a TV, and of course the wonderful historical and cultural attractions of Britain. Then also the friendships that have been forged between us players who had to play rugby under very difficult circumstances and while trying to control ourselves against the provocation of the demonstrators.'[13]

Back in South Africa, Tommy Bedford was thinking long and hard about the past tour and what it held for future Springbok tours:

Upon return to SA after the tour I was asked to be guest speaker at I don't know how many functions and occasions. I did not initially accept these invitations because I needed time to let the after effects of those difficult three months for me – having been very happy over there for three years as a student – sink in and, free from the demonstrators and the constant bombardment within me thinking about aspects of the tour.

In the cold light of day and out of the confines of the tour and what I had so hoped the Springbok team would glean from such a visit as I had previously had it was so that, as a few of us had discussed sitting on rocks in front of our hotel at Porthcawl in Wales overlooking the sea in the last week of the tour in February 1970, if there were going to be future international tours for the Springboks the rationale for sending them would require either the rugby, or the country, or both to change substantially. There was simply no way a tour such as what we had experienced was viable for the host country. At very least, in achieving this Peter Hain and the Anti-Apartheid lobby had succeeded, and this is what I further reflected on and which, unpalatable as it was to have to come to terms with, is what I in the talks I delivered eventually had to conclude. I stated that if we wanted to continue playing international rugby we therefore had to change as a people and as a country. Hain had tellingly made his point to emerge winner both on and off the field.[14]

15

AFTERMATH

Political Developments

In Britain, the Stop the Seventy Tour strengthened the Young Liberals' position on the extra-parliamentary left and reinforced their radical credentials. The STST also remained a touchstone for the Young Liberal Movement in forums such as their newspaper, the *Liberator*, through the 1970s, and provided inspiration for a new Stop the Apartheid Rugby Tour (SART) organisation in 1973, in which youth groups including the YLs, the National Union of Students, the Young Communists and the Labour Party Young Socialists made a concerted effort to stop the formidable British Lions of Willie John McBride from playing in South Africa in 1974. They failed, of course, and the British Lions returned home triumphant after an epic series in which they established themselves as arguably the best touring team to have ever visited the shores of South Africa.

For the Liberal Party, the Young Liberals' anti-apartheid activities in the UK provided an effective response to the appeal of single-issue campaigns for young people in the late 1960s. For the YLs, STST bolstered their existing credibility in protest campaigns, and fitted well with their combination of mainstream political activity, grassroots community politics and a commitment to direct action to achieve real change. Though rarely ideologically coherent, the YLs were deeply committed to racial equality and the eradication of racial segregation in South Africa.[1]

The year 1976 saw the infamous Soweto uprising, when thousands of black children in Soweto, the black township outside Johannesburg, demonstrated against the Afrikaans language requirement for black African students, and the police opened fire with tear gas and bullets. Violent protests and government crackdowns followed and drew more international attention to South Africa. Three years previously the United Nations General Assembly had denounced apartheid, and in 1976 the UN Security Council voted to impose a mandatory embargo on the sale of arms to South Africa. International economic pressure increased, and in 1985 the United Kingdom and the United States imposed economic sanctions on the country.

As unrest continued in black townships, an active worldwide anti-apartheid movement grew, focusing on the express aim of freeing Nelson Mandela and his fellow prisoners. Sanctions, demonstrations and music concerts, including one held on Mandela's 70th birthday in 1988, were some of the ways that his plight was kept in the public eye. Gradually South Africa became more isolated, businesses and banks refused to do business with the nation and the international demand for change increased.

By 1990 the South African government had begun to water down some aspects of apartheid legislation, including abolition of the pass laws and the ban on interracial sex and marriage. Finally, the South African government agreed to open negotiations resulting in the release of Nelson Mandela. Mandela's African National Congress easily won the election in 1994 and became South Africa's first black president, by which time apartheid had been dismantled. As mentioned earlier,

1969/70 Springbok tour captain Dawie de Villiers eventually served in Mandela's National Unity Cabinet.

However, after Mandela left the political scene, corruption and crime became rife. The country went into serious decline. The way things have been going in South Africa is therefore a big disappointment for Lord Peter Hain, who had fought so hard to break down apartheid and eventually achieve democracy. In an interview he reiterated the views he expressed in 2017, specifically that he and others felt betrayed in a way, as what they got was not what they had fought for during the 1960s, 1970s and 1980s. In an interview in the *Global Citizen* he said, 'Many others feel exactly the same way as I do ... some playing far more important roles than I did or my parents did. We feel deeply pained by the betrayal of the values of that struggle, and that's what motivates me. I still identify with SA very much, I'm a British citizen and I've lived in Britain for 51 years of my 67 years. I'm British but a big part of my heart is still in SA, and it's this betrayal of Mandela's legacy. It's the betrayal of the freedom struggle's values of justice, inequality, and integrity, human rights, and democracy, and probity – all of those values are just being completely traduced and ignored in a quite shameless way.' Lord Hain did add that all of this happened under the corrupt president Jacob Zuma, and that he thinks 'the country is back on track under [president Cyril] Ramaphosa'.[2]

The Rugby Front

On the rugby front, up to 1994, international sporting relations with South Africa, and also the non-integrated nature of rugby within South Africa, drew frequent controversy. South Africa, however, remained a member of the International Rugby Board (IRB) throughout the apartheid era. The Halt All Racist Tours (HART) campaign was established in New Zealand in 1969 to oppose continued tours to and from South Africa. Though contacts were restricted after the Gleneagles Agreement in 1977, there were still controversial tours – in 1980 by the British Lions and by France, in 1981 by Ireland, in 1982 and 1984 by South America (basically the Pumas in disguise) and in 1984 by England.

South Africa toured Australia in 1971, returning undefeated, and New Zealand in 1981. However, the Springboks were excluded from the first two Rugby World Cups, in 1987 and 1991, and only made their memorable debut in 1995. Racially selected New Zealand sports teams toured South Africa until the 1970 All Blacks rugby tour allowed Māori to go under the status of 'honorary whites'.

The All Blacks arrived in South Africa in 1970, having last been beaten in 1965 in the third Test by the Springboks on their tour of Australia – a world record at the time. It was a star-studded side, with the likes of captain Brian Lochore, Colin Meads, Ian Kirkpatrick, Sid Going, Chris Laidlaw, Earle Kirton, Bryan Williams among others. Looking at the Springboks' record on their 1969/70 UK tour, no one would give them a chance against these formidable rugby giants who had swept everything before them through five international seasons. This year, 1970, marked the end of the Springbok selectors' five-year plan by which time Springbok rugby was expected to be restored to its former glory. After their 1965 series defeat to New Zealand, they had beaten the French in 1967, the British Lions and the French again in 1968, and the Wallabies in 1969. But on the 1969/70 UK tour, they experienced an unexpected wobble. Of the players on the tour, 12 played in the Tests against the All Blacks (HO de Villiers was injured and Tommy Bedford allegedly overlooked for political reasons), and against all expectations the Springboks took the four-Test series 3-1, led by inspirational captain Dawie de Villiers.

The Springboks followed this historic win with an unbeaten tour of Australia in 1971, but with de Villiers having retired they were led by the experienced prop Hannes Marais. As in the UK two years before, they were welcomed by the sporting fraternity but incessantly harassed by demonstrators. They were 'just in time', because later in 1971 a proposed South African cricket tour was cancelled, and for two decades there would be no sporting contact between the two countries in rugby and cricket. Many of the rugby squad had been hardened by the experiences of the British tour, and this time around they were more prepared to accept and cope with the siege conditions at their hotels and the vicious demonstrations at rugby grounds. When they ran out onto the field at Melbourne, for instance, they found mounted police trying to chase protestors off the pitch. Showing that they had probably become immune to demonstrations, they casually jogged to the opposite side of the stadium and started their warmups. The tour signalled the emergence of a young future Springbok captain, Morné du Plessis, while at the other end of the spectrum there was the departure of Frik du Preez from the international scene after a record 38 Tests for the Springboks.[3]

With the release of Nelson Mandela in 1990, a reform process began that led to South Africa's readmission to the international community and the end of the sports boycott. South African sporting codes set about achieving internal unity by unifying the racially divided bodies from the apartheid era, and then resumed international competition. The rugby bosses, Danie Craven and Transvaal president and magnate Louis Luyt, had already embarked on this process as early as 1988 and met with the African National Congress in Harare. They were heavily criticised at the time for talking to a banned organisation, among others by F. W. de Klerk, then Minister of Education with responsibility to the sport portfolio. This 'African Initiative', as the meetings came to be known in the SARB, was facilitated by Tommy Bedford and Chris Laidlaw, the latter then New Zealand's ambassador to South Africa. It was usually chaired by future president Thabo Mbeki.

'There was preliminary contact in London and Frankfurt, because ANC people were not allowed into South Africa at the time,' Bedford recalls. 'It was a long journey that led to Harare, with many little journeys and many people spoken to along the way, but initially began after the Dakar Talks in July 1987 when later in Ouagadougou, Burkina Faso, when I put my thoughts and ideas about aspects of helping to change the South African situation, sport being one, which I felt I could personally do and achieve quietly and out of the glare of spotlights, to Thabo Mbeki and Essop Pahad.'[4]

Craven and Luyt returned to South Africa with a clear understanding that the South Africa Rugby Board would have to merge with the anti-apartheid South African Rugby Union (SARU) before the ANC would agree to the resumption of rugby tours. Craven, however, was suspicious of SARU, believing they were not driven by a love of rugby but by political ambition, and the merger only came about in 1992. That year signalled the return of the Springboks to the international arena, with Tests against New Zealand at Ellis Park and Australia at Newlands. Then, in 1995, the Rugby World Cup was hosted in South Africa, and won by the host nation in spite of the All Blacks having swept everything before them up to the final. Images of Springbok captain Francois Pienaar together with president Nelson Mandela – wearing the no. 6 Springbok jersey – will remain powerful for a long time to come.

For the record, with his South African background and ties with the late Nelson Mandela, Lord Peter Hain admits that he is also a Springbok supporter – but he qualifies this: 'Yes, I also support them if Wales is not playing!'[5]

Appendix

ITINERARY AND TEAM SHEETS

SPRINGBOKS VS OXFORD
5 NOVEMBER 1969, TWICKENHAM
FINAL SCORE: 3-6
HALFTIME SCORE: 3-6

	SOUTH AFRICA	OXFORD
Full back	P J Visagie	M G Heal
Wing:	A E van der Watt	O Jones
Centre:	O A Roux	P R Carroll
Centre:	E Olivier	D S Boyle
Wing:	J P van der Merwe	J L Cooke
Fly half:	M J Lawless	J R Williams
Scrum half:	D J de Villiers (capt.)	C R Laidlaw (capt.)
Prop:	R Potgieter	R R Speed
Hooker:	D C Walton	J Malins
Prop:	J L Myburgh	R Griffiths
Flank:	P J F Greyling	P J Torry
Lock:	F C H du Preez	R Davies
Lock:	M C J van Rensburg	A R Behn
Flank:	A J Bates	S James
No. 8:	M W Jennings	P Griffith

Referee: Mr M Titcomb (Bristol)
Attendance: 6 000

SCORERS
SOUTH AFRICA: Penalties: Visagie (1)
OXFORD: Penalties: Heale (2)

SPRINGBOKS VS EASTERN COUNTIES
8 NOVEMBER 1969, WELFORD ROAD, LEICESTER
FINAL SCORE: 11-9
HALFTIME SCORE: 6-9

	SOUTH AFRICA	EASTERN COUNTIES
Full back:	P J Durand	P G S Pulfrey
Wing:	A E van der Watt	G T Robertson
Centre:	P J van der Schyff	D J Small
Centre:	E Olivier	P R Sweet
Wing:	R N Grobler	R E Morris
Fly half:	P J Visagie	P D Briggs (capt.)
Scrum half:	D J J de Vos	J A Allen
Prop:	J F K Marais	D L Powell
Hooker:	G Pitzer	A G Johnson
Prop:	J B Neethling	P S Onyett
Flank:	P I van Deventer	R B Taylor
Lock:	A E de Wet	P J Larter
Lock:	G Carelse	J Harrison
Flank:	J H Ellis	B West
No. 8:	T P Bedford (capt.)	D J Matthews

Referee: Mr Ron Lewis (Wales)
Attendance: 20 000

SCORERS
SOUTH AFRICA: Tries: Van Deventer; Penalties: Visagie (1);
Drop goal: Visagie (1); Conversions: Visagie (1)
EASTERN COUNTIES: Tries: Robertson, Sweet; Penalties: Larter (1)

SPRINGBOKS VS NEWPORT
12 NOVEMBER 1969, RODNEY PARADE, NEWPORT
FINAL SCORE: 6-11
HALFTIME SCORE: 0-3

	SOUTH AFRICA	NEWPORT
Full back:	P J Durand	J. Anthony (capt.)
Wing:	S H Nomis	A. Skirving
Centre:	O A ROUX	D. Cornwall
Centre:	E Olivier	I. Taylor
Wing:	R N Grobler	L. Daniel
Fly half:	P J Visagie	W. Raybould
Scrum half:	D J de Villiers (capt.)	G. Treharne
Prop:	J B Neethling	B. Llewelyn
Hooker:	G Pitzer	V. Perrins
Prop:	J L Myburgh	G. Sutton
Flank:	P J Greyling	D. Haines
Lock:	M C J van Rensburg	L. Martin
Lock:	F C H du Preez	J. Watkins
Flank:	P I van Deventer	K. Poole
No. 8:	T P Bedford	P. Watts

Referee: Mr Robert Calmet (France)
Attendance: 23 000

SCORERS
SOUTH AFRICA: Penalties: Visagie (2)
NEWPORT: Tries: Skirving; Cornwall; Penalties: Anthony (1);
Conversions: Anthony (1)

SPRINGBOKS VS SWANSEA
15 NOVEMBER 1969, ST HELENS, SWANSEA
FINAL SCORE: 12-0
HALFTIME SCORE: 12-0

	SOUTH AFRICA	SWANSEA
Full back:	O A ROUX	S. Ferguson
Wing:	A E van der Watt	J. Davies
Centre:	J P van der Merwe	D. Morgan
Centre:	E Olivier	S. Davies (capt.)
Wing:	S H Nomis	L. Jones
Fly half:	M J Lawless	H. Brown
Scrum half:	D J de Villiers (capt.)	T. Pullman
Prop:	R Potgieter	A. Rutherford
Hooker:	D C Walton	R. Thomas
Prop:	J B Neethling	D. Bowen
Flank:	T P Bedford	C. Dyer
Lock:	G Carelse	M. James
Lock:	M C J van Rensburg	J. Joseph
Flank:	A J Bates	D. Winslett
No. 8:	M W Jennings	M. Henwood

Referee: Mr T F E Grierson (Scotland)
Attendance: 25 000

SCORERS
SOUTH AFRICA: Tries: Van der Watt; Penalties: D de Villiers (1);
Van Rensburg (2)
SWANSEA: Nil

SPRINGBOKS VS GWENT
19 NOVEMBER 1969, WELFARE, EBBW VALE
FINAL SCORE: 8-14
HALFTIME SCORE: 8-6

	SOUTH AFRICA	GWENT
Full back:	H O de Villiers	R. Williams
Wing:	S H Nomis	R. Jones
Centre:	O A Roux	A. Lewis
Centre:	P J van der Schyff	N. Edwards
Wing:	R N Grobler	R. Beese
Fly half:	P J Visagie	M. Grindle
Scrum half:	D J de Vos	T. Evans
Prop:	J F K Marais (capt.)	D. Williams
Hooker:	D C Walton	B. Wilkins
Prop:	J L Myburgh	G. Howls
Flank:	P I van Deventer	G. Evans (Geoff)
Lock:	F C H du Preez	E. Phillips
Lock:	G Carelse	S. Geary
Flank:	P J F Greyling	G. Evans (Graham)
No. 8:	M W Jennings	D. Hughes (capt.)

Referee: Mr D L Head (England)
Attendance: 12 000

SCORERS
SOUTH AFRICA: Tries: Jennings; Penalties: Visagie (1); Conversions: Visagie (1)
GWENT: Tries: Beese; Penalties: Williams (3); Conversions: Williams (1)

SPRINGBOKS VS LONDON COUNTIES
22 NOVEMBER 1969, TWICKENHAM
FINAL SCORE: 22-6
HALFTIME SCORE: 6-6

	SOUTH AFRICA	LONDON COUNTIES
Full back:	H O de Villiers	J. P. R. Williams
Wing:	A E van der Watt	R. Hiller
Centre:	O A Roux	S. J. Dawes (capt.)
Centre:	E Olivier	R. H. Lloyd
Wing:	S H Nomis	M. Bulpitt
Fly half:	P J Visagie	C. S. Hogg
Scrum half:	D J de Villiers (capt.)	N. C. Starmer-Smith
Prop:	R Potgieter	D. T. Bowen
Hooker:	D C Walton	P. C. R. Orr
Prop:	J B Neethling	O. C. Waldron
Flank:	P J F Greyling	A. J. Gray
Lock:	F C H du Preez	T. G. Evans
Lock:	G Carelse	C. W. Ralston
Flank:	A J Bates	A. L. Bucknall
No. 8:	T P Bedford	T. M. Davies

Referee: Mr M Joseph (Wales)
Attendance: 25 000

SCORERS
SOUTH AFRICA: Tries: Van der Watt (1); Roux (2); Bates; Bedford; Penalties: HO de Villiers; Conversions: Visagie (1); Carelse (1)
LONDON COUNTIES: Penalties: Hiller (1); Drop goal: Lloyd.

SPRINGBOKS VS NORTH WESTERN COUNTIES
26 NOVEMBER 1969, WHITE CITY STADIUM, MANCHESTER
FINAL SCORE: 12-9
HALFTIME SCORE: 12-3

	SOUTH AFRICA	NORTH WESTERN COUNTIES
Full back:	P J Visagie	B. J. O'Driscoll
Wing:	S H Nomis	C. P. Hanley
Centre:	O A Roux	C. Wardlow
Centre:	J P van der Merwe	D. Roughley
Wing:	R N Grobler	A. R. Richards
Fly half:	M J Lawless	J. Hayton
Scrum half:	D J de Villiers (capt.)	E. W. Williams
Prop:	R Potgieter	M. J. Hindle
Hooker:	J B Neethling	N. Coleclough
Prop:	J L Myburgh	B. S. Jackson (capt.)
Flank:	P I van Deventer	D. Robinson
Lock:	F C H du Preez	A. R. Trickey
Lock:	A E de Wet	M. Leadbetter
Flank:	A J Bates	E. T. Lyon
No. 8:	T P Bedford	A. Neary

Referee: Mr D P D'Arcy (Ireland)
Attendance: 6 500

SCORERS
SOUTH AFRICA: Tries: Van Deventer; Penalties: Visagie (2); Drop goal: Roux
NORTH WESTERN COUNTIES: Tries: Lyon; Penalties: O'Driscoll (2)

SPRINGBOKS VS NEW BRIGHTON/NORTH OF IRELAND
29 NOVEMBER 1969, LEASOWE, LIVERPOOL
FINAL SCORE: 22-6
HALFTIME SCORE: 8-3

	SOUTH AFRICA	NEW BRIGHTON/ N O IRELAND
Full back:	P J Durand	P. Townsend
Wing:	G H Muller	S. Maxwell
Centre:	P J van der Schyff	D. Ibison (capt.)
Centre:	J P van der Merwe	B. Turtle
Wing:	R N Grobler	A. McMurray
Fly half:	M J Lawless	S. Kirkwood
Scrum half:	D J de Vos	J. Dorman
Prop:	R Potgieter	D. J. K. Wilson
Hooker:	C H Cockrell	E. Flynn
Prop:	J B Neethling	J. Lander
Flank:	J H Ellis (capt.)	S. Dobbin
Lock:	I J de Klerk	N. Grainger
Lock:	A E de Wet	D. D. Boyle
Flank:	A J Bates	P. Bullivant
No. 8:	M W Jennings	M. Topping

Referee: Mr Chris Tyler
Attendance: 300

SCORERS
SOUTH AFRICA: Tries: Muller, Van der Schyff, Grobler, Ellis (2);
Penalties: Durand (1); Conversions: Durand (2)
NEW BRIGHTON: Tries: Wilson; Penalties: Kirkwood (1)

SPRINGBOKS VS NORTH OF SCOTLAND
2 DECEMBER 1969, LINKSFIELD, ABERDEEN
FINAL SCORE: 37-3
HALFTIME SCORE: 10-3

	SOUTH AFRICA	NORTH OF SCOTLAND
Full back:	H O de Villiers	P. Stott
Wing:	G H Muller	J. F. Carswell
Centre:	O A Roux	J. R. Rawlinson
Centre:	E Olivier	N. Fowlie
Wing:	S H Nomis	R. C. Brickley
Fly half:	M J Lawless	D. J. Loud
Scrum half:	D J de Villiers (capt.)	I. G. McCrae (capt.)
Prop:	J F K Marais	T. E. R. Young
Hooker:	C H Cockrell	A. S. Fraser (Stephen)
Prop:	J L Myburgh	D. M. D. Rollo
Flank:	P J F Greyling	S. G. Fowler
Lock:	F C H du Preez	I. C. Wood
Lock:	G Carelse	P. G. Kirkwood
Flank:	J H Ellis	H. A. McEwan
No. 8:	T P Bedford	A. S. Fraser (Allister)

Referee: Mr K D Kelleher (Ireland)
Attendance: 3 500

SCORERS
SOUTH AFRICA: Tries: Muller (4); Olivier (2); Marais, Ellis; Penalties: HO de Villiers (1); Conversions: HO de Villiers (5).
NORTH OF SCOTLAND: Tries: Carswell (1)

SPRINGBOKS VS SCOTLAND
6 DECEMBER 1969, MURRAYFIELD, EDINBURGH
FINAL SCORE: 3-6
HALFTIME SCORE: 3-0

	SOUTH AFRICA	SCOTLAND
Full back:	HO de Villiers	I. S. G. Smith
Wing:	G H Muller	A. J. W. Hinshelwood
Centre:	O A Roux	C. W. W. Rea
Centre:	E Olivier	J. N. M. Frame
Wing:	S H Nomis	A. G. Biggar
Fly half:	P J Visagie	I. Robertson
Scrum half:	D J de Vos	D. S. Paterson
Prop:	J K F Marais	J. McLauchlan
Hooker:	C H Cockrell	F. A. L. Laidlaw
Prop:	J B Neethling	A. B. Carmichael
Flank:	P J F Greyling	W. Lauder
Lock:	F C H du Preez	P. K. Stagg
Lock:	G Carelse	G. L. Brown
Flank:	J H Ellis	R. J. Arneil
No. 8:	T P Bedford (capt.)	J. W. Telfer (capt.)

Referee: Mr Meirion Joseph (Wales)
Attendance: 30 000

SCORERS
SOUTH AFRICA: Penalties: Visagie (1)
SCOTLAND: Tries: Smith; Penalties: Smith (1)

SPRINGBOKS VS ABERAVON & NEATH
10 NOVEMBER 1969, PORT TALBOT
FINAL SCORE: 27-0
HALFTIME SCORE: 0-0

	SOUTH AFRICA	ABERAVON & NEATH
Full back:	O A Roux	G. T. R. Hodgson
Wing:	A E van der Watt	I. Hall
Centre:	J P van der Merwe	J. Simonson
Centre:	E Olivier	F. Reynolds
Wing:	R N Grobler	R. Fleay
Fly half:	P J Visagie	D. Parker
Scrum half:	D J de Vos	M. Davies
Prop:	R Potgieter	D. Whitlock
Hooker:	D C Walton	A. Mages
Prop:	J L Myburgh	B. Thomas
Flank:	A J Bates	O. Jones
Lock:	I J de Klerk	J. Luff
Lock:	A E de Wet	W. T Mainwaring (capt.)
Flank:	P I van Deventer	D. Thomas
No. 8:	T P Bedford (capt.)	W. Lauder

Referee: Mr R F Johnson (England)
Attendance: 10 000

SCORERS
SOUTH AFRICA: Tries: Van der Watt; Olivier (2); Van der Merwe;
Visagie; Penalties: Visagie (1); Conversions: Visagie (3)
ABERAVON & NEATH: Nil

SPRINGBOKS VS CARDIFF
13 DECEMBER 1969, CARDIFF ARMS PARK
FINAL SCORE: 17-3
HALFTIME SCORE: 9-0

	SOUTH AFRICA	CARDIFF
Full back:	O A Roux	D. Gethin
Wing:	A E van der Watt	A. Finlayson
Centre:	J P van der Merwe	D. K. Jones
Centre:	E Olivier	A. D. Williams
Wing:	S H Nomis	S. J. Watkins
Fly half:	M J Lawless	B. Davies
Scrum half:	D J de Villiers (capt.)	G. Edwards
Prop:	J F K Marais	J. P. O'Shea
Hooker:	D C Walton	G. Davies
Prop:	J L Myburgh	C. H. Norris
Flank:	P J F Greyling	J. Hickey
Lock:	I J de Klerk	I. Robinson
Lock:	A E de Wet	L. Baxter
Flank:	A J Bates	M. John
No. 8:	T P Bedford	J. James

Referee: Air Cmdr G C Lamb (England)
Attendance: 28 000

SCORERS
SOUTH AFRICA: Tries: Roux; Van der Merwe; Nomis; Penalties: Lawless (1); Drop goal: Lawless (1); Conversions: De Villiers (1)
CARDIFF: Penalties: Gethin (1)

SPRINGBOKS VS COMBINED SERVICES
16 DECEMBER 1969, ALDERSHOT
FINAL SCORE: 14-6
HALFTIME SCORE: 3-6

	SOUTH AFRICA	COMBINED SERVICES
Full back:	H O de Villiers	I. S. G. Smith
Wing:	A E van der Watt	B. T. Neck
Centre:	J P van der Merwe	G. L. Jones
Centre:	E Olivier	D. S. Boyle
Wing:	R N Grobler	J. S. A. Jeffray
Fly half:	P J Visagie	G. B. D. Campbell
Scrum half:	D J de Vos	D. Spawforth
Prop:	J F K Marais (capt.)	R. D. H. Bryce (capt.)
Hooker:	C H Cockrell	R. L. Clark
Prop:	J B Neethling	T. A. Moroney
Flank:	A J Bates	A. D. H. Turner
Lock:	F C H du Preez	M. G. Molloy
Lock:	G Carelse	D. A. Hanna
Flank:	P I van Deventer	P. J. Bird
No. 8:	M W Jennings	A. J. Hoon

Referee: Mr C Durand (France)
Attendance: 6 000

SCORERS
SOUTH AFRICA: Tries: Van der Watt; Van der Merwe; Grobler; Marais; Conversions: De Villiers (1)
COMBINED SERVICES: Tries: Jeffray; Hoon

SPRINGBOKS VS ENGLAND
20 DECEMBER 1969, TWICKENHAM
FINAL SCORE: 8-11
HALFTIME SCORE: 8-3

	SOUTH AFRICA	ENGLAND
Full back:	H O de Villiers	R. Hiller (capt.)
Wing:	A E van der Watt	P. M. Hale
Centre:	O A Roux	D. J. Duckham
Centre:	E Olivier	J. S. Spencer
Wing:	S H Nomis	K. J. Fielding
Fly half:	P J Visagie	I. R. Shackleton
Scrum half:	D J de Villiers (capt.)	N. C. Starmer-Smith
Prop:	J F K Marais	K. E. Fairbrother
Hooker:	D C Walton	J. V. Pullin
Prop:	J L Myburgh	C. B. Stevens
Flank:	A J Bates	A. L. Bucknall
Lock:	I J de Klerk	P. J. Larter
Lock:	A E de Wet	A. M. Davis
Flank:	P J F Greyling	B. R. West
No. 8:	T P Bedford	R. B. Taylor

Referee: Mr K D Kelleher (Ireland)
Attendance: 60 000

SCORERS
SOUTH AFRICA: Tries: Greyling; Penalties: Visagie (1); Conversions: Visagie (1)
ENGLAND: Tries: Pullin; Larter; Penalties: Hiller (1); Conversions: Hiller (1)

SPRINGBOKS VS SOUTH WESTERN COUNTIES
27 DECEMBER 1969, EXETER
FINAL SCORE: 9-6
HALFTIME SCORE: 6-6

	SOUTH AFRICA	SOUTH WESTERN COUNTIES
Full back:	H O de Villiers	G. Bate
Wing:	A E van der Watt	K. C. Plummer
Centre:	O A Roux	J. Bevan
Centre:	J P van der Merwe	B. Davies
Wing:	R N Grobler	D. H. Prout
Fly half:	M J Lawless	R. Whitcomb
Scrum half:	D J de Villiers (capt.)	A. Pearn
Prop:	R Potgieter	C. B. Stevens
Hooker:	C H Cockrell	R. F. S. Harris
Prop:	J B Neethling	P. Baxter
Flank:	P J F Greyling	A. Cole (capt.)
Lock:	F C H du Preez	B. Ninnes
Lock:	M C J van Rensburg	J. Baxter
Flank:	P I van Deventer	R. George
No. 8:	M W Jennings	A. Hollins

Referee: Mr G A Jamison (Ulster)
Attendance: 15 000

SCORERS
SOUTH AFRICA: Tries: Lawless; Jennings; Penalties: HO de Villiers (1);
SOUTH WESTERN COUNTIES: Penalties: Bate (2)

SPRINGBOKS VS WESTERN COUNTIES
31 DECEMBER 1969, BRISTOL
FINAL SCORE: 3-3
HALFTIME SCORE: 0-3

	SOUTH AFRICA	WESTERN COUNTIES
Full back:	H O de Villiers	J. Waterman
Wing:	S H Nomis	M. R. Collins
Centre:	O A Roux	D. Tyler
Centre:	J P van der Merwe	G. P. Frankcom
Wing:	R N Grobler	P. Knight
Fly half:	P J Visagie	T. Hopson
Scrum half:	D J J de Vos	J. Morris
Prop:	J F K Marais	B. A. Dovey
Hooker:	D C Walton	J. V. Pullin
Prop:	J L Myburgh	A. J. Rogers
Flank:	P I van Deventer	P. Hayward
Lock:	A E de Wet	A. J. Brinn
Lock:	G Carelse	D. E. J. Watt
Flank:	A J Bates	R. Smith
No. 8:	T P Bedford	D. M. Rollitt (capt.)

Referee: Mr C Durand
Attendance: 10 000

SCORERS
SOUTH AFRICA: Tries: Bedford.
WESTERN COUNTIES: Penalties: Larter (1)

SPRINGBOKS VS NORTH EASTERN COUNTIES
3 JANUARY 1970, GOSFORTH
FINAL SCORE: 24-11
HALFTIME SCORE: 5-8

	SOUTH AFRICA	NORTH EASTERN COUNTIES
Full back:	H O de Villiers	L. Sheard
Wing:	A E van der Watt	E. J. H. Littlechild
Centre:	F Du T Roux	D. Murray
Centre:	J P van der Merwe	C. P. Carter (capt.)
Wing:	S H Nomis	W. Hartley
Fly half:	M J Lawless	A. G. B. Old
Scrum half:	D J de Villiers (capt.)	M. Young
Prop:	J F K Marais	M. McKenzie
Hooker:	C H Cockrell	S. B. Richards
Prop:	J B Neethling	B. Keen
Flank:	P J F Greyling	D. Parker
Lock:	I J de klerk	J. B. Wakefield
Lock:	A E de Wet	R. Uttley
Flank:	P I van Deventer	R. J. Arneil
No. 8:	M W Jennings	R. R. Tennick

Referee: Mr J. Young (Scotland)
Attendance: 6 500

SCORERS
SOUTH AFRICA: Tries: Van Deventer; Marais; HO de Villiers; D J de Villiers; Penalties: HO de Villiers (1); Conversions: HO de Villiers (3)
NORTH EASTERN COUNTIES: Tries: Littlechild, Parker; Penalties: Carter (1); Conversion: Carter (1)

SPRINGBOKS VS MIDLAND COUNTIES (WEST)
6 JANUARY 1970, COVENTRY
FINAL SCORE: 21-6
HALFTIME SCORE: 10-0

	SOUTH AFRICA	MIDLAND COUNTIES (WEST)
Full back:	H O de Villiers	P. Rossborough
Wing:	A E van der Watt	P. M. Hale
Centre:	O A Roux	D. J. Duckham
Centre:	F Du T Roux	R. E. Griffiths
Wing:	R N Grobler	K. J. Fielding
Fly half:	P J Visagie	J. F. Finlan
Scrum half:	D J J de Vos	J. G. Webster
Prop:	J F K Marais	J. M. Broderick
Hooker:	D C Walton	D. E. Lane
Prop:	J L Myburgh	K. E. Fairbrother
Flank:	J H Ellis	T. J. Cobner
Lock:	F C H du Preez	J. Lacey
Lock:	I J de Klerk	H. F. Prosser
Flank:	A J Bates	R. J. Phillips (capt.)
No. 8:	T P Bedford	L. J. Rolinson

Referee: Mr D M Lloyd (Wales)
Attendance: 10 000

SCORERS
SOUTH AFRICA: Tries: H O de Villiers, Du Preez, Van der Watt, F Du T Roux; Conversions: Visagie (3)
OXFORD: Penalties: Rossborough (1); Dorp goal: Rossborough (1)

SPRINGBOKS VS IRELAND
10 JANUARY 1970, DUBLIN
FINAL SCORE: 8-8
HALFTIME SCORE: 3-5

	SOUTH AFRICA	IRELAND
Full back:	H O de Villiers	T. J. Kiernan (capt.)
Wing:	A E van der Watt	W. J. Brown
Centre:	O A Roux	C. M. H. Gibson
Centre:	F Du T Roux	F. P. K. Bresnihan
Wing:	S H Nomis	A. T. A. Duggan
Fly half:	M J Lawless	B. J. McGann
Scrum half:	D J de Villiers (capt.)	R. M. Young
Prop:	J F K Marais	P. O'Callaghan
Hooker:	C H Cockrell	K. W. Kennedy
Prop:	J L Myburgh	S. Millar
Flank:	P J F Greyling	R. A. Lamont
Lock:	F C H du Preez	C. E. Campbell
Lock:	I J de Klerk	W. J. McBride
Flank:	J H Ellis	J. F. Slattery
No. 8:	T P Bedford	K. G. Goodall

Referee: Mr T F E Grierson (Scotland)
Attendance: 30 000

SCORERS
SOUTH AFRICA: Tries: Greyling; Penalties: H O de Villiers (1);
Conversions: H O de Villiers (1)
IRELAND: Tries: B J McGann; Penalties: Kiernan (1); Conversions:
Kiernan (1)

SPRINGBOKS VS MUNSTER
14 JANUARY 1970, LIMERICK
FINAL SCORE: 25-9
HALFTIME SCORE: 16-3

	SOUTH AFRICA	MUNSTER
Full back:	H O de Villiers	A. Horgan
Wing:	S H Nomis	J. Moroney
Centre:	O A Roux	G. O'Reilly
Centre:	M J Lawless	F. P. K. Bresnihan
Wing:	R N Grobler	J. Tydings
Fly half:	P J Visagie	B. McGann (capt.)
Scrum half:	D J de Villiers (capt.)	L. Hall
Prop:	J F K Marais	P. O'Callaghan
Hooker:	R W Barnard	T. Barry
Prop:	J L Myburgh	O. Waldron
Flank:	P I van Deventer	W. O'Mahony
Lock:	A E de Wet	S. Waldron
Lock:	G Carelse	E. Molloy
Flank:	J H Ellis	J. Buckley
No. 8:	M W Jennings	T. Moore

Referee: Mr R E Lewis (Wales)
Attendance: 10 000

SCORERS
SOUTH AFRICA: Tries: Nomis, Grobler, Myburgh, Van Deventer; Penalties: Visagie (1); H O de Villiers (2); Conversions: H O de Villiers (2)
MUNSTER: Penalties: Moroney (3)

SPRINGBOKS VS SOUTH OF SCOTLAND
17 JANUARY 1970, GALASHIELS
FINAL SCORE: 3-3
HALFTIME SCORE: 0-0

	SOUTH AFRICA	SOUTH OF SCOTLAND
Full back:	H O de Villiers	D. S. Cranston
Wing:	A E van der Watt	W. D. Jackson
Centre:	F Du T Roux	J. W. C. Turner
Centre:	E Olivier	J. N. M. Frame
Wing:	S H Nomis	J. D. Tweedie
Fly half:	M J Lawless	C. M. Telfer
Scrum half:	D J J de Vos	D. S. Paterson
Prop:	J F K Marais	N. J. Stevenson
Hooker:	C H Cockrell	F. A. L. Laidlaw
Prop:	J B Neethling	N. Suddon
Flank:	P I van Deventer	G. G. Lyall
Lock:	G Carelse	P. C. Brown
Lock:	M C J van Rensburg	I. Barnes
Flank:	A J Bates	T. G. Elliot
No. 8:	T P Bedford (capt.)	J. W. Telfer (capt.)

Referee: Mr D J F Ford (England)

SCORERS
SOUTH AFRICA: Tries: Marais
OXFORD: Tries: Tweedie

SPRINGBOKS VS LLANELLI
20 JANUARY 1970, LLANELLI
FINAL SCORE: 10-9
HALFTIME SCORE: 5-3

	SOUTH AFRICA	**LLANELLI**
Full back:	H O de Villiers	H. Jones
Wing:	A E van der Watt	R. Mathias
Centre:	M J Lawless	J. Thomas
Centre:	J P van der Merwe	G. Griffin
Wing:	G H Muller	A. Richards
Fly half:	P J Visagie	G. Ashby
Scrum half:	D J de Villiers (capt.)	G. Thomas
Prop:	J F K Marais	B. Gale
Hooker:	R W Barnard	A. Reynolds
Prop:	J L Myburgh	B. Butler
Flank:	P J F Greyling	C. John
Lock:	F C H du Preez	D. Quinnell
Lock:	I J de Klerk	S. Gallacher (capt.)
Flank:	J H Ellis	A. John
No. 8:	M W Jennings	H. Jenkins

Referee: Mr F Lovis (England)
Attendance: 20 000

SCORERS
SOUTH AFRICA: Tries: Ellis (2); Conversions: Visagie (1); H O de Villiers (1)
LLANELLI: Tries: Richards, Butler; Penalties: Jones (1)

SPRINGBOKS VS WALES
24 JANUARY 1970, CARDIFF ARMS PARK
FINAL SCORE: 6-6
HALFTIME SCORE: 3-3

	SOUTH AFRICA	WALES
Full back:	H O de Villiers	J. P. R. Williams
Wing:	G H Muller	I. Hall
Centre:	O A Roux	W. H. Raybould
Centre:	J P van der Merwe	S. J. Dawes
Wing:	S H Nomis	P. Bennett
Fly half:	M J Lawless	B. John
Scrum half:	D J de Villiers (capt.)	G. O. Edwards (capt.)
Prop:	J F K Marais	D. Williams
Hooker:	C H Cockrell	V. C. Perrins
Prop:	J L Myburgh	D. B. Llewelyn
Flank:	P J F Greyling	D. Hughes
Lock:	F C H du Preez	W. D. Thomas
Lock:	I J de Klerk	T. G. Evans
Flank:	J H Ellis	D. W. Morris
No. 8:	T P Bedford	T. M. Davies

Referee: Mr Air Cmdr G C Lamb (England)
Attendance: 42 000

SCORERS
SOUTH AFRICA: Tries: Nomis; Penalties: H O de Villiers
WALES: Tries: Edwards; Penalties: Edwards (1)

SPRINGBOKS VS SOUTHERN COUNTIES
28 JANUARY 1970, GLOUCESTER
FINAL SCORE: 13-0
HALFTIME SCORE: 0-0

	SOUTH AFRICA	SOUTHERN COUNTIES
Full back:	O A Roux	I. R. Moffatt
Wing:	G H Muller	P. Cadle
Centre:	F Du T Roux	J. L. Hewitt
Centre:	E Olivier	J. R. Donovan
Wing:	A E van der Watt	M. S. Simmie
Fly half:	M J Lawless	F. E. J. Hawkins
Scrum half:	D J J de Vos	D. Spawforth
Prop:	J B Neethling	W. J. Hannell
Hooker:	R W Barnard	D. M. Barry
Prop:	G Carelse	B. I. Clark
Flank:	T P Bedford	M. I. Player (capt.)
Lock:	A E de Wet	J. R. W. Harvey
Lock:	M C J van Rensburg	A. R. G. Else
Flank:	P I van Deventer	A. P. Hallett
No. 8:	M W Jennings	P. R Hall

Referee: Mr W K M Jones (Wales)
Attendance: 10 000

SCORERS
SOUTH AFRICA: Tries: Muller, De Vos, Neethling; Conversions: Van Rensburg (2)
SOUTHERN COUNTIES: Nil

SPRINGBOKS VS BARBARIANS
31 JANUARY 1970, TWICKENHAM
FINAL SCORE: 21-12
HALFTIME SCORE: 8-9

	SOUTH AFRICA	BARBARIANS
Full back:	H O de Villiers	J. P. R. Williams
Wing:	A E van der Watt	D. J. Duckham
Centre:	O A Roux	C. M. H. Gibson
Centre:	J P van der Merwe	J. S. Spencer
Wing:	S H Nomis	A. T. A. Duggan
Fly half:	M J Lawless	B. John
Scrum half:	D J de Villiers (capt.)	G. O. Edwards (capt.)
Prop:	J F K Marais	K. E. Fairbrother
Hooker:	C H Cockrell	F. A. L. Laidlaw
Prop:	J L Myburgh	D. B. Llewelyn
Flank:	P J F Greyling	J. J. Jeffery
Lock:	F C H du Preez	I. S. Gallacher
Lock:	I J de Klerk	A. M. Davis
Flank:	J H Ellis	R. J. Arneil
No. 8:	M W Jennings	T. M. Davis

Referee: Mr Air Cmdr G C Lamb (England)
Attendance: 25 000

SCORERS
SOUTH AFRICA: Tries: Ellis (2), Van der Watt; Penalties: D J de Villiers (1); Drop goal: Lawless (1); Conversions: D J de Villiers (3)
BARBARIANS: Tries: Duckham, Duggan, Arneil, Fairbrother

ENDNOTES

1. *Apartheid and a Time of Protest*

1. Nelson Mandela, *Lang Pad na Vryheid*, pp. 91–93. (*Long Walk to Freedom*); 'The Making of a "Traitor"'. *Sunday Times* 29 July 2018 (Interview with Lord Peter Hain)
2. Dawie de Villiers, *My Lewensreis: Springbok, politikus, diplomaat*, title page quotes
3. Ibid
4. 'The Native Question', F A W Lucas Papers AD 1769, 31 March to 6 April 1931. Wits University Historical Papers
5. P G Dickson, *The Natives Land Act 1913: Its Antecedent, Passage and Reception*, M.A. Thesis, University of Cape Town, 1970; Henry Kenney, *Power, Pride and Prejudice*, pp. 42–43
6. See Sol T Plaatje, *Native Life in South Africa*, Chapters 16 and 17
7. Henry Kenney, *Power, Pride and Prejudice*, Chapter 5: On the Road to Separate Freedoms
8. See Chris Schoeman, *District Six: The Spirit of Kanala*, Chapter 6: The Death of District Six
9. Henry Kenney, *Power, Pride and Prejudice*, pp. 71–79; 114–119
10. Ibid, pp. 138–146
11. L Strydom, *Rivonia*, pp. 131–136

12. John D'Oliviera, *Vorster: Die Mens*, pp. 200–201; Henry Kenney, *Power, Pride and Prejudice*, pp. 197–198; 211

13. Bruce Murray & Christopher Merrett, *Caught Behind*, pp. 117–122

14. Interview with Lord Peter Hain.

15. While major tours like the All Blacks to South Africa (1970 and 1976), South Africa to Australia (1971) and the British Lions to South Africa (1974 and 1980) did take place over the next decade, the Springboks became increasingly isolated, until South Africa's official return to international rugby in 1992.

16. See Peter Hain, *Outside In*, Chapter 2 for this background.

17. 'Not Playing Games.' *Journal of Liberal History*, No 74 Spring 2012

18. Dawie de Villiers, *My Lewensreis: Springbok, politikus, diplomaat*, p. 50

19. Ibid, p. 50

20. Frik du Preez interview

21. Tommy Bedford interview

22. 'Not Playing Games.' *Journal of Liberal History*, No 74 Spring 2012

2. A Proud Tradition

1. It has to be mentioned that South Africa suffered defeat to Ireland (6–9) and Scotland (5–8) on their short tour in 1965.

2. Chris Schoeman, *Seasons of Glory*, p. 37.

3. Paul Roos. One of South Africa's most famous rugby schools, Paul Roos Gimnasium (formerly Stellenbosch Boys' High), was named after him. He was headmaster of the school for a time.

4. Paddy Carolin captained the Springboks in the first Test of the tour against Scotland as Paul Roos had been ill. He was top scorer on tour with 75 points, including six tries and four dropped goals.

5. A C Parker, *The Springboks 1891–1970*, p. 32

6. The Thin Red Line, so called after their maroon Stellenbosch jerseys, consisted of the Western Province and Springbok

three-quarters Bob Loubser, De Villiers, the great Japie Krige and Anton Stegmann.

7. Chris Schoeman, *Seasons of Glory*, pp. 72, 74.
8. Bob Loubser, a Western Province 100 yards sprinter, also played for South Africa in the 1903 and 1910 series against the British Isles. He became Member of Parliament for Stellenbosch, following in the footsteps of his former captain, Paul Roos.
9. Chris Schoeman, *Seasons of Glory*, pp. 83–4.
10. Rev. George Daneel interview. Translated from the original Afrikaans.
11. *Western Mail*, 7 October 1958.
12. Ryk van Schoor interview.
13. Frik du Preez interview.

4. *Surprise, Surprise*

1. *Birmingham Daily Post*, 18 September 1969.
2. *The Journal*, 11 October 1969.
3. *The Journal*, 11 October 1969.
4. *Daily Mirror*, 24 October 1969
5. *Liverpool Echo*, 25 October 1969
6. *Daily Mirror*, 27 October 1969
7. Ibid
8. *The Birmingham Post*, 28 October 1969.
9. Interview with Tommy Bedford.
10. *The Daily Mirror*, 22 December 1966. 'Rugby in Britain? It's just a kick in the back.' By Peter Laker.
11. Ibid.
12. Interview with Johann van der Merwe.
13. Interview with HO de Villiers.
14. Interview with Eben Olivier.
15. British Pathé video 30 October 1969.
16. Interview with Avril Malan.
17. Interview with Johann van der Merwe.

18. Interview with Eben Olivier.
19. Interview with HO de Villiers.
20. Interview with Tommy Bedford.

5. *A Shaky Start*

1. Interview with Dawie de Villiers.
2. *Daily Mirror*, 31 October 1969. Rugby is our game – not politics, say Springboks; J. B. G. Thomas, *Springbok Invasion*, p. 47.
3. Personal interview with Avril Malan.
4. Interview with Johann van der Merwe.
5. Gerhard Viviers, *Rugby agter doringdraad*, pp. 16–17; J. B. G. Thomas, *Springbok Invasion*, pp. 47–48.
6. *The Rugby Paper*, August 31, 2014. 'Moment in Time: Oxford University beat South Africa in 1969.'
7. Chris Laidlaw, *Mud in Your Eye*, p. 186.
8. *The Rugby Paper*, August 31, 2014. 'Moment in Time: Oxford University beat South Africa in 1969.'
9. Interview with Dawie de Villiers.
10. *The Rugby Paper*, August 31, 2014. 'Moment in Time: Oxford University beat South Africa in 1969.'
11. Interview with Johann van der Merwe.
12. Ibid.
13. Ibid.
14. Ibid.
15. Chris Laidlaw, *Mud in Your Eye*, p. 6.
16. *The Birmingham Post*, 8 November 1969. 'Riot Squad for the Springboks' match.'
17. Ibid.
18. *The Times*, 10 November 1969. Letter to the Editor.
19. Interview with Lord Peter Hain.
20. *The Times*, 10 November 1969. Letter to the Editor.
21. Bill McLaren, *Talking of Rugby*, pp. 137–138
22. J. B. G. Thomas, *Springbok Invasion*, pp. 55–58.

23. Interview with Bob Taylor.

24. Interview with Peter Larter.

25. Ibid.

26. Ibid.

27. *The Birmingham Post* 10 November 1969. 'More effective protests planned for Springboks.'

28. Ibid.

29. *Belfast Telegraph*, 11 November 1969. 'Springboks, yes; Springboks, no.'

30. *Press & Journal* 11 Nov 69. 'Labour bid to cancel let of Linksfield for the Springboks.'

6. *A Welcome in the Vales*

1. *Birmingham Post* 11 Nov 1969. 'Dawie de Villiers returns.'

2. *Press & Journal*, 11 Nov 1969. 'Not a snub, says Lord Provost.'

3. Steve Lewis, *Newport Rugby Football Club 1950–2000*, pp. 46–47; J. B. G. Thomas, *Springbok Invasion*, pp. 61–64.

4. *The Journal,* 13 Nov 1969. 'Springboks beaten to a frazzle.'

5. *Daily Mirror,* 14 Nov 1969. 'Tourists switch Roux to key job.'

6. Swansea RFC official website http://www.swansearfc.co.uk

7. Ibid.

8. Ibid.

9. J. B. G. Thomas, *Springbok Invasion*, p. 64.

10. Translated from Gerhard Viviers, *Rugby agter Doringdraad*, pp. 24–26

11. Interview with Johann van der Merwe.

12. *Belfast Telegraph*, 15 November 1969. 'Police clash with demonstrators at Springboks match.'

13. *Coventry Evening Telegraph*, 15 November 1969. 'Springboks show best form of tour.'; J. B. G. Thomas, *Springbok Invasion*, pp. 66–68.

14. Team Manager's report; J. B. G. Thomas, *Springbok Invasion*, pp. 68–69.

15. *Evening Chronicle*, 17 November 1969. 'Callahan told of violence at Springboks match.'
16. *House of Commons Debates* 17 November 1969 Vol 791, p. 851.
17. Ibid.
18. Ibid.
19. Ibid.
20. Ibid.
21. *Coventry Evening Telegraph*, 19 November 1969. 'Police guards Springboks match ground.'
22. *The Rugby Paper*, 30 November 2018. 'Derek Morgan has the answer to Pichot's foreign rant.'
23. J. B. G. Thomas, *Springbok Invasion*, pp. 70–72.

7. *London & North West Counties, No Ulster*

1. *The Birmingham Post*, 21 November 1969. 'New lock forward joins Springboks.'
2. J. B. G. Thomas, *Springbok invasion*, pp. 75–79.
3. Team Manager's report; J. B. G. Thomas, *Springbok invasion*, pp. 80–81
4. Team Manager's report.
5. In 1985, Pahad was elected a National Executive Committee member of the ANC and in 1991, a year after he returned to South Africa from exile, he was appointed deputy head of the ANC Department of International Affairs. For the next three years, Aziz Pahad served as a member of the National Peace Executive Committee and of the Transitional Executive Council's sub-committee on Foreign Affairs. In 1994, he was elected a Member of Parliament and was appointed Deputy Minister of Foreign Affairs in the Government of President Nelson Mandela.
6. *Guild Gazette*, 25 November 1969. 'Liverpool supports the demo.'

7. J. B. G. Thomas, *Springbok invasion*, pp. 82–85.
8. *The Journal*, 12 December 1969. 'Springboks hit more trouble.'
9. Ibid.
10. *Belfast Telegraph*, 6 November 1969. 'Ulster stars WILL play Springboks.'
11. BBC One documentary *The Story of Willie John McBride*, 2015.
12. Ibid
13. *Belfast Telegraph*, 6 November 1969. 'Ulster stars WILL play Springboks.'
14. *Belfast Telegraph*, 7 November 1969. 'No Official Snub for the Springboks.'
15. *Belfast Telegraph*, 21 November 1969. 'Opposition MPS join fight to stop Springboks' visit.'
16. *Daily Mirror*, 25 November 1969. 'Callaghan curb on Springbok riot stewards.'
17. *The Birmingham Post*, 26 November 1969. 'Ulster calls off Springboks' visit.'
18. Team Manager's report; *The Journal*, 12 December 1969. 'Springboks hit more trouble.'

8. Troubles in Scotland

1. Gerhard Viviers, *Rugby agter doringdraad*, p. 34.
2. J. B. G. Thomas, *Springbok Invasion*, pp. 89–91.
3. Team Manager's report.
4. *The Birmingham Post*, 3 December 1969. '98 are arrested at Springboks' match.'
5. *Evening Express*, 19 November 1969. 'Why a double standards?'
6. *Daily Mirror*, 2 December 1969. 'New threat to the Springboks.'
7. Interview with Rodger Arneil.
8. Ibid.
9. Wallace Reyburn, *There was also some Rugby*, pp. 123–125; J. B. G. Thomas, *Springbok Invasion*, p. 93–97.

10. Ibid.

11. *The Scotsman*, 7 November 2012. 'Former Scottish captain Jim Telfer remembers victories and violence.'

12. *The Herald*, 1 January 2001. '30-year-old files reveal ugly side of Springboks tour that brought shame on our nation.'

13. Interview with Lord Peter Hain.

9. *Back to Wales*

1. J. B. G. Thomas, *Springbok Invasion*, pp. 98–101.

2. Team Manager's report.

3. Interview with Dawie de Villiers.

4. Team Manager's report.

5. *Coventry Evening Telegraph*, 10 December 1969. 'Quiet in Wales for Springboks.'

6. *Birmingham Post*, 11 December 1969. 'Springboks score 27.'

7. *Western Mail* 19 November 2002. Carolyn Hitt: 'Rebel with a cause Hain recalls his days on the rugby protest frontline.'

8. Match programme Cardiff vs South Africa, 13 December 1969.

9. Interview with John O'Shea.

10. Ibid.

11. J. B. G. Thomas, *Springbok Invasion*, pp. 104–107.

12. Ibid, pp. 107–108.

13. Interview with John O'Shea.

14. Team Manager's report.

15. Gerhard Viviers, *Rugby agter doringdraad*, p. 47.

16. J. B. G. Thomas, *Springbok Invasion*, pp. 109–112.

10. *England & Counties Galore*

1. *The Evening Telegraph*, 15 December 1969. 'Don't play the Springboks.'

2. *The Birmingham Post*, Saturday, 20 December 1969. 'England courage can lead to victory.'

3. Interview with Springbok Johann van der Merwe.

4. Interview with Frik du Preez.

5. Team Manager's report.

6. Gerhard Viviers, *Rugby agter doringdraad*, pp. 48–49.

7. Roelf Theunissen, *Springbokkaptein Dawie de Villiers*, p. 169.

8. Ibid, p. 171

9. Wallace Reyburn, There was also some Rugby, pp. 136–140; B.G. Thomas, *Springbok Invasion*, p. 120.

10. Roelf Theunissen, *Springbokkaptein Dawie de Villiers*, p. 171 (translated from Afrikaans).

11. Interview with Robert Taylor.

12. Interview with Peter Larter.

13. J. B. G. Thomas, *Springbok Invasion*, p. 120.

14. Ibid, pp. 121–122; Team Manager's report.

15. J. B. G. Thomas, *Springbok Invasion*, pp. 122–123.

16. *The Coventry Evening Telegraph*, 23 December 1969. 'Threat of more Springbok demos.'

17. Gerhard Viviers, *Rugby agter doringdraad*, p. 32.

18. Team Manager's report; Roelf Theunissen, *Springbokkaptein Dawie de Villiers*, p. 151.

19. J. B. G. Thomas, *Springbok Invasion*, pp. 125–127.

20. Team Manager's report.

21. Ibid; Gerhard Viviers, *Rugby agter doringdraad*, pp. 58–59.

22. J. B. G. Thomas, *Springbok Invasion*, pp. 129–132.

23. Interview with Lord Peter Hain.

24. Team Manager's report.

25. J. B. G. Thomas, *Springbok Invasion*, pp. 133–135.

26. *The Daily Mirror*, 5 January 1970. 'Old has a new cap look.'

27. Team Manager's report.

28. *Coventry Evening Telegraph* 4 January 1970. 'Springboks facing defeats again at Coundon Road.'

29. J. B. G. Thomas, *Springbok Invasion*, pp. 136–139.

30. Roelf Theunissen, *Springbokkaptein Dawie de Villiers*, p. 152–153.

31. *Coventry Evening Telegraph*, 7 January 1970. '£9000 Bill for the Springboks operation.'

32. *Coventry Evening Telegraph*, 7 January 1970. 'Police say thanks for cuppas.'

33. *Coventry Evening Telegraph*, 10 January 1970. 'No harm' in treating injured Springboks.'

34. Team Manager's report. *Come Here to Me!*, 3 February 2015. 'The controversial visit of the Springbok team to Dublin.'

35. Ibid; Roelf Theunissen, *Springbokkaptein Dawie de Villiers*, p. 155–156. *Come Here to Me!*, 3 February 2015. 'The controversial visit of the Springbok team to Dublin.'

11. *Dublin Demos*

1. *Irish Times*, 9 November 2017

2. *Sunday Independent*, 7 Nov 2004. 'Our greatest threat to South Africa.'

3. *Come Here to Me!*, 3 February 2015. 'The controversial visit of the Springbok team to Dublin.'

4. Ibid.

5. Ibid.

6. Kader Asmal, *Politics in my Blood*, pp. 53, 57.

7. Ibid, p. 49.

8. Personal interview with Dawie de Villiers. Asmal resigned from Parliament in 2008 in protest against the ANC's disbanding of the elite Scorpions anti-crime unit. He felt it was improper that politicians who had been investigated and found by the Scorpions to be engaged in corruption, then took part in the vote to disband the unit.

9. Team Manager's report.

10. A. C. Parker, *Springboks 1891–1970*, pp. 313–315; J. B. G. Thomas, *Springbok Invasion*, pp. 141–144.

11. *Daily Mirror*, 12 January 1970. 'Boks robbed by the luck of the Irish.'
12. Interview with Roger Young.
13. Interview with Dawie de Villiers.
14. Team Manager's report.
15. Ibid.
16. J. B. G. Thomas, *Springbok Invasion*, pp. 151–153.
17. *Daily Mirror* 15 January 1970, 'Springboks' skipper dazzles the Irish.'
18. Team Manager's report.
19. Interview with Dawie de Villiers.
20. Interview with Eben Olivier.
21. Interview with HO de Villiers.
22. Personal interview with Hannes Marais.
23. Edward Griffiths, *The Captains*, p. 219.
24. Gerhard Viviers, *Rugby agter doringdraad*, pp. 41–42.
25. Ibid.
26. *Birmingham Post*, 16 January 1970. 'Springboks wing out of tour.'
27. Personal interview with Johann van der Merwe.

12. *Wales & 'Wait For Llanelli'*

1. J. B. G. Thomas, *Springbok Invasion*, p. 157.
2. Team Manager's report.
3. Gerhard Viviers, *Rugby agter doringdraad*, pp. 84–86; J. B. G. Thomas, *Springbok Invasion*, p. 160.
4. Evening Telegraph, 20 January 1970. 'Springboks rally after early shock.'; J. B. G. Thomas, *Springbok Invasion*, pp. 157–162.
5. J. B. G. Thomas, *Springbok Invasion*, p. 163.
6. Interview with Dawie de Villiers.
7. Gerhard Viviers, *Rugby agter doringdraad*, p. 90.
8. *Wales Online* 17 October 2015. 'The day Wales ended decades of South African dominance.'

9. Interview with Dawie de Villiers.
10. Interview with Avril Malan.
11. A.C. Parker, *Springboks 1891–1970*, pp. 315–317; J. B. G. Thomas, *Springbok Invasion*, p. 165–168;
12. *The Birmingham Post*, 26 January 1970. 'Injury time try denies Springboks.'
13. Gerhard Viviers, *Rugby agter doringdraad*, p. 94.

13. A Grand Finale

1. J. B. G. Thomas, *Springbok Invasion*, p. 172–174.
2. *The Birmingham Post*, 31 January 1970. 'Classic – British backs vs. Springbok pack.'
3. *The Independent*, 30 May 2009. 'John Taylor: Rebel with a Cause.'
4. Nigel Starmer-Smith, *The Barbarians*, pp. 188–190; J. B. G. Thomas, *Springbok Invasion*, pp. 178–181.
5. Interview with Rodger Arneil.
6. Gerhard Viviers, *Rugby agter doringdraad*, p. 97.
7. Interview with Dawie de Villiers.
8. *The Birmingham Post*, 2 February 1970. 'Tradition is downfall of Barbarians.'
9. Gerhard Viviers, *Rugby agter doringdraad*, pp. 98–99.
10. *Coventry Evening Telegraph*, 2 February 1970. 'Boks leave their best to the last.'
11. *Farmer & Stockbreeder*, 6 January 1970, pp. 83–90.
12. Team Manager's report.
13. Ibid.
14. Ibid.
15. Ibid.
16. Ibid.
17. Interview with Avril Malan.
18. Interview with John O'Shea.
19. Interview with Peter Larter.
20. Interview with Roger Young.

21. Interview with Robert Taylor.
22. Interview with Dawie de Villiers.
23. Gerhard Viviers, *Rugby agter doringdraad*, pp. 110–111.

14. *Looking Back*

1. Gerhard Viviers, *Rugby agter doringdraad*, pp. 70–71.
2. Interview with Ray Mordt.
3. Interview with Tommy Bedford.
4. Ibid.
5. Interview with Avril Malan.
6. Interview with Eben Olivier.
7. Interview with Lord Peter Hain.
8. Ibid.
9. Interview with Tommy Bedford.
10. House of Commons Debates 27 January 1970, vol. 794 cc1503-91503
11. Interview with Dawie de Villiers.
12. Interview with HO de Villiers.
13. Interview with Johann van der Merwe.
14. Interview with Tommy Bedford.

15. *Aftermath*

1. *Journal of Liberal History* 74, Spring 2012.
2. Interview with Lord Peter Hain; *Global Citizen*, 7 December 2017 with Alec Hogg.
3. Interview with Hannes Marais.
4. Interview with Tommy Bedford.
5. Interview with Lord Peter Hain.

BIBLIOGRAPHY

Books, Theses

Asmal, Kader, *Politics in my Blood* (Auckland Park: Jacana Media, 2011)

Bennett, Phil, *Everywhere for Wales* (London: Stanley Paul, 1981)

Clayton, Keith, *The Legends of Springbok Rugby 1889-1989: Doc Craven's Tribute* (Cape Town: KC Publications, 1989)

Craven, Dr D. H., *Die Groot Rugbygesin van die Maties* (Stellenbosch: University of Stellenbosch, 1980)

Craven, Dr D. H., *Ek Speel vir Suid-Afrika* (Cape Town: Nasionale Pers, 1949)

De Villiers, Dawie (with Chris Schoeman). *My Lewensreis. Springbok, Politikus, Diplomaat* (Cape Town: Penguin Random House, 2018)

De Villiers, HO (with Neville Leck), *HO: A Biography of Courage* (Cape Town: Don Nelson Publishers, 1977)

Dickson, P.G., *The Native Land Act 1913: Its Antecedent, Passage and Reception*. M.A. thesis, University of Cape Town, 1970

D'Oliviera, John, *Vorster: Die Mens* (Johannesburg: Perskor, 1977)

Du Preez, Frik (with Chris Schoeman), *Frik: The Autobiography of a Legend* (Cape Town: Don Nelson Publishers, 2004)

Edwards, Gareth, *100 Great Players* (London: MacDonald Queen Anne Press, 1987)

Edwards, Gareth, *Gareth* (London: Stanley Paul, 1978)

Gainsford, John (with Neville Leck), *Nice Guys Come Second* (Cape Town: Don Nelson Publishers, 1974)

Gouws, Leon, *Frik du Preez: Rugbyreus* (Pretoria: Janssonius & Heyns, 1971)

Greyvenstein, Chris, *Springbok Saga* (Cape Town: Don Nelson Publishers, 1989)

Greyvenstein, Chris, *20 Great Springboks* (Cape Town: Don Nelson Publishers, 1987)

Griffiths, Edward, *The Captains* (Cape Town: Jonathan Ball, 2001)

Hain, Peter, *Don't Play with Apartheid* (London: Allen & Unwin, 1971)

Hain, Peter, *Inside Out* (London: Biteback Publishing, 2011)

John, Barry, *The Barry John Story* (Glasgow: William Collins Sons, 1974

Laidlaw, Chris, *Mud in your Eye* (Cape Town: Howard Timmins, 1974)

Kenny, Henry, *Power, Pride and Prejudice:The years of Afrikaner nationalist rule in South Africa* (Cape Town: Jonathan Ball, 1991)

Lewis, Steve, *Newport Rugby Football Club 1950-2000* (Stroud: Tempus, 2000)

McBride, Willie John (with Peter Bills). *Willie John: The Story of My Life* (London: Portrait, 2004)

McLaren, Bill, *Rugby's Great Heroes and Entertainers* (London: Hodder & Stoughton, 2003)

McLaren, Bill, *Talking of Rugby* (London: Hutchinson, 1991)

Murray, B & Merrett, C., *Caught Behind: Race and Politics in Springbok Cricket* (Johannesburg: Wits University Press, 2004)

Muller, Hennie, *Totsiens to Test Rugby* (Cape Town: Howard Timmins, 1953)

Parker, A. C., *The Springboks 1891-1970* (London: Cassell, 1970)

Plaatje, Sol T., *Native Life in South Africa* (Johannesburg: Wits University Press, 2016)

Raeburn, Wallace, *There was also some Rugby* (London: Stanley Paul, 1970)

Schoeman, Chris, *Legends of the Ball: Rugby's Greatest Players*. Chosen by Willie John McBride, Frik du Preez & David Campese (Cape Town: CJS Books, 2007)

Mandela, Nelson, *Lang Pad na Vryheid* (Midrand: Macmillan Academic S.A., 2007)

Schoeman, Chris, *South Africa's Rugby Legends: The Amateur Years* (Cape Town: Penguin Random House, 2015)

Schoeman, Chris, *The No.10s: South Africa's Finest Flyhalves 1891-2010* (Cape Town: Random House Struik, 2010)

Schoeman, Chris, *Seasons of Glory – The Life and Times of Bob Loubser* (Cape Town: CJS Books, 1999, revised edition 2006)

Schoeman, Chris, *District Six: The Spirit of Kanala* (Cape Town: Human & Rousseau, 1994)

Shnaps, Teddy, *A Statistical History of Springbok Rugby* (Cape Town: SARB, Don Nelson, 1989)

Starmer-Smith, Nigel, *The Barbarians* (London: Macdonald & Janes Publishers, 1977)

Strydom, Lauritz, *Rivonia: Masker Af!* (Johannesburg: Voortrekkerpers, 1964)

Theunissen, Roelf, *Springbokkaptein Dawie de Villiers* (Cape Town: Tafelberg, 1972)

Thomas, J. B. G., *Springbok Glory* (London: Stanley Paul, 1961)

Thomas, J. B. G., *Springbok Invasion* (London: Stanley Paul, 1970)

Viviers, Gerhard, *Rugby agter Doringdraad* (Pretoria: Van der Walt en Seun (Edms) Bpk, 1970)

Williams, J. P. R., *JPR: An Autobiography* (Glasgow: William Collins Sons, 1979)

Official Documents

Springbok Manager Corrie Bornman's Official Tour Report, 10 February 1970

Letter from Department of Sport & Recreation to Secretary SA Rugby Board on Wilf Isaacs cricket tour. 15 September 1969

House of Commons Debates 17 November 1969 Vol. 791

House of Commons Debates 27 January 1970 Vol. 794

Interviews

Former Springboks

Avril Malan

Dawie de Villiers

Eben Olivier

Frik du Preez

Hannes Marais

HO de Villiers

Johann van der Merwe

Piet Greyling

Piet Visagie

Ray Mordt

Rev George Daneel

Ryk van Schoor

Sid Nomis

Stephen Fry

Tommy Bedford

Other

Lord Peter Hain

Bob Taylor (England)

John O'Shea (Wales)

Peter Larter (England)

Rodger Arneil (Scotland)

Roger Young (Ireland)

Newspapers, Magazines & Journals
Belfast Telegraph 1969–70
Birmingham Daily Post 1969–70
Coventry Evening Telegraph 1969–70
Daily Mirror 1969–70
Evening Chronicle 1969–70
Guild Gazette 1969–70
Liverpool Echo 1969–70
Press and Journal 1969–70
The Journal 1969–70
The Scotsman 1969–70

Later Single Articles
Journal of Liberal History No. 74 Spring 2012. 'Not Playing Games.'

The Old Limerick Journal Summer edition 2009. 'The 1970 Springboks tour and local politics in Limerick.'

Western Mail 19 November 2002. 'Rebel with a cause Hain recalls his days on the rugby protest frontline.'

The Sunday Independent 7 November 2004. 'Our greatest threat to South Africa.'

The Independent 20 November 2011. Alec Hogg: 'Peter Hain: The retiring hero who changed the course of history.'

The Rugby Paper 31 August 2014. 'Moment in time: Oxford beat South Africa in 1969.'

Come Here to Me 3 February 2015. 'The Controversial Visit of the Springbok team to Dublin.'

Global Citizen 7 December 2017. 'Meet Peter Hain: The British Lord obsessed with exposing Zupta corruption.'

The Sunday Times (South Africa) 29 July 2018. 'The Making of a traitor.'

The Rugby Paper 30 November 2018. 'Derek Morgan has the answer to Pichot's foreign rant.'

Journal of Southern African Studies Vol. 27, No. 4 2001. 'The D'Oliveira Affair of 1968.'

Farmer & Stockbreeder 6 January 1970. Magazine cutting on the Springboks' life on tour (title and author missing)

Videos

'Springboks Arrive.' British Pathé 1969.

'Scotland vs Springboks.' British Pathé 1969.

'Scotland vs South Africa.' Archivo DiFilm 1969.

'To be black in South Africa.' British Pathé 1969.

'Springboks Demonstration.' British Pathé 1969.

'Springboks vs London Counties.' Archivo DiFilm 1969.

'England vs South Africa.' Archivo DiFilm 1969.

'Ireland vs South Africa.' Archivo DiFilm 1970.

Wales vs South Africa.' Archivo DiFilm 1970.

'Barbarians vs South Africa 1970.' TeeKay 1970.

'Springboks vs Barbarians.' Archivo DiFilm 1970.

'The Story of Willie John McBride.' BBC, 2015.

INDEX